THE MANAGER'S HANDBOOK FOR BUSINESS SECURITY

THE MANAGER'S HANDBOOK FOR BUSINESS SECURITY

SECOND EDITION

GEORGE K. CAMPBELL, Contributing Editor

ELSEVIER

AMSTERDAM • BOSTON • HEIDELBERG • LONDON • NEW YORK • OXFORD
PARIS • SAN DIEGO • SAN FRANCISCO • SINGAPORE • SYDNEY • TOKYO

Security
Executive Council

Elsevier
225 Wyman Street, Waltham, MA, 02451, USA
The Boulevard, Langford Lane, Kidlington, Oxford, OX5 1GB, UK

Originally published by the Security Executive Council, 2009

Notices
Knowledge and best practice in this field are constantly changing. As new research and experience broaden our understanding, changes in research methods, professional practices, or medical treatment may become necessary.

Practitioners and researchers must always rely on their own experience and knowledge in evaluating and using any information, methods, compounds, or experiments described herein. In using such information or methods they should be mindful of their own safety and the safety of others, including parties for whom they have a professional responsibility.

To the fullest extent of the law, neither the Publisher nor the authors, contributors, or editors, assume any liability for any injury and/or damage to persons or property as a matter of products liability, negligence or otherwise, or from any use or operation of any methods, products, instructions, or ideas contained in the material herein.

Library of Congress Cataloging-in-Publication Data
Campbell, George, 1942-
    The manager's handbook for business security / George K. Campbell. – Second edition.
       pages cm
    ISBN 978-0-12-800062-5
1. Business enterprises–Security measures. 2. Risk management. I. Title.
    HD61.5.C36 2014
    658.4′7–dc23

                                                                        2013045269

British Library Cataloguing-in-Publication Data
A catalogue record for this book is available from the British Library

ISBN: 978-0-12-800062-5

For more publications in the Elsevier Risk Management and Security Collection, visit our website at store.elsevier.com/SecurityExecutiveCouncil

This book has been manufactured using Print On Demand technology. Each copy is produced to order and is limited to black ink. The online version of this book will show color figures where appropriate.

  Working together to grow libraries in developing countries

www.elsevier.com • www.bookaid.org

Printed and bound by CPI Group (UK) Ltd, Croydon, CR0 4YY

CONTENTS

Acknowledgments xi

Introduction xiii

Chapter 1 Understanding the Business of Security.........................1
Introduction 1
The Security Program Review 7
Build the Business Case for Crafting a Measurably Effective
Security Program 9
Highlights for Follow-Up 16

Chapter 2 Security Leadership 19
Introduction 19
Leadership Competencies 20
Keys to Organizational Influence and Impact 21
The Next Generation Security Leader 24
Highlights for Follow-Up 26

Chapter 3 Risk Assessment and Mitigation.................................29
Introduction 29
Assessing Viable Threats 30
Vulnerability Assessment 31
Board-Level Risk and Security Program Response
Research 32
A Risk Quantification Process 33
A Risk Management-Based Concept of Operations 36
Highlights for Follow-Up 38

Chapter 4 Strategic Security Planning 41
Introduction 41
Strategic Security Program Focus 43
Eight Key Strategic Issues 44
The Security Planning and Program Development Process...44
Business Alignment and Demonstrating Security's Value 45
Highlights for Follow-Up 47

Chapter 5 Marketing the Security Program to the Business....................49
Introduction 49
The Essentials 49
A Marketing Strategy..49
Brand Recognition 50
The Mission Statement...51
Policies and Business Practices 51
Applying Standard Security Practices to Business Objectives...............53
Highlights for Follow-Up 57

Chapter 6 Organizational Models 59
Introduction 59
Baseline Elements...60
Program Characteristics 61
What Organizational Model Works Best in Your Company.....................62
Alternative Organizational Models 62
Consolidated Service Model 64
Seriously Explore the Potential Advantages of a Security
Committee 64
Unified Risk Oversight..65
Access Is the Fundamental Essential 66
Highlights for Follow-Up 72

Chapter 7 Regulations, Guidelines, and Standards.........................75
Introduction 75
Typical Regulatory Elements 76
How Many Security Regulations Apply to Your Company?.....................76
The Legislation, Regulations, Voluntary Compliance,
and Standards (LRVCS) Breakdown 78
The Security Professional's Role 79
The Implications of Noncompliance.................................90
Highlights for Follow-Up 93

Chapter 8 Information Security 95
Introduction 95
Critical Importance of Information Security.....................96
Core Information Assurance Requirements.......................97
Information Has Value...97

Information Moves at Warp Speed 98
Key Assessment: What Is the State of Control? 98
Organizing the Information Security Program 100
Information Security Infrastructure and Architecture 101
Day-to-Day Operational Security 101
Cyber Incident Response Planning...102
Highlights for Follow-Up 103

Chapter 9   Physical Security and First Response.........................**107**
Introduction 107
Your Objective: An Integrated Solution 110
Physical Security at a Glance 111
Alignment with the Threat 111
Security Operations 115
The Quality of First Response 116
All Space Is Not Created Equal 117
Physical Security as a Force Multiplier 117
Equipment Removal and Value of Risk Assessments..............118
Security Riding on the Corporate Network................................118
A Note on Convergence 119
Highlights for Follow-Up 119

Chapter 10   Security Training and Education **121**
Introduction 121
Objectives of Security-Related Training and Education 122
Training Options 122
In-House Training 123
Certificate Programs 123
Academic Programs...124
Development Plan...124
Contractors and Vendors..125
Training Business Units in Security-Related Responsibilities...............125
Tracking Training Administration 126
Highlights for Follow-Up 127

Chapter 11   Communication and Awareness Programs............**129**
Introduction 129
Strategies...131

Tactics 131
Security Awareness Approaches 131
Tailoring the Message 136
Highlights for Follow-Up 137

Chapter 12 Safe and Secure Workplaces...............................**139**
Introduction 139
Predictability of Risk 140
The Policy Framework 140
Workplace Violence Policy 140
Protecting Key Executives and Key Individuals...................... 142
Highlights for Follow-Up 146

Chapter 13 Business Conduct..**149**
Introduction 149
Know Your Adversary... 149
Corporate Hygiene 150
Learning from Business Conduct Cases................................... 152
High-Level Policy or Guideline Statement 152
Checklist for Conduct of Internal Misconduct Investigations 156
Highlights for Follow-Up 160

Chapter 14 Business Resiliency...**163**
Introduction 163
Your Focus.. 163
High-Level Policy or Guideline Statement 164
Track Business Continuity Readiness....................................... 165
NFPA Standard 1600.. 166
National Response Framework 166
Regulatory Requirements... 167
Highlights for Follow-Up 167

Chapter 15 Securing Your Supply Chain **169**
Introduction 169
An Example of the Elements of Supply Chain Risk Oversight:
Customs Trade Partnership Against Terrorism, Shipment
Guard (C-TPAT) Security Criteria for Importers 170

A Focus on Supply Chain Security Has Multiple Benefits 174
Highlights for Follow-Up 175

Chapter 16 Security Measures and Metrics **177**
Introduction 177
What Are Measures and What Are Metrics? 177
What Are the Key Objectives for Our Metrics? 178
Why Measure? What Are the Benefits of Measures
and Metrics? 179
Roles and Responsibilities 180
It's about Communication and Risk Management 182
Where Do I Find the Data for My Measures and Metrics? 182
Business Alignment—Demonstrating Value to Management 183
Pitfalls to Avoid 184
Five Metrics You Might Consider 185
Conclusion 195
Highlights for Follow-Up 196

**Chapter 17 Continuous Learning: Addressing Risk
with After-Action Reviews** **197**
Introduction 197
After-Action Review (AAR) and Incident Post-Mortem 197
Know Your Audience 198
Outline for the Incident Post-Mortem Management Plan
and Briefing 198
Highlight for Follow-Up 199

Appendix A: Risk Review Elements 201
Appendix B: Security Devices, Equipment, and Installation
Labor Costs 211
Appendix C: Request for Proposals for Contract
Security Services at [Specific Company Location(s)] 219
Appendix D: Workplace Violence Incident Response Guideline 225
Appendix E: Code of Business Conduct and Ethics Template 241
Appendix F: Corporate Incident Reporting and Response Plan 255

Appendix G: Considering the Essentials: Questions
                for People and Program Development 269
About the Contributing Editor 279
About Elsevier's Security Executive Council
Risk Management Portfolio...281
Index 283

ACKNOWLEDGMENTS

Concept: Bob Hayes
Content: Security Executive Council members, faculty, and staff
Contributing Editor: George K. Campbell
Development Editor: Kathleen Kotwica

INTRODUCTION

The *Manager's Handbook for Business Security* represents the collective knowledge of the Security Executive Council's members, faculty (former security executives and subject matter experts), and staff. It has been developed to provide current best practices in security for new security managers, current security managers who are in transition from public to private or one corporate profile to another, and business executives with an interest in or responsibility for corporate security. We have sought to provide the reader with short, focused topics with a view to validate, fine-tune, or overhaul existing programs; create new programs; and assist in their growth.

While it is nearly impossible to cover the subject matter here without some clear recollection of the available literature, this is not a rehash of the many fine, comprehensive security management publications that are available through a variety of qualified sources. Instead, we have sought to provide a series of short subjects that we hope will assist readers to lead and inspire more effective security programs within their organizations.

Our goal is to challenge readers to critically evaluate their programs, better engage their business leaders, provide tools for planning and enhancing security programs, pass along some lessons learned, and, we hope, generate value-added ideas.

Our Vision for the Value of This Publication

The Security Executive Council seeks to serve current and emerging corporate security leaders with knowledge-based tools that will enhance their abilities to positively influence their companies' protection. This book contains many examples from strategic initiatives the Council has undertaken and the experiences of established security leaders. It is intended to guide the security manager with actionable essentials that our experience has shown will add value to the company and aid in the perception of the incumbent as an effective leader.

Every enterprise has its own unique culture and expectations for management and leadership. This book represents the experiences of several of your predecessor colleagues, who believe passing this knowledge on is a way to stay engaged in the profession in which we have invested much of our lives.

If you find here a lesson or two or three that help you better navigate the often stormy corporate waters, achieve an objective, or adeptly avoid a hazard, we have more than accomplished our mission.

Sincerely,
George K. Campbell, Contributing Editor

UNDERSTANDING THE BUSINESS OF SECURITY

Introduction

There is an old saying about new leaders: *For the first six months you are part of the solution, and after that you are part of the problem.* Management expects you to identify the strengths and weaknesses in the security program. If you immediately get caught up in the minutia, you will invariably lose the opportunity to craft an objective assessment and set goals for reinforcement and improvement. You need to understand where your program stands in management's plus and minus columns.

Unless you have spent significant time inside the company, you need to get grounded early on in a thorough understanding of the business. How does management convey the company mission and values, what makes it succeed, what risks could impact its value, and what metrics does it use to measure its performance?

If you fail to understand what really moves your business and its top management, you risk assessing and defining the wrong security mission and priorities.

Who Are the Key Constituents?

To succeed, there are several relationships you need to understand and develop. Who are your customers? What moves them? How do they view security? Your definition of service begins with the perceptions of these often conflicting constituencies:

- public and investor relations
- shareholders and customers
- board of directors

- senior management
- line business unit managers
- chief financial officer
- chief information officer
- general auditor
- legal counsel
- chief compliance/ethics officer
- chief risk officer
- chief marketing officer
- facilities and real estate
- employees
- security teams
- third-party vendors
- supply chain participants
- insurance carriers
- regulators and law enforcement

Many of these offices may have conflicting views of the mission and value of the security function. It is this diversity of perception that must be understood and managed.

What Issues Move Your Constituents?

All corporate organizations have a history, both pro and con. Outstanding service is an expectation, but you need to understand how prior engagements with the business have framed opinions of the competency of your team and their mission within the enterprise.

Don't miss the potentially long-held bias from a prior incident that left a bad taste. You may start out with a label that, while admittedly undeserved, requires a new understanding going forward. This is your program. Regardless of history, establishing your style versus your predecessor's is critical.

Each of these constituents has a different perspective and agenda regarding security, which mark their individual views of the following:

- What could bite? What keeps them awake at night, and what role does security play in their comfort or discomfort?
- What are the regulatory and situational environments that may impact their view of protecting the brand, the supply chain, and shareholder interests?
- What is their perspective on corporate culture, what is "right," and the shared view of "corporate integrity."
- How does security influence or fail to influence its contribution to business value?

- What are the costs of security programs versus the measurable return?[1]
- Do they see themselves as a champion or sponsor of an internal corporate service model that includes security?
- How might security be tied to their success?

Regardless of your industry or risk profile, there is a daunting array of relationships that you will have to develop and maintain to understand your constituents' needs and to know who can be your "go to" customers. It's important to understand who has no clue about security but should, who is a supporter and mentor, and who would welcome the program's untimely end—and to establish relationships with all these individuals.

Knowing if your venture has an enterprise risk management (ERM) framework may prove helpful to you in building partnerships and gathering insights from others with the same charge but a different discipline. Understanding the scope and boundaries of the security function and where it fits into an ERM framework would be helpful. Security would likely fall into the operational risk bucket of an ERM structure, as in the model depicted in Figure 1.1.

Where to Start?

Whether you have come from within the organization or just arrived from a prior job, you must thoroughly examine the organization you are leading and assess where the program is headed and where you and your constituents think it should be.

The need to assess the strengths and weaknesses of the security organization.

---

[1] In the years since the global recession began, we find ourselves challenged on all sides by this cost/value equation. Your mandate may well be to evaluate every security program from top to bottom to determine where real value is being delivered at a competitive cost. What would be the consequences of elimination? You will need to have a clear picture of the hierarchy of risks confronting the business and the levels of effort required to manage them, and failing that, to maintain a baseline of resources to respond effectively enough to minimize the consequences of a security event. There is a threshold below which you can no longer have confidence that you are prepared to respond to what you know has an increasing potential to occur. From your analysis of vulnerabilities and risk trends (see Chapter 3), you should focus on demonstrating that at various levels of security resource reduction, combined with the likely increase of risk, your ability to prevent, detect, and adequately respond will not be possible.

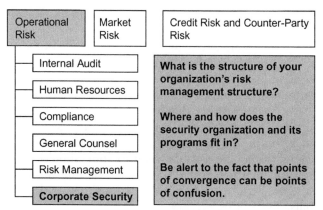

Figure 1.1 Enterprise Risk Management (ERM) Structure. An example of an ERM structure with security as part of the operational risk bucket.

Research by the Security Executive Council (SEC) has highlighted key areas that define a leading-edge security program, as listed below:

- The program is risk based.
- Services provided correspond with risks of concern to senior management and the board of directors (board-level risks).[2]
- Comprehensive program elements have been defined.
- The program has definitive costs and resource requirements that may be tracked to specific risk management and service-level objectives.

Programs are driven by at least four or more of the following defined catalysts:

- regulations
- products or brand
- incidents
- sponsors
- geography
- corporate culture
- return on investment (ROI) or value
- combinations of the above

The desired maturity model of your program needs to be consistent in all markets, business units, and functions; be sustainable in leadership[3] and executive support; provide for measurable security programs; and provide access to executive management and the board of directors when necessary. Periodic peer review assessment and validation is highly desirable. The guiding service-delivery strategy should incorporate the elements of

---

[2]See the complete description of these business risks in Chapter 3.
[3]See Chapter 4 for the desired next-generation leadership and service categories.

Unified Risk Oversight (URO)™. URO is a method of approaching risk whereby any corporate peril is identified by a team of executives or managers who represent the company's various business units and is then managed with the best interests of the business and its goals in mind. By "corporate risk" we mean not just the compiled risks of individual business units, but also the new picture created when different departments' risk considerations are brought together and compared, combined, and prioritized.

URO does sound similar to another popular term—enterprise risk management (ERM).[4] However, there is one crucial difference: oversight. While ERM identifies all risks that may impact the corporation at the board level, URO is about who or what entity is watching over it all. It calls for one centralized overseer, a component that is not necessarily an integral part of enterprise risk management. When risk is managed by the URO method, all decisions to transfer, avoid, mitigate, or accept risk are made in full consideration of their impact on all business units. Of course, this means not every decision will reflect what you may feel is the best option for security, but every decision will take security into account and seek to provide the best possible outcome for the business as a whole.

What Is the Real Cost of Security?

There are potentially significant security-related costs across the company, which are not directly attributable to your oversight. These costs tend to be obscured and accountability can be diluted. You should endeavor early on to probe and understand the scope and "ownership" of these expenses. They may more appropriately be under your control, or perhaps you should at least have some policy-based input. However, you may be perfectly happy having these expenses elsewhere, if this lowers your visible expense profile. Use Table 1.1 to calculate these costs as closely as possible. Seek out support from a trusted colleague in risk management, internal audit, or the CFO's office to capture these budgeted items.

---

[4]The rating agency Standard & Poor's (S&P) announced in 2008 a new policy requiring a review of "enterprise risk management" (ERM) practices for all corporations that it rates. Management from all companies rated by S&P in the United States now have to present and discuss their ERM practices at regular meetings with ratings analysts. ERM requires a firm to address all its risks on a firm-wide basis; this includes the full range of risks, including credit risks, market risks, as well as hazards to a firm's operations (operational risks).

Task Assignment: Assess Where Your Program Is and Where You Want It to Be

1. What clues on top management's assessment of the security program did you gather from the interview process? What expectations were expressed and how do you intend to get to the bottom of these perceptions?

2. Is there a discernable legacy that you perceive and/or are expected to address?

3. What are the key stakeholders' views of security? List your major security functions and rank their level of support among *knowledgeable consumers*. Are there common threads of positives and negatives?

4. To what extent are security programs integrated into strategic business planning?

5. How well does your—and others'—early assessment view the ability of the program to anticipate and respond to the risks it is expected to understand and address?

6. To what extent is your department proactively assessing risk and using the results of these assessments to influence policy and modify behavior?

7. What do you know of the competencies and needs of your key subordinates? What are the priorities here?

8. If you use contract services, how competent and responsive are they, both from the record and from your knowledgeable constituents' opinions? Are they cost-effective?

9. If you were told to reduce your budget by 10% or 25%, which programs would you select to cut with what anticipated consequences? If you could increase your budget by 10% or 25%, what programs would you create or enhance, and what positive results would you anticipate?

10. Given your understanding of the business and the risks confronting it, what issues most need attention in your early days? Would your conclusion surprise senior management? If so, build the business case for addressing it.

11. The security program is one of many business enablers; and, to some extent, it may serve as a guardrail. What does top management see as the culture they want to create or maintain? What is the tone they want to set?

12. How do you assess your program's ability to deliver services that contribute to management's vision in growing the business, setting behavioral standards and tone, and clearly defining a risk appetite?

13. How well does your staff understand what they are doing, how they are doing, and why they are doing it?

14. Armed with your results, what is your plan for addressing your program's shortcomings and optimizing its strengths?

Table 1.1 Security Budget Cost Elements

Cost Element	$
Direct security expenses for the most current 12 months to include all cost center items assignable to any organizational unit with security-related responsibilites. Include guard services if assignable to Facilities or some other non-security cost center.	
Estimated indirect expense by non-security personnel in support of security-related activities.	
Fire and life safety equipment required by codes and policy.	
Estimated time associated with internal and external investigations by non-security personnel.	
Annual expenses for security and compliance-related software.	
Time for security-related audits by internal/external auditors.	
Cost of unrecovered losses, business interruption, and insurance premiums.	
Average daily time for all employees to comply with physical and logical access and other required security procedures.	
Capitalization expenses for security hardware, software, vehicles, etc.	
Business unit staff time engaged in security-related risk analyses, awareness, and other training.	
Expenses associated with regulatory compliance not included above.	
Other—specific to your company.	
Total =	

Use this table to calculate the real costs of corporate security within an organization.

The Security Program Review

One of the earliest discussions you should have with your boss is to indicate your intention to do a top-down review of the security program to include interviews with internal customers. If you have been brought in to fix perceived problems, your objective need analysis be expected. If they think nothing is broken, you still need to find the weak spots and strengths, because they are there regardless of opinions on high. Part of this discussion should cover your flexibility to address needs with new resources, your ability to increase employee headcount if needed, and other support for "making adjustments" with existing staff. If you are going to build a team, management needs to be on board from day one.

If your program is largely outsourced, convey your intentions to the vendor(s). Get feedback from knowledgeable internal parties. Assess cost against demonstrable performance. Review any existing contracts with your legal department to determine your ability to modify terms or make necessary adjustments.

Keep in mind that the only contact the average employee or visitor will ever have with security is that security officer or contract guard at some access point, on the phone when their access badge doesn't work, or when there is a minor incident. If this first line of response fails to represent the professionalism expected of a company representative, your organization has a problem. Particularly where low-bid guard force vendors are employed, this potential should be assessed early and be high on your list of issues. See Chapter 5 for some thoughts on this.

This is an ideal time to supplement your own time with an internal detailee, perhaps from the internal audit group, human resources, or a business unit resource with experience in organizational reviews. The alternative is to use a qualified consultant with whom you are familiar and who will provide objective credibility to your conclusions. Plan to get this initial review done in your first 90 days, because you will get overwhelmed with normal business if you wait.

It's important that you let your team know your objectives early on, and that they will be key players in whatever steps you will employ to take the program to the next level.

What Is the "Next Level?"

The assessment process reveals a documented baseline. If expectations are high for incremental improvements, you will have some targets set for you. This is also true if downsizing is the expectation. However, when you are seen as the "expert," the next level is about bringing about perceived value, delivering measurably improved performance, and connecting in substantive ways with the company's real business objectives.

If you were seen as really successful in connecting security mission to fundamental corporate value, isn't it possible that you might be challenged to take a broader and, perhaps, more business-centric set of responsibilities?

Build the Business Case for Crafting a Measurably Effective Security Program

If you poll your management and stakeholders as well as a sample of line employees, you will likely get a variety of answers to the question, "Why do we have a security program here?" The good news is that your selection for the job is a clear statement that senior management understands the need for a security program on some level. Nevertheless, they may not have a full appreciation for the breadth and depth of contributions your organization may, or should, offer. Your business plan will need to take into consideration each of these benefits and the degree to which they are prioritized and delivered with competence. Consider the list of potential benefits from a proactive security program (see Table 1.2), and ask selected stakeholders to rank them and comment on their opinion(s).

We acknowledge the size and scope of the list. That goes with your portfolio of responsibilities, regardless of the degree to which you share leadership for "corporate security' with others in the governance team. These are the issues that signify the degree to which your programs are seen as an integral part of the business by those who are paying for the services you offer. If these customers do not perceive a benefit, it may be that they have never been prompted to consider where they could see value. If others see a benefit, how can you leverage that understanding to the doubting constituency? Remember, in the great game of corporate reorganizations, you never know who your next boss might be.

Consider the checklist in Table 1.2 and commence filling in where the security program contributes to each of these areas in *measurable* ways. Keep track of areas in need of improvement. Test the results with colleagues in the business. Work towards an understanding of your mission and their needs. The result of this analysis is an assessment of your program's alignment with the business. Critically evaluate the feedback. Take heed of where they see you to be *unconnected* with their concept of value. Also, take note of where some see you as very connected and why.

Given the possibility that many of those managers you have selected to be interviewed have never thought about or been challenged on the security program value connection, you may need to be prepared to provide a brief summary of how your programs deliver on each of the potential benefits in this list. Be prepared with real, measurable examples. If you have the

Table 1.2 Perceived Benefits of Corporate Security Programs

Perceived Benefits of Corporate Security Programs	High			Low		Comments
	5	4	3	2	1	
Enhance investor, shareholder, and customer or market confidence						
Promote integrity in business						
Preserve financial success						
Provide a competitive edge by enabling peace of mind						
Maintain an informed, engaged senior management						
Reduced risk in business process reduces loss experience						
Regulatory/legal requirements met at optimum cost						
Reduced scrutiny by regulators						
Proactively eliminate vulnerability in business process						
Deter threats						
Reduce the likelihood of events with the potential for adverse impact						
Reduce risk of service disruption						
Identify, mitigate, and/or avoid risky relationships						
Maintain a safe, secure, and productive work environment						
Fiduciary responsibility protection						
Recapture lost assets						
Reduce insurance costs						
Enhance community standing						
Educate employees						
Protect and enhance the brand						
Other? (keyed to your industry)						

Use this table to measure and track how security contributes to an organization in a quantifiable way.

metrics, lay them out so the manager can be more informed and honest in his or her response. Use the time to educate managers on the potential for a real business engagement.

Steps in Building the Business Case

It is highly likely that your company requires an annual or multi-year business plan of its various units, nevertheless you will need one to identify your priorities and chart your course. Demonstrate to senior management that you have a vision for what needs to be done in your core programs and to be more aligned with key business issues. Set forth why and with what resources you will take essential first steps in gaining their confidence and buy-in for your plans.

One approach to developing your plan is through the use of a business strategy map, which is commonly used in many businesses today. If you are not familiar with a strategy map, the *Harvard Business Review* published an article entitled "Having Trouble with Your Strategy? Then Map It" in its October 2000 issue. It serves as a helpful overview of the process. The attached map[5] (see Figure 1.2) is one developed from the many messages contained in this thesis, and your unique company requirements and program schedule should drive its contents.

Another approach to business planning is portrayed in Figure 1.3. Each step is described as follows.

1. *Assess the program:* You are in this job because management has concerns, seeks a new level for the program, or has some other agenda that you should understand at this point. This first step sets the stage and provides the foundation for the business plan.

   1.1. Your business strategy must reflect and demonstrate an understanding of the overall business strategy and how your plans will align and support the overarching corporate strategy.

   1.2. Many of your priorities will focus upon the issues raised in customer feedback sessions. Having sought them, there will be an expectation that your plan will address them on some level.

   1.3. Corporate culture and management style represent tremendous and often overlooked influences on the success of the security program and the individual who leads it.

---

[5]Thanks to Michael Ennis, formerly of Fidelity Corporate Security, for this diagram.

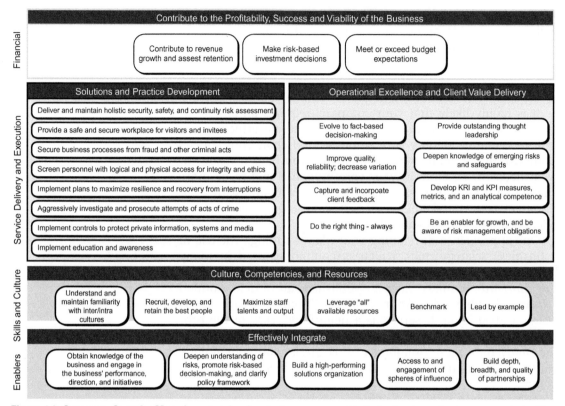

Figure 1.2 Corporate Security Map. An example of a strategy map used to help develop a business case to justify a security program within an organization.

1.4. The competencies and shortcomings of your inherited staff (or vendors) obviously require your honest assessment, as will your approach to filling any gaps. Consider utilizing your human resource contact to assist in this process.

1.5. This initial assessment of risk clearly will place the process set forth in Chapter 3, "Risk Assessment and Mitigation," the core of your way forward. Your intent here is to ensure that the business plan addresses prioritized risks on your watch. Note any shared risks—those where security partners with one or more other organizational units for risk management.

1.6. Your assessment of the policy infrastructure is a critical step, inasmuch as this provides the legal framework and a good measure of the business case for security programs. "Policy" is a dirty word in many corporate cultures. However, in these cultures, there still are rules,

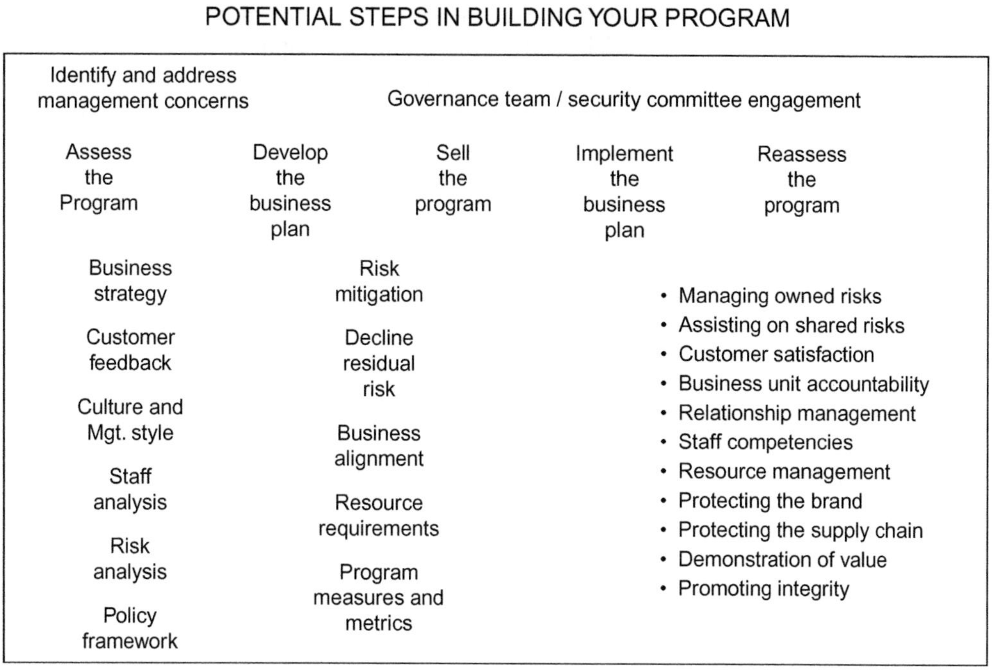
POTENTIAL STEPS IN BUILDING YOUR PROGRAM
Identify and address management concerns
Governance team / security committee engagement
Assess the Program
Develop the business plan
Sell the program
Implement the business plan
Reassess the program
Business strategy
Customer feedback
Culture and Mgt. style
Staff analysis
Risk analysis
Policy framework
Risk mitigation
Decline residual risk
Business alignment
Resource requirements
Program measures and metrics
• Managing owned risks
• Assisting on shared risks
• Customer satisfaction
• Business unit accountability
• Relationship management
• Staff competencies
• Resource management
• Protecting the brand
• Protecting the supply chain
• Demonstration of value
• Promoting integrity

Figure 1.3 Potential Steps in Building Your Program. An alternative approach to building a security program.

practices, or guidelines. Use whatever term works in your culture.

2. *Develop the business plan:* As noted above, there may be a preset format to follow, but this high-level view may accommodate almost any approach. As we note throughout, you are here because the company needs your special expertise to address a family of risks they appreciate but may not fully comprehend. This plan will affirm those they recognize and introduce and prioritize those you have uncovered in your review.
   - **2.1.** Your risk mitigation strategy is structured to address the risk analysis set forth in Step 1.
   - **2.2.** A cautionary note on *residual risk*. These are risks on the playing field that you are choosing to tell management are *not* on your watch but should be assigned elsewhere. Clearly, you need to assign the management of these risks to others in better positions (in terms of ownership, via resource or accountability) to effectuate responsive risk-mitigation tactics. For example, you may understand that poor site selection and

equipping of property are contributing to security risks, but the facilities organization neither consults nor desires your contributions to site protection—at least until a crisis occurs. You will find a number of these examples in various corners of the business; but without the charter and resources to deal with them, decline to involve them in your plan and lay out your rationale.

2.3. As we will discuss in many instances in this book, aligning your program with the overall corporate business strategy is a key element in delivering real value to the enterprise. Your understanding of the company business strategy and culture provide direction on how to focus your priorities for strengthening and improving the program. Clearly, your varied constituents' perceived value of security programs as gleaned earlier must influence your plan in responsive ways. This is especially true if those perceptions demonstrate an ignorance of risk that must be addressed in your marketing strategy. Do not miss the opportunity to consider the value of engagement of a security committee or, at a minimum, partnering with the corporate governance team as an integral part of the plan. When you both demonstrate a willingness to collaborate, the common sense conclusion is that managing risk is a shared responsibility.

2.4. Resource requirements and program measurements are obvious elements of any plan and particularly critical for the new security leader crafting the way forward. Resources apply to the budget strategy you select at this stage of business planning. You may want to use your findings to make a strong move for additional resources, where they clearly support improved risk management and security value. Alternatively, you might want to consider a year of positioning the program and moving existing resources in ways that better serve your priorities.

2.5. Whatever you select for program content, having measures and metrics to support progress and results against specified objectives are absolutely essential. See Security and Metrics chapter for more on metrics.

3. *Sell, implement, and re-assess:* These are the key ingredients of any business plan. Remember that you are in competition for scarce resources and annually (at a minimum) you have to convince management of the necessity of security's products and services.

3.1. Sell the program: Regardless of format, develop your plan in sufficient detail to incorporate the tactics of selling your conclusions and solutions. *Do not tie success to objectives that have not been fulfilled by the availability of new or redirected resources.* In Chapter 5 we discuss marketing the security program and the many aspects of execution. Again, note the potential relationship to a security committee, which you may formally establish with key stakeholders or which may be a bi-directional advisory body.

3.2. Implement the plan: This step involves your ability to effectively utilize the resources you have been able to retain or enhance. There is also the requirement to prioritize execution to match available resources. *At the heart of your plan must be a principle of shared responsibility for protection with line business units and other governance bodies.* Invariably, the risks you have targeted in your plan must be addressed at several levels of execution, often with the business unit comprising the front line of defense. The multiple plan-implementation topics at the lower right of the chart in Figure 1.3 are recommended elements of any comprehensive security strategy, but you likely will decide to focus on some more than others in the shorter term.

3.3. Reassess the program: Your assessment of the security team developed in Step 1 will identify both the potential stars and those with whom you have concerns. Drill down with HR on the latter. Review prior performance reviews, and potential voids in them, for all individuals. Determine where you need to fill gaps, and probe the competencies and desires of the standouts. Build a working relationship with HR now, and it will pay dividends as you build your team. You will also benefit from a trusting relationship with HR when those challenging internal business-conduct cases arise.

In your assessment of strengths and weaknesses in programs and personnel, you will invariably identify the need for new, improved, or different skills. Prioritize and build them into your plan. Make the business case for each one. This is an opportunity to absorb some additions with headcount reductions in other programs.

Also, when you are doing your initial feedback sessions with business unit leaders, encourage them to suggest one of their stars who they think would make a good coach for those on your team in need of this support. If there is a particular program you need to fix or want to launch, consider reaching into a business unit or other governance organization for an intra-business temporary duty yonder (TDY) assignment. These are effective ways to build bridges with the business without adding to budget or headcount.

Identify, test, and develop your successor(s). You owe yourself a bench that finds several motivated and increasingly qualified personnel in line for key positions. Push succession planning downward across the organization. Combine planning with competency analysis to emphasize the development plans for high-profile successors.

If you are reliant upon contractors, take ownership for succession. If you identify an especially effective leader in the vendor team, guarantee that that individual is slated to be assigned to a new, potentially high-value target. Make your contract protect key individuals or be prepared to offer them employment.

If your early feedback from the boss has been supportive of additional headcount or contract resources, carefully lay out your prioritized needs and the business case for each one. Otherwise, make this part of your longer-term plan. Don't be afraid to give "stretch" assignments to those on board whom you have identified as part of the future team. On the other hand, if your program assessment uncovers work of nominal value, consider redeployment of those individuals to priority assignments where skills and jobs match. Your ability to incorporate appropriate measures of success will influence the quality of the reassessment process.

THE BOTTOM LINE: If you don't know your company's business and what makes it successful, you don't understand the risks and cannot adequately define your mission. Define it and then build your business strategy around adding real and perceived value.

Highlights for Follow-Up

- Who are the two or three senior people you have met who see value in corporate security and understand what you want to accomplish? What is your plan for developing these relationships?

- Based on your review and feedback from constituents, what is the most serious shortcoming of the program? What is your plan to address this, and on what schedule?
- Who are the two strongest players on your team, and how do you propose to use them to measurably improve the program?
- Who are your weakest players, and what is your plan to address their weaknesses?
- Who among your constituents are going to be the most difficult to satisfy, and why? How are you going to address this need?
- If you had to identify one learning experience from your first 90 days, what would it be, and how will it influence your business plan and priorities?

2

SECURITY LEADERSHIP
Establishing Yourself and Moving the
Program Forward

Introduction

What produces an effective leader in your particular company? There are competencies and styles that work well in one culture and are less effective in others. Do you understand yours? Where is a model you could emulate? Is there a positive or negative legacy you need to address? What are your team's expectations for a leader they can respect?

Business Value

A good leader will manage a team that is respectful, knowledgeable and committed to service excellence. Leadership in anticipating and responding to risk, influencing policy, and communicating on the shared responsibility for asset protection are success factors for the shareholders of the company.

The Essentials

This chapter focuses on three interrelated, high-level views of security leadership: leadership competencies, keys to organizational influence and impact, and the "next generation security leader." Each grouping focuses on security leadership through a different lens of personal impact, organizational impact, and next generation security skills.

The first view offers nine competencies the individual should bring to the job and further develop as part of a planned growth strategy. The second view of security leadership summarizes five measures of influence that are clearly reflective of organizational leadership, and the third displays 65 knowledge elements and skills that serve to enhance corporate leadership. This latter inventory enables rating yourself against a next generation model as well as allowing you to outline the knowledge and skills you seek to hire in order to complement the team.

Leadership Competencies

The successful security executive is a leader in a variety of critically important ways:

1. Team leader—First and foremost, you are the leader of the security team. Inspire them to learn, excel, and be customer focused. Hire the best. Avoid those who seek to be the corporate cop. Only engage those contractors who are capable of understanding the corporate culture and your vision for the program.
2. Thought leader and subject matter expert—Our profession brings unique expertise to the organization. You need to consider how this knowledge can be blended into corporate strategy and tactics.
3. Business enabler and creative problem-solver—We need to support corporate efforts in succeeding in the competitive marketplace. We do this by enabling the business to engage in processes that might otherwise be too risky.
4. Business strategist and advisor—You must understand the businesses you support! Security's goals reflect the goals and plans of the company, and your ability to lead will be tied to your ability to engage business management on their own terms.
5. Risk management guide—Risk is why you have a job. You have a unique perspective; you see gaps in controls from your risk assessments and incident post-mortems. Your programs provide an ability to connect the dots on risk-related issues that others do not have. Anticipate! Operate the security risk radar and use your pulpit to assure awareness.
6. Influencer of enterprise policy—As a leader, you will be in a position to influence the scope and content of a core set of risk management policies or guidelines. Communicate! Act as a positive change agent on behalf of organizational protection.
7. Relationship manager—An effective working relationship with business unit managers at all levels is a key element in your protection strategy. From this collaborative foundation, you may influence business strategy and better ensure issue resolution.
8. Risk group and security committee leadership—You are a member of the corporate governance team and see risk in unique ways. Work closely with legal, audit, human

resources, risk management, and others to gain perspective on risk and to influence risk management strategy.

9. Management model—You model the behavior essential to a company that believes and acts with integrity. You lead your team to excel and practice quality in their craft.

Note the absence of characteristics that resemble a command and control orientation. While knowledgeable command is essential in a crisis, security is effective only when it is embedded in business process and ownership for secure operations is shared with business unit managers and an aware employee population. Your perceived authority is embedded in your corporate accountability; and, when security assumes a posture of "corporate cop," you may stray from being seen as a teammate and enabler. Leadership that proactively aligns security with business objectives and brand protection will add measurable value and have strong management support for its programs.

> "Leadership is the art of accomplishing more than the science of management says is possible." —Former secretary of state Colin Powell

Keys to Organizational Influence and Impact

If we were able to boil success down to a few factors that will most likely assure your ability to be an influential leader and make results happen because you have a responsive audience, consider the following (which we will discuss further in Chapter 5, "Marketing the Security Program to the Business," and Chapter 6, "Organizational Models").

1. *A framework of security policies explicitly endorsed by senior management*—Sell a manageable set of high-level policy statements to senior management. For example, "We will provide safe and secure workplaces for our employees and visitors." Engage the CEO and others. Who can argue against that statement, which is based in employment law? The follow-up question is, what programs at what cost will ensure that this policy will be met? You may find yourself in a culture that abhors the perceived strictures of "policy." In that case, label these factors as business principles, jurisdictions, guidelines, or program objectives. The point is that you get buy-in for those few high-level statements that enable goal-setting and a foundation of expectations. See

Chapter 6, "Organizational Models," for a more complete discussion on this factor.

Why is this valid?

An accepted policy framework articulates management expectations. As such, it supports your definition of the work to be performed in order to deliver on each one. An understanding of the work supports defensible alternatives to staffing and budget development.

2. *A core management philosophy that holds line managers accountable for protecting the firm*—Security is everybody's job, and you are there to provide leadership, expertise, a workable infrastructure, and the tools to enable line managers to share this important responsibility. Furthermore, management must understand that protecting the company and its shareholders is everyone's job.

Why is this valid?

If they expect you to protect the company, update your resume. You are an enabler of their fiduciary responsibility to protect the shareholders of the company. You are the expert, the first responder, but the rest of management are the custodians of corporate assets.

What tone has management set with regard to responsibility for managing risk? This notion of delivered and accepted accountability is critical to any security executive's success. Where the tone across the business is one of shared responsibility and accountability, security becomes the navigator and guide, providing tools and leadership while anticipating risk and being prepared.

3. *A clearly established role in the corporate risk management program*—Risk is why they hired you. You know about risks that the rest of the governance team likely hasn't ever considered. Get on the team and lead in your area(s) of expertise. Use metrics to track trends and measure the results of security strategies. Collaborate on solutions with your colleagues.

Why is this valid?

Consider this: there is a high-level discussion of the risks confronting the company and nobody thought to invite you or ask for your input. "Security" is about the absence of risk! Without your perspective, they don't have an actionable handle on risk.

4. *A qualitative risk analysis and reporting program*—Security generates lots of data on a variety of risks. Organize it. Analyze it. Learn what contributed to incidents and identify the

vulnerabilities. Inform management and identify what steps should be taken to mitigate future problems. "Qualitative" means your findings are *actionable*. This is where you learn to influence managers and determine what their individual hot buttons are in order to make results happen.

Why is this valid?

You cannot lead if you are not aware of what could happen, given the presence of vulnerability in business process. You are not leading if you fail to understand how to inform your various constituencies. This is about your ability to influence policy and behavior with the quality information you possess.

5. *A comprehensive communication and risk awareness program*—The notion of delegated responsibility for secure operations is introduced above. This completes the circle by assuring that corporate security takes what it learns and passes it on to the accountable people who are in the position to take action. Remember that communication is a two-way street. Provide the means for comfortable reporting of concerns by your constituents to your organization.

Why is this valid?

This closes the loop. You have a framework for expectations, the means to learn where the risks reside, a venue to communicate your concerns and advice, and now you need to give accountable personnel the tools to execute *their* responsibilities. Your influence is measured by the willingness of the business to understand these responsibilities and to accept the work that supports the protection strategy.

6. *Engagement of the C-suite*—You have access to the top, you see the results of your services or messages implicitly or explicitly in business plans, and you see responsive behavior from the top and elsewhere in the organization.

Why is this valid?

Without top management's engagement, the security program is an orphan.

7. *The value of partnerships*—You have positive relationships with control groups (legal, HR, risk, and audit) and business unit line management.

Why is this valid?

Alliances and collaboration with the governance team yields far better knowledge of risk and maximizes the potential for results. Partnering with line business managers builds trust and enables the notion of shared responsibility for asset protection.

The Next Generation Security Leader

The Security Executive Council (SEC) polled successful security managers—members and faculty—and discovered six factors that frame a security leadership profile (see Figure 2.1). These are highlighted in the following discussion, which provides a comprehensive view of the knowledge, competencies, and skills we bring to our role as business security leaders and those we must cultivate to maximize our value and impact within our organization. This picture graphically displays the diversity and complexity of our leadership roles and challenges us to evaluate our strengths and opportunities for growth. Obviously, the nature of the businesses you serve will influence your assessment, since some elements may be more critical to success than others.

Government backgrounds, for example, provide knowledge of leadership, the legal framework, investigations, and responsiveness. Information technology (IT) security skills help in protection of critical information in both digital and printed formats. Business backgrounds help to align security value and business goals. A career in corporate security ensures a security leader's intimate knowledge of a company. Executive leadership skills produce a focus on business results. Awareness of emerging issues helps to maintain situational readiness.

How well do you and your staff measure up to the security leader of the future? Try this self-test. Evaluate yourself against each of the skills identified in Figure 2.1. Give yourself 3 points for skills that you already possess (rate *E* for expert). Give yourself 2 points for skills that you can brush up on pretty quickly (rate *A* for adequate). For a skill that needs improvement, score 1 point (rate *I* for needs improvement). If there is a skill that you have no experience with and know nothing about, mark down a zero (rate *M* for missing).

When you finish count up your points. Give yourself an additional point, up to a maximum of 5 points, for every year of experience you have in one of the following fields: law enforcement, IT, business, and security.

Divide your score by 2 to get your "Next Generation" score. Those scoring 90 to 100 points should consider themselves ready to take on the challenges of 21st century security. A score from 80 to 89 points limits the role and level of your position in

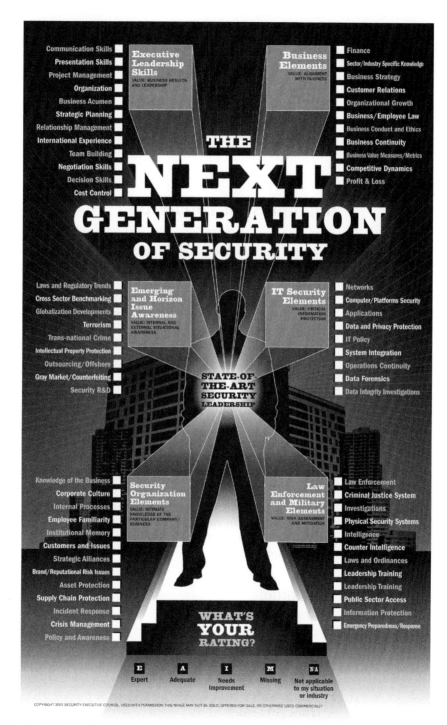

Figure 2.1 The Next Generation Security Leader. Six factors that frame a security leadership profile.

the organization. If you scored below 80, you may be risking your future. You should take steps now to expand your range of skills.

THE BOTTOM LINE: Management involves power by position. Leadership involves power by influence.

Highlights for Follow-Up

- If you accept the leadership competencies discussed above, where do you see your strengths and weaknesses? Which of these represents your best opportunity for influence and leadership in your first six months to a year on the job?
- If you have arrived at this position on your own merits, you know where you need to grow and how to commence leading while this growth unfolds. Find a mentor who knows the business and has a reputation for being a real leader that people want to follow. What characteristics does he or she possess that you might emulate?
- Keep your eye on the target. Listen and learn how to get things done in your corporate culture. A successful security program leverages results from its understanding of the culture.
- Never forget that those you lead are watching.
- Where does the program stand with regard to the five keys to leadership and influence? Which of these do you believe are the most important for your business planning? Which are most important for your personal development?
- What did you learn about yourself and your needs from your Next Generation score?

Key Terms

- Effective leader
- Core competencies
- Security model
- Communication policy
- Next generation security leader
- Team leader
- Thought leader
- Business enabler

- Risk management
- Security policies
- Framework
- Qualitative analysis
- Program management
- Risk awareness
- Security leadership
- Leadership competencies
- Organizational influence and impact

3

RISK ASSESSMENT AND MITIGATION

Introduction

If management, your directors, and insurers did not see the need to manage the types of risk they see—under your watch—you would not be here.

Business Value

Business unit management likely does not fully appreciate the depth and breadth of risk that you will understand. Your department's programs will enable the business to do what would otherwise be too risky. Measure and communicate that value.

The Essentials

Depending on the scope of your security responsibilities, there are several relatively common business-based vulnerabilities and risk exposures that you should consider in your risk assessment strategy:

1. Absence or weakness of effective business controls—combined impact of employee empowerment, business velocity, and growth on reliability of controls and effective care
2. Ethical lapses by employees in key positions—maintenance of reputation and avoidance of corporate liability
3. The corporation as a property owner—crime, workplace violence, and premises liability
4. Business interruption—failure to plan and be effectively prepared
5. Adequacy of logical and physical access controls—unauthorized access to our facilities and proprietary information
6. Connectivity and reliability of safeguards—the company's reliance on technology and critical pathways
7. Lack of business—process-based ownership of security

8. Globalization of the business—internationalization of risk
9. Corporate visibility—the company and key executives as high-profile targets
10. Inadequate focus on security-related risk—maintenance of awareness on risk dynamics

Assessing Viable Threats

You can find any number of well-done articles on threat assessment. The challenge is defining which threats are real for your organization now and based on where they are going in their evolving business plan. Threat assessment is a critically important product of the security organization, because nobody else has a clue, and no one is doing it in your space. On-line threat-reporting security resources are numerous, but they can only generalize and do little that is specific to your company, unless you have a tailored and contracted service at your disposal.

Threat is the source of the risk. The diverse threats confronting our businesses are dynamic, not static. They may be natural events beyond our control, man-made errors, accidents, or criminal acts, and there are deficiencies in your system of internal controls or other risky business practices. When we talk about threats, we often hear, *But it hasn't happened here.* This may be true, but as you see in Figure 3.1, there are incremental steps in threat likelihood, and the more exposed you are to *exploitable vulnerabilities*, the greater the likelihood of a threat

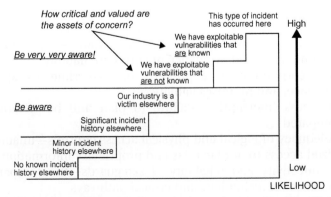

Threat assessment–measuring likelihood

Figure 3.1 A representation of the incremental steps in measuring threat likelihood.

becoming a reality. That situation underscores the critical need for on-going risk and vulnerability assessments, with particular attention to the threat from the knowledgeable insider.

Vulnerability Assessment

Drilling down within risk assessment finds the real focus of a follow-up strategy: nailing down how exposed or vulnerable a critical process or asset is to compromise or loss. Vulnerabilities are flaws in protection that may be exploited by an adversary, or a set of conditions that contribute to protection system failure. If there is a single compulsory exercise for the asset custodian and the security team, it is to have an on-going program of identifying vulnerability to critical assets and business processes from specified threats. It's an interesting exercise to sit with a business process owner and ask, "If you wanted to [name the attack] this asset, how would you do it and avoid detection?" The incident post-mortem is an ideal opportunity to identify vulnerability with one very notable exception: *it's too late.*

Vulnerability is broad in scope and may be measured outright or with opportunities for compromise estimated. Building weaknesses are exploitable and measurable. Access to the asset (s) is measurable. Probability of detection is measurable. Protection systems can be disarmed, bypassed, or simply overlooked. People in key positions make mistakes, may be compromised, or have dishonest objectives of their own. If redundancies are not in place, you can measure the ability of employee response to pre-planned events. You can apply covert and overt tests to measure effectiveness of safeguards. In some cases, you may want to employ trusted outside experts to test your security measures under carefully controlled conditions.

Risk within business activities comes in many flavors. The keys to controlling these varied risks are to understand the source of the threat to specific assets, where the gaps in protection may be found, and what kinds of controls need to be in place to address these vulnerabilities and mitigate these risks.

> The probability of experiencing a major incident is primarily determined by the strength of the controls applied to an environment. —Information Security Forum

Board-Level Risk and Security Program Response Research

Enterprise risk assessments (ERA) are becoming more common. Soon, every major corporation will have conducted an internal review or will have engaged outside contractors to conduct an assessment. Inevitably, this assessment will be presented to the board of directors or the executive management team. Internal executives will be assigned to each risk and will be required to report periodically to the board on progress to mitigate the risk. This pattern is being repeated across the United States and across the globe, and both members and non-members of the Security Executive Council have observed it. The Council wanted to address this trend by creating a tool that members could use in presentations to the board of directors or senior management.

This project has resulted in a successful graphic representation of the board-level risks an organization may face, and the security processes and programs designed to mitigate them. The Board-Level Risk Diagram sample that follows (see Figure 3.2) facilitates executive management's understanding of board risk and the role security plays in reducing it.

The methodology employed involved numerous completed ERAs provided by both member and non-member companies, and several other ERA examples were found through research. All ERAs were analyzed for commonality, and their content was categorized into eight Council-identified board-level risk topic areas. Faculty and staff were asked to review the risk areas and report on any security programs or services provided to their companies, which would remove or reduce the board-level risk.

The Board-Level Risk Diagram can be modified to present the overall ERA security response to the board in a succinct and quickly understandable manner. The concept chart can also be used to quickly position the value of security on par with any other staff group addressing major risks to the corporation. It may also be used for staff and departmental training and awareness of the board-level risks, as well as the role the department plays removing or reducing them. For companies in which an ERA has not been completed, security directors have reported this chart has been effective in establishing security as a leader in identifying and communicating how departmental services add to board-level value.

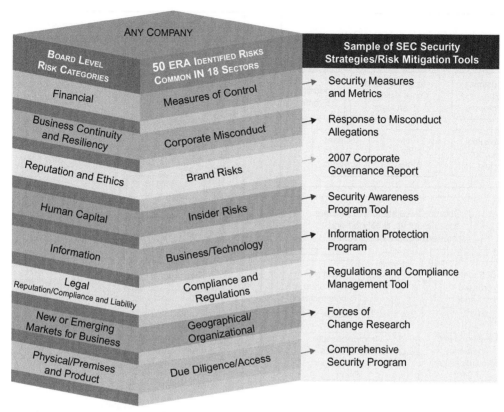

Figure 3.2 Solutions to Reduce Board-Level Risk. A graphical representation of the eight board-level risk categories.

A Risk Quantification Process

Having a list of security-related business risks and their associated countermeasures is an essential part of the risk management process. However, understanding how to quantify those risks to set priorities is equally important. The flow chart in Figure 3.3 lays out one approach to the analytical process associated with risk exposure quantification.

In Step 1 of the diagram in Figure 3.3, the process commences with an inventory of business risk information available from internal risk management (values and volume impacts, and insurance data), industry risk data, security's risk and hazard data, known incident data from all governance functions, and incident post-mortem outputs. These profiles enable selection of a more likely set of single-incident risk scenarios. Based on their unique consequences, you now have one or several types of incidents you can value.

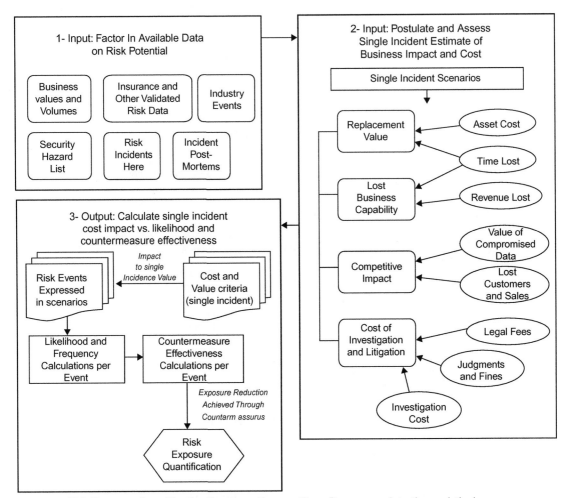

Figure 3.3 Risk Exposure Quantification Strategy—Process Flow. One approach to the analytical process associated with risk exposure quantification.

These scenarios are forwarded to the second step to postulate multiple factors related to the potential consequences and impact of a single incident of the specified type. Estimates of cost may be made for each scenario using a worst-case baseline, such as total loss of a known valued asset, or a less-consequential result, such as an outage for a specified time. Impact costs may be estimated by engaging the business unit, which typically has loss-impact data calculations as part of the contingency planning baseline. Other estimates may be merely logical plug-ins supported by prior-event data.

The single-incident cost estimates are then processed through the filter of the effectiveness of the countermeasures that are in place for each risk event. For example, backup resources are in place to respond to a natural disaster outage, and the time to recover may be reliably estimated through prior tests. That recovery time and other impacts may also be reliably cost estimated. You will find your CFO and risk management or insurance offices most helpful in identifying insurance industry data associated with various security incidents, scoping single incident costs to risk impacts, as well as approaches to potential cost to various security scenarios.

Likelihood of an incident is a measure of knowledge of your vulnerability to specific breaches based on test data, known downtimes, audit data on unresolved business process deficiencies, and increased frequency of similar events within your industry or nearby. Effectiveness of countermeasures is also based on test data. The known resilience or identified weaknesses of the countermeasures available in your scenario will drive your likelihood estimates. For example, what if this process were to postulate a much wider impact of the disaster that limited or eliminated the backup capability in our outage scenario above?

You will find that your best likelihood measure used for influential impact will be your periodic testing of the effectiveness of various safeguards applied by your resources and those employed within business units, particularly where they are required by standard or policy. Several key areas of measurement include:

- the perceived value or attractiveness of the object of protection;
- the degree of probable success in penetrating a specific countermeasure; and
- the greater the knowledge of that vulnerability within the population, the greater the likelihood of successful attack.

Each of these concepts may be verified by testing.

There are a variety of risk-quantification tools available through risk-management organizations and vendors. This is but one exercise that may be engaged in by a governance team approach or in cooperation with the potentially affected business units.

The bottom line is the need to understand the potential impact of the higher-likelihood risk events in financial and other relevant terms.

More in-depth discussions may be found in the ASIS International *General Security Risk Assessment Guideline*[1] and in the Institute of Internal Auditors booklet *Business Risk Assessment*.[2]

---

[1]ASIS International, Alexandria, VA, 2003.
[2]David McNamee, Institute of Internal Auditors, Altamonte Springs, FL, October, 1998.

The chart in Table 3.1, developed by Sandy Sandquist, director of global security at General Mills, provides an excellent way to spell out sets of risk scenarios and estimate impact in financial and operational terms. Use it to specify your estimate of risks appropriate to your assessment of likely exposure to the business. In this example, "High" is equal to or greater than $100 million; "Medium" is between $10 and $100 million; and "Low" is equal to or less than $10 million. Use different impact values to suit your own risk concerns.

A Risk Management-Based Concept of Operations

A simple and straightforward way to approach security risk mitigation is to think of it in three progressive levels: anticipation, preparation, and execution.

1. *Anticipation*—Risk is dynamic. Perhaps more than another business executive, the CSO is paid to anticipate risk, to think and understand "what if," and to have in place a credible program to qualify viable threats. This program involves the following elements:

    the ability to maintain an actionable threat profile utilizing credible local and international resources and assets;

    the ability to install and maintain an integrated set of security controls that provide real-time indications of risk—key risk indicators (KRIs);

    the ability to *reliably* document and analyze security/risk events to identify and mitigate vulnerabilities and develop improved response capabilities that are tracked and monitored—key performance indicators (KPIs);

    the ability to be thoroughly knowledgeable in the capabilities and competencies of security assets; and

    the ability to attract and retain a customer-responsive cadre of protection assets.

2. *Preparation*—There are three ways we learn the presence of risk: (1) an unanticipated event; (2) we probed and discovered conditions that could result in an event, and we did not follow-up; and (3) we probed, discovered, and closed the gap. Credible anticipation imposes an obligation to be prepared for the "what ifs." Preparation involves, but is not limited to, the following:

    the ability to influence the organization and its leadership so that response capabilities are in place and tested;

Table 3.1 Corporate Security Potential Impact/Cost

Corporate Security Issues/Risks with Potential Impact Greater Than $X Million Prior to Any Mitigation Efforts		
Major Issue/Risk	*Select Impact**	*Possible Outcome*
Catastrophic loss of key staff in single event	☐ High ☐ Medium ☐ Low	☐ Loss of key personnel ☐ Delay or loss of new product launch ☐ Lawsuits ☐ Loss of investor confidence
Terrorism—regional event	☐ High ☐ Medium ☐ Low	☐ Loss of use of business-critical facility and employee logistics ☐ Possible loss of employee lives ☐ Loss of regional workforce ☐ Evacuation of all nearby businesses/residences ☐ Long recovery time with major business interruption
Workplace violence	☐ High ☐ Medium ☐ Low	☐ Possible loss of employee lives ☐ Temporary interruption with certain products if facility is sole supplier ☐ Negative publicity ☐ Adverse litigation
Nationalization of operation (international)	☐ High ☐ Medium ☐ Low	☐ Loss of use of production facility ☐ If plant is sole supplier, out of market with certain products ☐ Loss of business with minimum compensation ☐ Loss of proprietary business process to competition
Product tampering resulting in death or serious injury	☐ High ☐ Medium ☐ Low	☐ Negative brand impact ☐ Possible loss of employee lives ☐ Possible loss of life by general public ☐ Public lawsuits ☐ Negative publicity
Product tampering—non-Company product but in associated category	☐ High ☐ Medium ☐ Low	☐ Negative brand impact ☐ Possible loss of life ☐ Slow business process recovery ☐ Public lawsuits ☐ Negative publicity
Theft and publication of customer lists with private data	☐ High ☐ Medium ☐ Low	☐ Negative brand impact ☐ Cost to protect customer privacy going forward ☐ Adverse litigation ☐ Regulatory sanctions
Loss of IT systems from malicious act	☐ High ☐ Medium ☐ Low	☐ Interruption to market share ☐ Major impact on manufacturing, sourcing, and sales ☐ Loss of investor confidence ☐ Major cost of alternate site and restoration of data

an integrated set of security elements keyed to the unique and likely threats previously identified;

the ability to train the dispersed safety or security assets to a level consistent with planned standards of incident response; and

the ability to *objectively* test all critical defenses and response capabilities and implement corrective actions.

3. *Execution*—This phase of the concept of operations relies on the tested competence of security assets you have established to respond to risk events:

the ability to lead as a risk event unfolds;

the ability to respond in such timely and effective ways that the risk event is mitigated with minimal loss or damage to corporate assets;

the ability to learn from the execution phase, to confirm what was anticipated, or to understand why contributing vulnerabilities were not previously identified; and

the ability to examine objectively plans, preparations, and response.

THE BOTTOM LINE: You have a broad and unique view of enterprise risk. Link that knowledge to the business alignment strategy, educate, and then take steps to ensure that your ability to respond is competent and prepared.

When there is an obligation to address resource reductions in response to adverse business conditions, use your knowledge to establish a threshold of risk tolerance, below which you no longer have confidence that the company is prepared to respond to what you believe has an increasing potential to occur.

Highlights for Follow-Up

- Understand the risks you own and those in which you share responsibility for some phase of management or elect to defer.
- Anticipate! Understand the potential source of the risk event(s) and how it would likely occur.
- Be aware of the impacts of emerging economic and strategic pressures on the business, and how developing corporate plans may impact the risks you should understand better than others in the management team.
- Advertise advice and requirements.
- Establish ownership for risk management and response.
- Offer assistance in installing and training on protection measures. Test their effectiveness frequently. Provide feedback on

results. Escalate if you don't see measurable improvement, then repeat the test.
- Establish key performance indicators appropriate to your programs.

Key Terms
- Risk assessment
- Risk mitigation
- Effective business controls
- Corporate liability
- Security program elements
- Response research
- Vulnerability assessment
- Risk quantification

4

STRATEGIC SECURITY PLANNING

Introduction

Would you invest in a business that lacked well-established goals and/or failed to have a thorough understanding on where it was going and what it is going to take to get there? Management has the same question for the security program.

Business Value

Successful businesses organize and deliver their products and services based on a combination of long-term and annual plans. These plans seek to maximize profit for the shareholders (or achieve some specific objective) while minimizing risk. Absent a plan effectively aligned with the strategic objectives and likely risks confronting the enterprise, how can management decide to allocate scarce resources to what will be seen as a cost center?

The Essentials

Today, our needs are greater than ever to create and enhance business goals to reduce costs, to increase profitability, and to protect brand image. Moving from traditional security thinking to business leadership thinking has already begun.

There are several business drivers that should frame your strategic philosophy, including:

- Security issues are clearly on the CEO's and board of director's agendas. Security executives must thoroughly understand business strategy and the place of the security program in that strategy.
- Traditional security programs and informational security programs are seeing an increase in convergence in their goal

to protect, prevent, and mitigate risks; the issue is not competition but coordination.

- Security leaders engaged in turf battles run the risk of being viewed as short-sighted and not thinking strategically or in the company's best interest.
- Global supply chains, business open architecture,[1] just-in-time parts and services delivery, and outsourcing all point to changing security risks and thinking beyond the fence. Your company's plant behind the fence can be secure, but if supplies are disrupted or your partner cannot provide contracted support, the safe plant becomes vulnerable.
- The creation of the Department of Homeland Security (DHS) and the increased focus on private sector security standards will result in a significant growth in regulations impacting corporate security departments for many years.
- Brand exposure is increasing in importance. Adverse publicity from clients, customers, the media, or regulators can reduce shareholder value, result in lost contracts, reduce revenue, and result in senior management termination. However, a good investigative capability can turn negative client or customer issues into positive events by a solid, timely, professional response. Mitigation of the risk is critical.

The goals of security are to:
- develop and manage security programs that enhance profitability;
- make the company a tougher competitor;
- enhance the company's ability to reduce shrinkage, reduce attrition of employees, and create a safer, more efficient workplace;
- assist in the creation of "peace of mind" for the consumer, employees, directors, and investors; and
- be in continuous dialogue with our business leaders to ensure that security strategy complements business strategy in order to accomplish the company's goals.

If success only comes from the security department acting in isolation, it does nothing to ensure the company's future. The linkage to the business side is crucial. A successful set of security programs must "bring value" to the company, or they will be viewed only as a cost by business leaders.

---

[1]Business open architecture refers to shared systems, customers, partnerships, controls, etc.

Strategic Security Program Focus

When developing a security program, the following must be considered:

- The security program aligns with business objectives.
- The benefits of the security program outweigh the cost of the program.
- Security costs and performance are managed and measured on a program basis.
- Relevance is articulated.
- Programs are constantly evolving.
- Cross-pollination is an opportunity for improvement.

Figure 4.1 displays the high-level strategic management process and the more action-oriented steps in security planning and program development.

Using this model of understanding strategic management, the work has been broken down into six major milestones:

Milestone	*Maps to*
Start-up	Strategic analysis
Examine existing strategy	Strategic analysis
Compare best practice	Strategic analysis
Strategic options	Strategic choice
Strategy and road map	Strategic implementation
Close down	Strategic implementation

Figure 4.1 Strategic Management Process. The high-level strategic management process and the more action-oriented steps in security planning and program development.

Some managers find it difficult to craft a way forward in measurable steps. Milestones provide the navigation points from start to finish in order to guide the plan's progress. Milestones must be related to the complexity, proposed duration, and resource availability for each specific objective in the plan.

Eight Key Strategic Issues

The following eight key issues need to be addressed by the strategy work:

1. Alignment of security strategy with organization's business objectives.
2. Risk appetite and attitude to protection and legislation.
3. Asset protection coordination and mutually supporting business processes.
4. Approach to asset-protection investment.
5. Structure and organization of the corporate security group.
6. Future resources and skills mix.
7. Integration and assimilation of security strategy throughout the organization.
8. Sustaining the security strategy.

Do you have a contingency plan for responding to management plans for incremental reductions in cost? Always have a 10% plan, a 20% plan, and a 30% plan in your bottom drawer that you have developed with your management team. Include impact assessments for specific line items you believe will increase business risk as a result of security program reduction or elimination.

The Security Planning and Program Development Process

Look at Figure 4.2, which graphically displays the steps in a strategic planning process. Adopting a model like this shows that you have carefully selected a proven process to:

- modify the security program to existing or new environments;
- align services and support with business objectives;
- validate and measure our results and value;
- identify risks, get management input, and develop priorities and consensus on risk mitigation; and
- align services and support with business objectives.

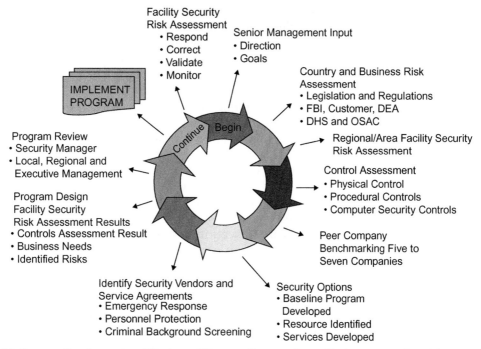

Figure 4.2 Program Development and Business Alignment Process. A graphical representation of the steps in a strategic planning process.

If this process is new to the organization, you can add target dates around the circle.

The security program targets the following six measures to reduce risk:

1. assignment of security responsibility within the business unit and site;
2. development of security policies, procedures, and guidelines;
3. employee security awareness, documentation, and training;
4. controlling access to people, property, product, information, and facilities;
5. reporting security-related incidents and responding to reported incidents; and
6. annual validation of security systems and services.

Business Alignment and Demonstrating Security's Value

How effectively are we aligned with the businesses we serve? In 2007, the Conference Board published a survey of several hundred business executives that revealed a serious disconnect between these business leaders and the value of the security functions they perceived within their organizations. *How can we expect support for our programs, especially in the more challenging economic times, when many of our constituents believe we bring no value to the bottom line?*

There are multiple buckets of security-program objectives and activity results that may be brought to the table to support our alignment and value contributions. Consider these:

- *Increased level of protection with improved controls and less cost:* When we learn from incidents and develop improved methods of protection, we can identify less labor-intensive controls and innovative applications of technology.
- *Increased engagement of employees in securing corporate assets:* A more security-aware employee population enables faster notification and improved engagement in protection. Pushing security, awareness, and tools into the population maximizes protection and accountability. Reductions in employee interaction with time-consuming security measures pay dividends in increased compliance.
- *Enhanced ability to satisfy customers with improved methods of protection:* Reduced risk to customers in sensitive transactions and relationship management contributes to brand loyalty and sales. A good example is in the resilience of protection measures around confidential customer information. Without effective security tools, business could not do what it does in cyberspace. Advertised and demonstrably effective security measures not only enable customer satisfaction but may also be a draw for new customers and sales. Being "the secure choice" is a plus to the bottom line.
- *Increased recovery time to critical process interruption:* Well-planned and tested security and business continuity programs reduce loss and enable faster recovery from an incident.
- *Reduced risk and increased integrity to revenue-generating activities:* Well-planned and integrated security capabilities enable profit centers to conduct their activities with improved efficiency and less cost. Reduced notable audit findings attributable to security defects build support for measurably effective security controls. Pre-contract examination of risk potential in third-party vendor security measures prospectively identifies vulnerabilities to enable favorable contract terms and post-contract inspections, thereby reducing risk and consequence of loss.
- *Increased confidence in effectiveness and need for security controls:* Where integrated security measures succeed in

preventing loss and reducing impact, and thus demonstrate their value to the business, constituents understand and lend support. Similarly, revenue-producing business activities benefit due to more efficient or constraining means of protection.

- *Reduced risk of attack through more measurably effective protective measures:* When security measures visibly succeed in reducing risk, the cost of doing business is measurably reduced through faster recovery and less cost of insurance. Penetration testing yields data on safeguards effectiveness and supports claims of reduced opportunity for attack. Examination of incident trends, and probing post-incident lessons learned produces metrics that enable affirmation or redirection of internal controls, which then yield improved risk-management practices.

THE BOTTOM LINE: Your strategic plan is focused on two related targets—addressing risk and adding value.

Highlights for Follow-Up

- Are your services seen as a cost or value center? Go back and review the stakeholder statements you collected during the Task Assessment in Chapter 1. Don't rely on your frequent customers, and look for feedback from executives where security is less known.
- What is your candid appraisal? If you have results that demonstrate aligned value, how have you missed telling the story? If you see a real lack of alignment with business objectives, what steps might you take to better deliver?
- How would you approach a proposal to outsource the current portfolio of proprietary security services to achieve potentially significant savings?
- Do any of the alignment examples noted in this chapter resonate with you? Using these topics as a starter, how do your security programs provide clear indications of alignment with the business?

Key Terms

- Strategic security plans
- Minimizing risk
- Business drivers

- Strategic philosophy
- Security planning
- Program development
- Security strategy alignment
- Risk appetite
- Legislation
- Asset protection

5

MARKETING THE SECURITY PROGRAM TO THE BUSINESS

Introduction

Security is in the business of enabling enterprise asset protection. This involves engaging internal customers to accept responsibility for protection. Just as the company requires a marketing strategy, so too does the security organization. The cornerstone of this strategy is the definition of the security organization's purpose and the policy framework for delivering the work.

Business Value

A proactive marketing strategy informs the enterprise population of its security-related responsibilities and the risks that require their awareness and attention. "Selling" security underscores the reliance that the security organization has for aware and engaged employees and maximizes the reach of the policy infrastructure and its related safeguards.

The Essentials

Your unique perspective on risk requires a plan on how to inform and engage employees, vendors, and others. Your culture and internal communication infrastructure both provide direction on how to communicate the messages you deem timely and essential.

A Marketing Strategy

The goals and related business objectives that follow in this chapter offer multiple targets for your marketing strategy. Work with your governance team colleagues to select content for the strategy based on current risk exposure. If your company has a corporate communications group, they can be very helpful in crafting delivery tactics.

Don't overdo it! Break rooms filled with security messages, monthly brochures extolling good practices, or the corporate intranet constantly barraging employees with advice and admonitions are similar to watching ads on TV—we tune them out. Pick your targets. If you know a business unit that is doing a bad job at access control, tailor a program for them. Pick a specific problem with security information that requires broad engagement and deliver a message at desktop sign-on. Develop an annual marketing plan that addresses the most risky issues and those the population can impact with your well-crafted messages. Avoid scare tactics; they invite less than serious responses from employees. If you are heavily into outsourcing of high-risk processes, engage the vendor with a program to underscore their responsibilities to protect your assets. Make every security employee or contractor representative a *knowledgeable* sales agent.

Brand Recognition

Does your company's mix of products and services imply any measure of risk to the shareholders or the consumer population? Are you moving into risky territory? Are you incredibly dependent upon uptime reliability of online systems and protection of customer data? Are you in a "trust me" business? Is *product safety* your middle name? Go to your marketing people and find out what criteria they are using to poll customers on brand recognition and expectations. Is there anything there that could offer your programs an entrée to supporting the reliability of the brand message? This is about aligning your services with business objectives.

When you craft your marketing strategy, you have to carefully consider how it reflects the picture of the brand your company is conveying. If their tagline is "Protecting your hard-earned assets," you might think about "Share the responsibility" for the internal risk ownership message. Every company carefully develops and protects the image it conveys to the consumer. Explore how your security programs fit with that mission. Focus on how security programs might better enable the business to convey a "secure" message to the customer base. In these times, with the diversity of risk facing global business, there may be multiple opportunities here.

The Mission Statement

A well-crafted mission statement allows you to focus the program on more specific and action-oriented objectives. Engaging and obtaining consensus from senior management on your concept of mission enables buy-in and gives a basic structure to security's program plans. First, think about what makes your company tick and how you want security to connect the brand and its corporate objectives to enterprise success. Second, think about how your mission statement can motivate the security team and contribute to making the business more aware of roles and responsibilities.

Policies and Business Practices

Many companies dislike the notion of *policy*, but they all have a set of rules and formalized expectations, especially in these times of regulatory and board-level oversight. *Guidelines*, *business practices*, *business objectives*, or *management principles* may be reasonable substitute terms in these environments and may contain the essential expectations that serve to frame implementing procedures and the security programs that enable them.

Learning from experience is great. However, what is the *real* cost of policy or procedure that has been created in response to crisis or litigation? There are multiple benefits to a policy infrastructure accepted by senior management, including the following:

- Policies establish the legal framework for the security program. They become key components in the system of internal controls.
- Policies communicate management's approach to governing the enterprise and define what behavior is and is not allowed.
- Policies set expectations, clarify roles, and establish accountability.
- A policy statement enables goal setting; compliance requires planning and resource allocation. Thus, policies providing a rationale for the security budget process.
- Policies and related procedures provide a measure of protection from litigation.

Figure 5.1 offers several ideas for mission statements and related high-level policies, and the eight high-level policy statements form the framework of a comprehensive corporate security program. Consider the implications of a CEO or senior

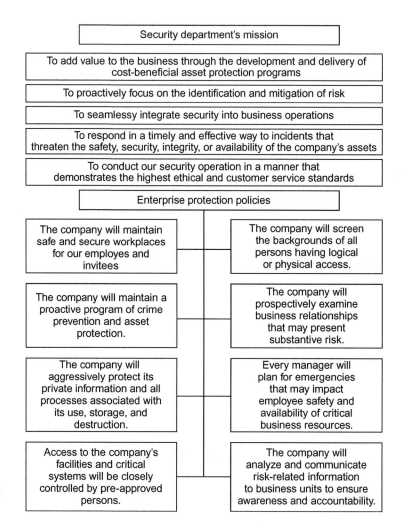

Figure 5.1 Security Department Mission Statement. Several ideas for mission statements and related high-level policies.

management team's denying the validity of any of these, especially in these days of risk-sensitive boards of directors and external regulators.

Do you want to "sell" these high-level expectations? In your discussions with senior managers, ask them if they accept the common-sense business principle embedded in each statement. You may get pushback on a couple, so be prepared to discuss the risks and business consequences associated with the absence of some form of safeguards like these.

Applying Standard Security Practices to Business Objectives

Depending upon the internal business control orientation of your company, security practices may be referred to as *standards, procedures, guidelines, business practices*, or whatever term suits the culture. The point to be remembered is that high-level policy or goal statements have to translate into elements of work that can be planned, resourced, organized, and delivered.

Business Objective 1: To Proactively Identify and Monitor Risks to the Security, Safety, and Continued Business Operations of the Company.

To achieve business objective 1, the following standard practices should be implemented:

- Assess risk to the assets and business activities of the company. This will include the clarification of the nature and likelihood of the hazard event occurring and statements of hazard consequences. A full threat evaluation for key business processes and assets will identify the scope and cost-effectiveness of possible countermeasures. Significant expenditures will include a return-on-investment analysis.
- Define the process relating to the evaluation of employee and insider threats.
- Monitor workplaces for hazards to health and safety.
- Proactively identify risks of workplace violence.
- Conduct a business-risk analysis for major disasters or other business interruption scenarios.
- Ensure that all investigations and incidents conclude with a review, and that appropriate lessons are derived and fed back into the business.

Business Objective 2: To Take Positive Actions to Provide a Safe and Secure Place of Work for Our Employees and Visitors.

To achieve business objective 2, the following standard practices should be implemented:

- Control access to company work and business space.
- Apply physical security measures in support of asset-protection strategies.
- Set guidelines for the use of manpower in a protective-services role.
- Plan and apply emergency services in support of employees' safety and business continuity.

- Define the minimum accepted security measures applicable to the protection of critical business areas.
- Define the minimum accepted level of security monitoring of critical business assets.

Business Objective 3: To Take Appropriate and Cost-Effective Measures to Secure Our Business Processes from Fraud and Other Criminal Acts.

To achieve business objective 3, the following standard practices should be implemented:
- Define the scope of proactive programs designed to ensure timely reviews of current business processes. Measure and add business controls that contribute materially to the early identification and mitigation of fraud or other crimes.
- Outline the role of security in the overall process of providing compliance to the U.S. Patriot Act and other regulations.
- Outline the contribution that can be made by security to customer identification programs and knowledge of your customers' requirements.

Business Objective 4: To Ensure that Our Staff and Others With Free Access to our Property and Systems Meet the Highest Standards of Integrity and Ethical Conduct.

To achieve business objective 4, the following standard practices should be implemented:
- Define the process by which security provides timely support to human resources for the process of pre-employment background investigation for all new hires.
- Define the extent to which background checks will be carried out on persons with access to company space and systems who are not full-time employees.
- Define those activities that, in the domain of security, will fall into the category of unethical conduct and practices.
- Define the procedures and mechanisms by which company employees and outsiders may report unethical behavior for subsequent investigation.

Business Objective 5: To Put Appropriate Security Controls and Mechanisms Into Place to Protect Our Private Information and Systems Used to Process Such Related Data.

To achieve business objective 5, the following standard practices should be implemented:

- Assure accurate *identification* by ensuring that each entity is uniquely identified in all transactions and that we ask for credentials.
- Assure *authentication* by ensuring that identities are accurately confirmed and credentials are verified.
- Assure *authorization* by controlling and limiting access to resources. Access is based on the concepts of "need to know" and "appropriate to role."
- Assure *confidentiality* by keeping private information securely private. We can keep a secret.
- Assure *data integrity* by maintaining proof that no unauthorized changes have been made and accurate records are kept.
- Assure *nonrepudiation* by ensuring that parties are bound to their actions—a deal is a deal.
- Assure *accountability* by making sure actions are auditable—we know who did what.
- Assure *effective administration* by making sure all the practices listed above are carefully managed. It is people who make or break security.

Business Objective 6: To Have Plans and Appropriately Structured Business Resources to Maximize the Resilience of the Company from Disasters and to Enhance the Recovery from any Business Interruption.

To achieve business objective 6, the following standard practices should be implemented:

- Define the scope and content of plans developed by business units for the mitigation of damage in the event of a disaster and the subsequent timely restoration of business.
- Define the role of and give support from security to business units in the planning and execution of business contingency plans.
- Define the scope of testing for and rehearsal of business contingency plans.
- Define the protection to be applied to critical business resources against all forms of business interruption.
- Define the minimum backup and standby facilities to be prepared by business units for critical business facilities and processes.
- Define a standard security practice to outline the organization, planning, training, and response actions to be taken in support of safety issues in all occupied space.
- Define a standard security practice to report the *actual* status of testing and preparedness.

Business Objective 7: To Investigate Aggressively and Prosecute Attempts or Acts of Crime Against the Company and Its Resources.

To achieve business objective 7, the following standard practices should be implemented:

- Outline the scope and responsibilities for investigation and prosecution of all suspected criminal acts against the assets of the company: human, physical, and intellectual.
- Define the scope and procedures for recording, investigating, and reporting to the appropriate authorities—or competent bodies—criminal acts or suspected infringement of regulatory rules in the security domain.

Business Objective 8: It Is the Primary Responsibility of Professional Security Staff to Plan, Manage, and Monitor Security Practices, But it is the Responsibility of Every Member of the Company to Positively and Responsibly Support Them and for Managers to Ensure that Security Is a Normal, Everyday Part of Managing the Business.

To achieve business objective 8, the following standard practices should be implemented:

- Outline the responsibilities of managers and staff to report suspected, intended, or actual acts of crime or security violations against or involving the company.
- Define the responsibility of security to provide a proactive program of security awareness, which will inform all employees of security risk and the steps they should take to assist in the protection of corporate assets.

In evaluating the applicability of each of these practices, you will see the clear implication that where management accepts the high-level principle there are a series of corresponding business processes that enable accomplishment of the work. Therein lies the essence of your business plan, the focus for your financial requirements, and your marketing strategy for engaging business units in their responsibilities for asset protection.

THE BOTTOM LINE: Leadership involves the power of leadership. Influence is shaped and focused by a marketing strategy.

Highlights for Follow-Up

- Has your security mission been articulated and accepted by senior management?
- What approach within your corporate culture would best enable implementation of a set of high-level security policies?
- Which standards or practices under the eight business objectives is the security program currently performing? Which ones do you think would be value-added for your program and the company?
- What constraints would exist for the implementation of each one?
- How might those barriers be overcome? Of those services currently being delivered, to what extent are they at a standard of performance acceptable to you?
- Are you satisfied that the security program is being effectively marketed and sold within the company?
- How are you measuring program acceptance or buy-in and knowledge of shared responsibilities?
- Where are the biggest gaps in the security program's marketing strategy, and what would be required to fill these gaps?

Key Terms

- Enterprise asset protection
- Internal customers
- Marketing strategy
- Legal framework
- Brand recognition
- Mission statement
- Policies and procedures
- Internal controls
- Governing the enterprise
- Roles and accountability
- Standard security practices
- Business objectives
- Appropriate practices

6

ORGANIZATIONAL MODELS

Introduction

As you move among your colleagues in other organizations, you will learn quickly that there are no established security model templates.[1] History with regard to management's view of culture, acknowledgement of risk, regulatory influence, or corporate whim will often determine reporting relationships and the portfolio of programs assigned to a specific security responsibility. When management decides to rearrange offices, we are often caught up in the "who goes where" game. This is another very good reason to have effective working relationships with a variety of key senior managers. You never know who your next boss might be.[2]

Business Value

Value lies in a combination of what works in the corporate culture and the competencies that the incumbent security manager brings to the table. It is likely that you will propose one alignment of security functions early on and then discover interdependencies that make more sense for proposals later on. The value is in the wisdom of your rationale with regard to improved cost and risk management, business alignment, ability to better enable the business to compete, or a combination of these or other purely local objectives.

[1] Highly centralized organizations will tend to hold security policy, headcount, and service delivery solid-line reporting to the chief security officer. A decentralized model would tend to retain strategic security leadership, policy, and oversight in headquarters while service delivery would be the responsibility of each applicable business unit.

[2] Thus, the potential dilemma of "letting the chips fall where they may." You may conduct a sensitive investigation today that might shine a harsh light on a manager who one day becomes your supervisor. So be it. If this manager fails to understand your responsibility to corporate integrity, you should escalate when and if that history impacts your performance or that of your organization. Carefully clarify the history as the handoff takes place so you can gauge their objectivity.

The Essentials

As most practitioners know, there is no one "best" security program, which is why we see so many variations based on sector, type of business, centralized versus decentralized, domestic versus global, and so on. It is impossible to have one program that is universally accepted as a best practice. However, by utilizing the collective knowledge of the Security Executive Council faculty and members, we have identified all the characteristics that this group of successful practitioners, companies, and programs embody:

- *Baseline program elements*, which define the program that, members and faculty agree, should be in place to mitigate major risks.
- *Business-aligned program elements*, which faculty and membership define as programs that are above and beyond baseline and unquestionably add measurable value to the company's bottom line.
- *Program characteristics*, which are the elements most frequently identified in successful programs or that lead to the success of programs and executive support. These characteristics are most often the items included in benchmarking studies, since they are readily observable and often most similar in company sector comparisons.

Baseline Elements

Baseline elements for consideration should include the following:

- an established security department (internal and/or outsourced)
- incident reporting
- risk assessments
- access control and site protection
- information security
- emergency response and disaster recovery
- awareness and education
- investigations
- travel security
- workplace violence
- personnel screening, background investigations, and due diligence
- law enforcement liaison
- product protection

Program Characteristics

Some or all of the following characteristics should define your security program(s):

- risk-based
- services correspond to board-level risks (BLR); risk committee ties to BLR
- defined programs with comprehensive elements
- programs have definitive costs and resource requirements (e.g., full-time equivalents, or FTEs)
- there is a positive correlation between the number of catalysts that drive a program and program success:
  - regulatory driven
  - product driven
  - brand protection driven
  - incident driven
  - sponsor driven
  - geographically driven
  - corporate culture driven,
  - ROI/value driven
- corporate security is the subject matter expert (SME) group that provides risk mitigation-related consulting to the rest of the organization
- measure and communicate the impact and value of services to the senior executive level of the organization
- monitor and identify emerging security-related issues that can significantly impact the organization; create and develop strategies to mitigate the impact
- consistently focus on services that positively impact the financial business performance
- effectively communicate to executive management the level of residual risk they are accepting if the risks are not mitigated or transferred
- both the risks and the risk mitigation strategies are well-documented and transferable
- validate strategies periodically through peer review
- access to executive management and the board of directors when necessary
- consistent delivery in all markets, business units, and functions
- demonstrate leadership and receive continual executive support
- maintain an inventory of security key risk indicators

You may want to use this checklist to evaluate where your program now stands and where your planning seeks to take it.

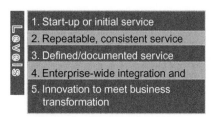

Levels
1. Start-up or initial service
2. Repeatable, consistent service
3. Defined/documented service
4. Enterprise-wide integration and
5. Innovation to meet business
   transformation

Figure 6.1 Maturity of the Corporate Security Program. The five levels of maturity for the corporate security program.

These characteristics are also useful as a means to engage management on their vision for the security function and how these capabilities and characteristics may enable security programs to better contribute to company goals.

The Security Executive Council outlines five levels of maturity for the corporate security program (see Figure 6.1). Comprehensive security programs start at Level 4.

What Organizational Model Works Best in Your Company

The illustration in Figure 6.2 provides a representation of the potential mix of services in a corporate-wide security program potentially representing Level 4 or better. Within a box of global business risk, we array a perimeter of global response services and an inner core providing a wide array of security programs aligned against current threats and global business risks. No one is favored over another, since many risk profiles, cultural influences, and demonstrated competencies of the incumbent security executive will define the configuration that best serves the company. As seen in the response to 9/11 or after a specific legislative or regulatory initiative, events will often determine placement and portfolio of services assigned to the security organization(s).

Alternative Organizational Models

The illustration in Figure 6.3 represents one example of the diverse range of services that may be found under the "corporate security" umbrella. Here we have a set of core services existing within a global risk framework and surrounded by a perimeter of proactive security operations that may be proprietary or contractual. Ownership of any of these services may be

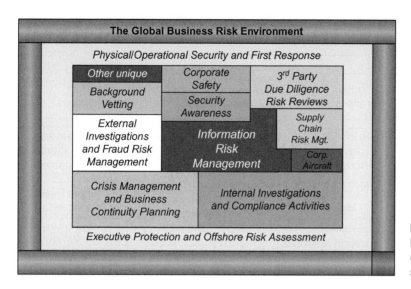

Figure 6.2 The Global Risk Environment. The potential mix of services in a corporate-wide security program.

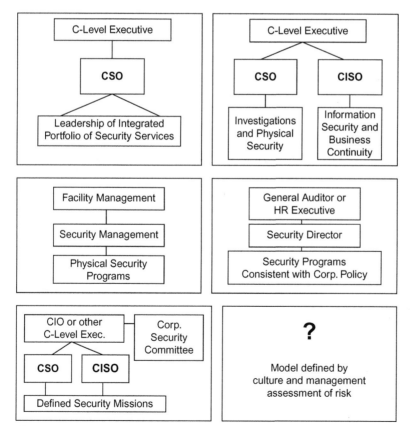

Figure 6.3 Alternative Organizational Models. One example of the diverse range of services that may be found under the "corporate security" umbrella.

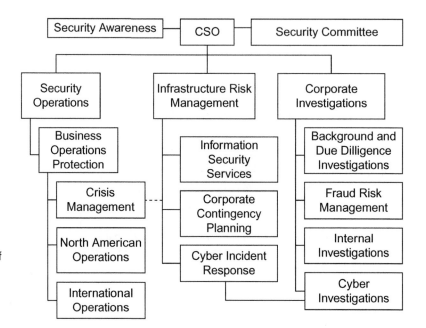

Figure 6.4 The Consolidated Service Model. An example of a consolidated or converged security organization consistent with a CSO's portfolio of responsibilities.

centralized or distributed across business-unit activities or governance functions. Using this illustration as a jumping off point, we cannot possibly encompass the inventory of organizational models that may be reflective of the diverse cultures and risk profiles represented in the readership of this book. Perhaps there is a challenge in that lesson that encourages a serious evaluation of the mix of services appropriate to a service model in your organization.

Consolidated Service Model

Where an organization adopts an approach that desires to assure that corporate security responsibilities are unified under an accountable chief security officer (CSO), the example in Figure 6.4 is one of a consolidated or converged security organization consistent with a CSO's portfolio of responsibilities.

Seriously Explore the Potential Advantages of a Security Committee

It should be evident that security programs are interdependent and benefit from (if not rely on) strategic planning and program integration under single-executive management. This fact argues in compelling ways for a full-service corporate security organization. If they are under separate organizational functions *and* there is no established means to share and analyze risk data, a consolidated view of security-related risk will be lost. The resulting picture of risk is likely to be very different from one that emerges from a single, uncoordinated source. This is too often a difficult lesson learned from tragic or business-threatening circumstances.

If the consolidated model is not adopted, a security committee should be established and chartered by the CEO or COO and supported by a corporate board of directors. Membership should include all senior executives engaged in managing the governance infrastructure and at least one senior executive from a business line. Where security programs are administered internally to a business unit (fraud risk management, business continuity planning, and distributed information security functions are examples), they should be represented as well. If more broadly chartered, as with a governance committee, a security subcommittee should be considered to more clearly gather and analyze risk exposure data unique to their functions. Typical membership of the security committee would include the chief security officer (CSO) and senior management of corporate security, the chief information security officer (CISO), the chief auditor, general counsel, the chief risk officer, and the HR employee relations designee engaged in business conduct matters. A senior business line executive with more extensive risk exposure is a good candidate as well.

The business of the security committee should be to develop a set of results-oriented measures and related metrics that achieve the following:

- Assist the board and senior management in understanding security-related risk and framing the parameters of risk tolerance.
- Ensure that the dots are being effectively connected with regard to a reliable picture of risk exposure.
- Enable follow-up recommendations and actions and track the results of risk-mitigation activities.
- Provide a framework for assessing security's value as a core element of business strategy in an increasingly risky world.

Unified Risk Oversight

A particularly responsive way to effectively comply with the mountain of legislation, regulation, and voluntary guidelines—let alone to ensure cost-effectiveness in meeting the dynamics of business security threats—is to approach it in the context of unified risk oversight, which is a method of approaching risk whereby the corporate risk is identified by a team of executives or managers who represent the company's various business units, then manage with the best interests of the business and its goals in mind. By "corporate risk" we mean not just the compiled risks of individual business units, but the new risk picture created when different departments' risk considerations are brought together and compared, combined, and prioritized. When risk is managed by this method, all decisions to transfer, avoid, mitigate or accept risk are made in full consideration of their impact on all business units. This means not every decision will reflect what you may feel is the best option for security, but every decision will take security into account and seek to provide the best possible outcome for the business as a whole.

Access Is the Fundamental Essential

Regardless of the configuration of reporting and alignment, security management must be able to have unfettered access to the CEO and other key executives. Whether for routine updates or crisis management, translation through multiple layers of superiors will significantly inhibit awareness of risk, decision-making, and the perceived value of security. There is no set or best model for reporting other than to *state clearly that you need to report to someone who provides you with supportive access to the top*. If your important messages are being choked off or unduly edited, you need to find a host who is secure in his or her job and accepts the importance of your role in the governance infrastructure. Is there a "best" home? No, it depends on your culture and corporate reporting desires. There are as many combinations out there as there are corporate structural models, which are most often influenced by how the top sees your role in the risk management priority scheme.

Several potential organizational models are displayed in the following discussion. No one is favored over another since many risk profiles, cultural influences, and demonstrated competencies of the incumbent security executive will define the configuration that best serves the company.

A Corporate Security Work Breakdown Structure

Regardless of how your organization decides to align security programs organizationally, there is a significant inventory of services typically found in one degree or another in most global businesses. Table 6.1 is a representative listing of work elements involved in the administration of a full-service corporate security function. Note that the list of tasks only delegates a few levels downward. If you were to break each of these activities down to a full work structure, it would take several pages. The point is to understand the complexity of every work activity that you propose, may accept, and adopt. It's all about the relevance of the work to mitigating the identified risk(s), and the time each activity takes to accomplish at a level of targeted competence. Time is money, and that time must be measured against the return on managed risk.

"Rightsizing"

Periodic adjustments in the expense column are inevitable. Stock analysts watch the quarterly numbers, and the typical corporate move when those numbers fail to meet expectations is to slash expenses. The further you are from the customer, the more likely your budget will be targeted. This is the time when we are clearly seen as "cost" centers. Always have a 10% to 20% downsized plan in your file for when the call comes.

Table 6.1 is a good starting point for the exercise. Table 1.2 in Chapter 1 outlines the perceived benefits of corporate security programs and should support the value measures in Table 6.1. Those services that have a clear legal or enterprise protection requirement need to be protected. On the other hand, you will always have some measure of "nice to have" services in the portfolio that will be the first candidates for cuts. Management's expectation will be firm, but you still need to have the opportunity to make your case on where cuts in a lean budget will unnecessarily expose the company to unacceptable risks. Be prepared to demonstrate with your risk assessment the potential impact of specific cuts.

A modified version might be to replace the "Xs" with headcount increments. For example, Plan and Program Development might be 1.75 full time equivalents (FTEs). This will serve as a high-level staffing model of sorts and ensure the program is properly balanced.

How This List Might Be Useful

As you plan or assess your program, you need to think about the range of activities associated with the work you deem important. Programs are comprised of subactivities, all of which

Table 6.1 Full Service Corporate Security Work Functions

Responsibilities for Primary Corporate Security Services Security Program Element	Where is there Clear Value in the Service?					
	Enterprise Required	Bus. Risk Mitigation	Life Safety	Regulatory or Legal?	Volume Related?	Cost Mgt.?
1. Program Administration						
1.1 Budget and finance	X					X
1.2 Plan and program development	X	X				X
1.3 Policy and standards	X	X	X	X		
1.4 Personnel management	X					
1.4.1 Performance measurement	X	X	X	X		X
1.4.2 Personal development	X	X				
1.4.2.1 Core competency analysis	X	X				X
1.4.3 Job analysis and recruiting	X					X
1.4.4 Skills training		X	X	X	X	X
1.4.4 Time tracking						X
1.5 Data analysis and reporting		X	X	X		X
1.5.1 Lessons-learned analysis		X		X	X	X
1.5.2 Management reporting	X	X		X		X
1.5.3 Trend analysis and metrics		X	X	X	X	X
1.5.4 Specific incident analysis	X	X	X	X	X	
1.6 Inspection and review	X	X	X	X		X
1.7 Contract management	X					X
2. Technology Management						
2.1 Research and development		X				
2.2 System design guidelines	X	X	X	X		X
2.2 Project management	X				X	
2.3 Equipment procurement	X					X
2.3.1 Inventory management	X					X

(Continued)

Table 6.1 (Continued)

Responsibilities for Primary Corporate Security Services	Where is there Clear Value in the Service?					
Security Program Element	Enterprise Required	Bus. Risk Mitigation	Life Safety	Regulatory or Legal?	Volume Related?	Cost Mgt.?
2.4 System design and engineering	X	X	X	X	X	X
2.5 System installation	X		X	X	X	X
2.5.1 System maintenance	X	X	X	X	X	X
2.6 Fire and life/safety systems	X	X	X	X	X	
3. Access Administration						
3.1 Logical access administration	X	X		X	X	
3.2 Physical access administration	X	X	X	X	X	
3.2.1 Credentials and badging	X	X		X	X	
3.3 Vendor/other special access administration	X	X		X	X	
4. Risk Management						
4.1 Single point of failure analysis	X	X				X
4.2 Alarm abatement	X	X	X	X	X	X
4.3 Vulnerability, strengths, weaknesses, opportunities, and threat analyses	X	X	X	X		X
4.4 Risk/cost analysis	X	X	X			X
4.5 Risk reporting and metrics	X	X	X	X	X	X
4.6 Risk mitigation activities	X	X	X	X	X	X
4.6.1 Fraud prevention		X		X		X
4.6.2 Practice risk identification		X	X	X		X
4.6.3 After-action review process	X	X	X	X		X
4.6.4 Life and safety program	X	X	X	X	X	X
4.6.5 Alarm monitoring	X	X	X		X	
4.6.6 Central dispatching	X	X	X		X	
4.6.7 Emergency management	X	X	X	X	X	X
4.6.8 Computer virus response	X	X				X

(Continued)

Table 6.1 (Continued)

Responsibilities for Primary Corporate Security Services	Where is there Clear Value in the Service?					
Security Program Element	Enterprise Required	Bus. Risk Mitigation	Life Safety	Regulatory or Legal?	Volume Related?	Cost Mgt.?
4.6.9 Response to computer-based threats	X	X		X	X	X
4.6.10 Executive protection program	X	X	X		X	
5. Investigation						
5.1 Background investigation	X	X		X	X	
5.2 Due diligence examination	X	X		X	X	X
5.3 Criminal investigation	X	X	X	X	X	
5.4 Incident response	X	X	X	X	X	X
5.4.1 Incident reporting	X	X	X	X	X	
5.5 Sensitive case administration	X	X		X	X	X
5.6 Case management	X	X			X	X
5.6.1 File management	X	X		X	X	
5.7 Law enforcement liaison	X	X				
5.8 Workplace violence threat assessment	X	X	X	X	X	
5.9 Cyber incident investigation	X	X			X	
6. Risk Communication and Business Unit Skills						
6.1 Measures and metrics	X	X	X	X	X	X
6.2 Employee security orientation	X	X		X		
6.3 Security communication		X	X	X		
6.4 Business unit communication	X	X	X	X	X	
6.5 Security committee liaison	X	X	X		X	
6.6 Information security skills development		X				
6.7 Development of security awareness material	X	X		X		
6.7.1 Security awareness program		X	X	X		
6.8 Fraud prevention training		X				

(Continued)

Table 6.1 (Continued)

Responsibilities for Primary Corporate Security Services	Where is there Clear Value in the Service?					
Security Program Element	Enterprise Required	Bus. Risk Mitigation	Life Safety	Regulatory or Legal?	Volume Related?	Cost Mgt.?
6.9 Floor warden training	X	X	X	X	X	
6.10 Business continuity training and awareness	X	X	X	X		
7. Business Contingency Planning						
7.1 Emergency notification listing	X	X		X	X	X
7.2 Plan development and maintenance	X	X	X	X	X	
7.2 Plan review and administration	X	X	X	X		
7.3 Business function criticality lists	X	X	X	X		X
7.4 Plan testing	X	X		X	X	X
7.5 Alternate site support	X	X				X
7.6 Crisis management testing and maintenance	X	X	X			X
8. Information Security Administration						
8.1 Information security consulting	X	X				
8.2 Information security engineering	X	X				
8.3 Proprietary Information Program administration	X	X	X	X		
8.4 Information security risk assessment	X	X		X		X
8.5 Compliance monitoring	X	X		X		X
8.5.1 Safeguards installation and maintenance	X	X		X		X

A representative listing of work elements involved in the administration of a full service corporate security function.

involve elements of cost for a person's time or other resources. Why is this activity important? Where is the anticipated value? What business objective drives the need for these resources to be allocated? Each of the columns identifies a potential business driver such as a business-directed activity, risk management, activity volume, the need to manage cost, or a legal requirement. Depending on your industry, corporate mission, and resource management priorities, you may want to modify the business drivers as well as the unique activities to better tailor this list to your needs.

Use this higher-level checklist in your assessment of status and planning for program development.

THE BOTTOM LINE: Organize your resources and services for responsiveness to risk and clear connection to your customers.

Highlights for Follow-Up

- Using whatever criterion you believe is appropriate to your company, how would you rate your ability to access senior management for nonemergency communications?
- Do you believe your current organizational model yields the best results for influence and senior management access? Why or why not? If not, what would be required to make this model more impactful?
- If one does not currently exist, would a security committee work in your company? If so, how might it be organized and sold?
- How does your management react to the receipt of bad news? How does this or other factors influence your preference regarding placement of the security organization?
- Considering Table 6.1, do you accept the value columns as appropriate to your organization? If so, how would you check the appropriate line of work? If not, which ones would you include?

Key Terms

- Organizational model
- Alternative organizational models
- Consolidated services model
- Unified risk oversight
- Program characteristics

- Baseline elements
- Business-aligned security program
- Global risk environment
- Regulatory driven
- Product driven
- Incident driven
- Governance committee
- Program administration
- Technology management

REGULATIONS, GUIDELINES, AND STANDARDS

Introduction

Since 9/11 virtually every industrial sector and related regulatory agency has been actively examining potential vulnerabilities to terrorism in its many forms and consequences. The response has been a virtual glut of regulations and security guidelines.

Business Value

Security executives are expected to be knowledgeable of the potential impacts of security-related legislation and resulting regulations. This enables them to advise management and applicable trade associations on political, legal and economic strategies. They also need to develop plans to support cost-effective compliance.

Regulations are often enacted as a legislative or executive branch knee-jerk response to a single incident. Think of the acts of terrorism on September 11, 2001 and the Patriot Act, or the Enron scandal and the Sarbanes-Oxley Act of 2002. Importantly, these responses reveal inattention to known vulnerabilities, or failure to be appropriately aware of emerging threats. Standards are quantitative or qualitative assessments employed by industry and professional groups to provide measures and targets of comparison. Some take on the impact of codes such as those of the National Fire Protection Association where, like regulations, noncompliance may involve serious sanctions.

Essentials

As legislative, executive, or industry action unfolds, you should work with corporate general counsel and legislative affairs to assess impact and provide input to your trade association and political representatives. You need to be the resident expert for impact analysis and thoughtful compliance.

Typical Regulatory Elements

There are several elements that are typically involved in security, safety, privacy, and ethics regulations, including

- on-going risk assessment process coupled with a periodic regulatory focus;
- demonstrated willingness to open doors to independent review of controls;
- metrics to demonstrate degree of compliance or variation outside of prescribed guardrails;
- communication to inform and empower employees and vendors on their responsibilities;
- measurable risk mitigation plans in place and effective;
- verifiable reporting upward and externally, as required;
- verifiable engagement of senior management in compliance;
- process for confidential reporting of suspected infractions;
- appropriate positioning of a qualified individual to oversee compliance;
- appropriate funding of on-going compliance programs; and
- support for regulatory reviews or inquiries.

As you approach assessment of the potential impact of proposed regulations or conformance with current ones, each of these elements should be evaluated and implemented appropriate to your organization's regulatory requirements and your company's status regarding compliance. Remember that installing any one of these contributes to some measure of compliance with others.

How Many Security Regulations Apply to Your Company?

Few security executives today can call their security organizations unregulated, and those who do are probably in for an unpleasant surprise.

Since 9/11, a hyper-charged interest in national security has propagated a spate of new laws, regulations, and voluntary guidelines that impact the operations of security programs in both the private and public sectors. Growing concerns about the privacy of information, business conduct and ethics have also helped to boost the number of rules landing in the hopper.

The effect of regulation on the U.S. and international aviation industry has been headline news for more than five years. Additionally, there have been the types of corruption scandals that led to the development of accountability rules like Sarbanes-Oxley. Legislation to increase the security of sensitive government information, the critical U.S. infrastructure, and the national food supply has similarly received a great deal of public attention. However, not all such legislation is high profile. There are numerous rules with security significance that appear to have slipped under the radar, not only of the general public but of many security professionals.

The Security Executive Council has compiled a comprehensive database of international security laws, regulations, and guidelines—both for corporations in general and for specific industries. As of 2013, the Council's list of U.S. federal legislative actions (including executive orders and statutes) sits at 43, the list of U.S. federal regulations at 23, and the list of voluntary guidelines or standards numbers 58. This current list only scratches the surface.[1]

For one thing, security professionals have more than federal mandates to contend with. For example, as of April 2012, 46 states, the District of Columbia, Puerto Rico, and the Virgin Islands have laws requiring notification of any security breach involving personal information.[2] States also develop their own rules, dealing with such varied issues as critical infrastructure protection, employee and workplace security, and identity theft. For global corporations, international law also plays a major role in security operations.

The length and breadth of legislative and regulatory coverage poses a significant challenge for many security professionals, a challenge complicated all the more by the fact that they are often unaware of many of the rules that apply to their operations. New rules are being developed all the time, new amendments are changing older rules, and some regulations that would appear to apply to a specific industry group sometimes carry a longer reach than their creators intended. The Chemical Facility Anti-Terrorism Standards of the Department of Homeland Security (DHS) are an example. Their stated intent is to provide tighter security for high-risk chemical facilities, but they are proving to be a thorn in the side of the food industry, because the thresholds of many of the regulated chemicals are

[1]See the Council's library at www.securityexecutivecouncil.com/public/lrvc/.
[2]Stevens, Gina, "Data Security Breach Notification Laws," Congressional Research Service, April 10, 2012, 7–5700, R42475, http://www.fas.org/sgp/crs/misc/R42475.pdf.

undefined. This problem is putting many facilities that use, for refrigeration purposes, even small amounts of a certain type of ammonia under the thumb of the regulations.

Security professionals needn't feel entirely helpless in the face of this onslaught of governmental activity. By understanding how these regulations and laws are made and knowing how and when to take action, security professionals can become agents of change for the good of their organizations, their industries, and their nation.

The Legislation, Regulations, Voluntary Compliance, and Standards (LRVCS) Breakdown

It's critical to understand the differences in the nature and development of legislation, regulations, and industry voluntary guidelines.

Legislation encompasses both executive directives and statutes. An executive order, sometimes called a presidential directive, is issued by the executive branch and may deal with such matters as internal operations, national security, or foreign policy. Executive orders are binding on their own, but they are often accompanied or followed by congressional statutes that make them indisputable law. Statutes are the approved legislative acts that are developed by Congress, such as the Federal Anti-Tampering Act and the Homeland Security Act. These begin as proposed bills in either the House of Representatives or the Senate. For example, if a bill is introduced in the House, it is first sent to committee for research and consideration, amended and sent up for debate, and finally voted upon. The approved act is then sent to the Senate, which also puts it through committee and votes before returning it to the House. The final step is the signed approval of the president.

Legislation is generally broad in scope. It mandates that certain objectives be achieved, but it doesn't often dig into the details of who, what, when, where, and how. Instead, legislation appoints certain federal agencies to develop and enforce specific regulations that will accomplish the stated goals. The appointed agencies carefully research the issue and then develop rules that are intended to be fair to the regulated group by identifying multiple options and requesting public comment.

Voluntary guidelines may be created by federal and state agencies or by industry organizations and associations.

Government entities may issue guidelines where regulation would be unfeasible for an entire industry, or where strict regulation could impose an unbalanced business or economic risk.

C-TPAT, the Customs-Trade Partnership Against Terror, is a good example of voluntary guidelines. Organizations that follow it earn the reward of easier, quicker international shipping. Industry organizations often create guidelines to avoid future legislation; if they police their own members through voluntary compliance, the government may see no need to step in and mandate change. Often, this strategy is successful, as is the case with C-TPAT. Other times it is not a success, and the need for regulation surfaces again. Industry and government standards created by organizations such as National Institute of Standards and Technology (NIST), International Organization for Standardization (ISO), ISACA (previously known as the Information Systems Audit and Control Association), National Fire Protection Association (NFPA), and American Institute of Certified Public Accountants (AICPA) also fit in this category.

The Security Professional's Role

It is imperative that the first obligation of the security executive is to understand completely the elements of compliance and the means to cost-effectively demonstrate conformance with applicable regulations.

Developing a Regulatory Compliance Strategy

Based on a review of several security-related government regulations, there are multiple elements involved in conformance to their respective requirements. While you may want to track your organization's compliance with the specifics of those regulations that apply to your operations, you may find the chart in Figure 7.1 to be useful in preparing management for the common elements found in most regulatory compliance exercises.

Preparing for Regulation

Regulations and standards do not arrive overnight. They often take years to discuss, refine, and gain support from key constituencies. Security professionals and their corporations can play a part in the creation and modification of any legislation or regulations that may impact their business. It's just a matter of knowing how to do it and recognizing when the window of opportunity is opened.

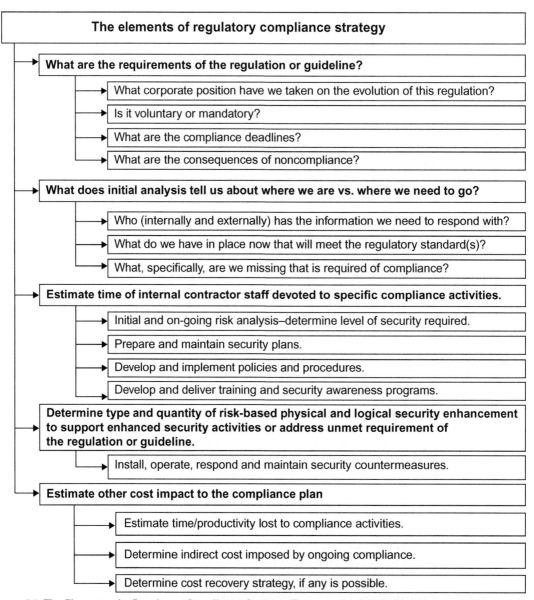

Figure 7.1 The Elements of a Regulatory Compliance Strategy. The examples in this figure are useful in preparing management for the common elements found in most regulatory compliance exercises.

Legislation

A bill receives its most intense scrutiny when in committee. Committees request multiple reports on differing views for all proposed legislation, and they are also authorized to hold hearings that incorporate testimony from qualified experts on the subject in question. In the legislative process, there are a few ways to ensure that your voice is heard when it matters:

Make Contact

It's important to make your views known to your senators and representatives if or when you become aware of proposed legislation that may impact your organization's security operations. You can reach members of Congress by phone, mail, or e-mail. Complete directories are available at www.house.gov and www.senate.gov. When contacting a member of Congress, keep your comments clear and concise. If appropriate, request an in-person meeting with the congressperson, or offer yourself as an on-call resource.

Build Relationships

If you're in a heavily regulated industry, it will be particularly useful for your organization to build ongoing relationships with legislators. There's no reason to wait until a significant bill comes along. Actually, if your legislators already know your organization, they may be more inclined to give weight to your concerns when it really counts. Advanced notice of legislative hearings is sometimes sent to relevant individuals and organizations, so it's a good idea to do what you can to get yourself on that list. Introduce your business early in the relationship. Some organizations even invite legislators for facility tours to build a more lasting impression.

Become Active in Industry and Security Organizations

Industry associations can amplify your voice by joining it with the voices of others. They also have their own resources dedicated to monitoring legislative and regulatory proposals, as well as their own government-relations teams with existing legislator relationships. Speaking through an association also allows your organization to work against sometimes publicly popular legislation without suffering a PR hit for doing so.

Regulation

When a government entity has created a draft regulation, it is required to allot at least 30 days for public comment. Typically, agencies allow 90 days of public comment on proposals. The web site www.regulations.gov provides an up-to-date list of all proposals that are up for public comment and that is searchable by agency and keyword.

Make Your Own Comments

Generally, you may submit comments on behalf of yourself or your organization through www.regulations.gov or by mail. (Be sure to provide three copies of comments and reference the appropriate docket number in your notice).

Comment Through an Industry Organization

As noted above, associations provide a unique opportunity to approach an issue with a loud and unified voice. Regulatory agencies carefully evaluate all public comments and execute revisions before drafting final regulations for approval.

Voluntary Guidelines

As in legislative development, it is important to approach government agencies and industry organizations with your input on proposed voluntary guidelines. This means maintaining strong relationships and being active in your association's meetings and committees where appropriate. Voluntary guidelines or industry standards are the most frequent starting point for new regulations.

If you decide to take any of the above actions, you will find success only if you act as a knowledgeable representative of your enterprise, having coordinated with all relevant corporate entities and keeping the best interest of the business in mind.

Standards

Standards are grounded on juried industry best practices that set measurable targets for those who choose to comply. Just as regulations have an independent review of compliance, so too do standards, and there is usually a certification process upon successful conformance review. Good examples are ISO 17799, the information security standard, NFPA 1600 Standard on Disaster/Emergency Management and Business Continuity, and Control Objectives for Information and Related Technology

(COBIT). More recent examples are from ASIS International, which has transformed its guidelines program into a more formal standards effort, and the American National Standards Institute's Homeland Security Standards Panel (ANSI/HSSP).

Know When to Act

Unfortunately, it doesn't help to know how you can impact new rules if you are unaware of them. You can't change anything if you don't know what's on the docket and what it might mean to you.

While a security department can try to keep track of all security-significant legislation, the complexities of proposed rules and regulations make this a sometimes-insurmountable challenge. It takes some digging to get to the security impact of many regulations, and often that impact isn't explicitly stated. Unfortunately, it might not be recognized until the rule is put into action.

Organizations would do well to make law-watching a coordinated, enterprise effort. Most large companies already rely on their government affairs department to watch laws that affect their business, such as taxes, EPA issues, and FDA issues. Security must partner with other corporate entities, such as government affairs, legal, quality, safety, and human resources, to jointly track and understand the import of proposed rules. An enterprise view helps individual departments more clearly understand when it's important to act and when it's important not to act. Some legislation affects numerous aspects of an enterprise, some positively and some negatively. Only with a business mindset can the benefits and drawbacks be accurately measured.

Regulation Management Worksheet

Using the Responsible, Accountable, Consulted, Informed (RACI) methodology (see Table 7.1), determine which of these regulations and voluntary guidelines affect your organization, either directly or indirectly, who should be involved, to what extent, and who should carry them out. For each item, place the responsibility in the appropriate title cell as either: R = Responsible, A = Accountable, C = Consult, or I = Inform (i.e., RACI). When completed, an additional exercise of replacing the RACI letters with FTE estimates will serve as both a high-level staffing model and provide insight as to how much labor is going to be needed to support a given process or program.

If your company chooses to ignore any of these or the myriad of other regulations or voluntary guidelines, you'd better have a good reason why.

Table 7.1 The Responsible, Accountable, Consulted, Informed (RACI) Methodology

Regulation or Guideline	CSO	Legal Counsel	SVP of Supply Chain	CIO	Dir. of HR	Other
Control Objectives for Information and Related Technology (COBIT) Issued by the IT Governance Institute, this guideline has been developed as a standard for good information technology (IT) security and control practices that provides a reference framework for management, users, and information systems, audit, control, and security practitioners. http://www.itgi.org/ http://www.isaca.org/0						
Customs-Trade Partnership Against Terrorism (C-TPAT) A voluntary government/business initiative developed to strengthen and improve the overall international supply chain and U. S. border security. http://www.cbp.gov/xp/cgov/import/commercial_enforcement/ctpat/						
Executive Order 13224: Blocking Property and Prohibiting Transaction, with Persons Who Commit, Threaten to Commit, or Support Terrorism Prohibits government agencies, contractor, and financial institutions from sponsoring,						

(Continued)

Table 7.1 (Continued)

Regulation or Guideline	CSO	Legal Counsel	SVP of Supply Chain	CIO	Dir. of HR	Other
supporting, or otherwise funding terrorists. Enforced by the U.S. Treasury Department's Office of Foreign Asset Control. http://www.treas.gov/offices/ enforcement/ofac/sanctions/ terrorism.Shtml						
Gramm-Leach-Bliley Act (The Financial Modernization Act of 1999) (GLBA) A federal law that requires financial institutions to ensure the confidentiality and security of their customers' personal information. http://www.ftc.gov/privacy/ privacyinitiatives/glboct.html						
Health Insurance Portability and Accountability Act of 1996 (HIPAA) Regulation that provides patients with greater access to their medical records and more control over how personally, identifiable health information is used. The regulation also addresses the obligations of healthcare providers and health plans to protect health information. http://www.hhs.gov/ocr/hipaa/						
ISO 17799 A code of practice for information security management developed by the International Organization for Standardization. The objectives outlined provide general guidance on the						

(Continued)

Table 7.1 (Continued)

Regulation or Guideline	CSO	Legal Counsel	SVP of Supply Chain	CIO	Dir. of HR	Other
commonly accepted goals of information security management. http://www.iso.org/iso/en/ ISOOnline.frontpage http://en.wikipedia.org/wiki/ISO/ IEC_17799						
ISO 27001 Published by the International Organization for Standardization (ISO) on October 15, 2005, this standard establishes best practice for an information security management system and complements ISO 17799. The two standards are related but perform distinctive roles. http://www.iso.org/iso/en/ commcentre/pressreleases/2005/ Ref976.html						
Maritime Transportation Act (MARSEC or MTSAct) Regulations for U.S. port facilities and vessels requiring the development of security plans and implementation of security measures and procedures. http://www.uscg.mil/hq/g-m/mp/ mtso.shtml						
National Strategy for Physical Protection of Critical Infrastructures and Key Assets Voluntary guidelines to protect physical infrastructures from						

(Continued)

Table 7.1 (Continued)

Regulation or Guideline	CSO	Legal Counsel	SVP of Supply Chain	CIO	Dir. of HR	Other
terrorist attacks. Like its counterpart cyberspace strategy (see immediately below), it emphasizes public/private partnership as the way to protect critical infrastructures. http://www.whitehouse.gov/pcipb/physicol.html						
National Strategy to Secure Cyberspace Voluntary guidelines make official long-established best practices for protecting information security. http://www.whitehouse.gov/pcipb/						
Public Company Accounting Reform and Investor Protection Act of 2002 (Sarbanes-Oxley) The federal Sarbanes-Oxley Act was created to protect investors by improving the accuracy and reliability of corporate disclosures. The Act covers issues such as establishing a public company accounting oversight board, auditor independence, corporate responsibility, and enhanced financial disclosure. http://en.wikipedia.org/wiki/Sarbanes_Oxley						
Public Health Security and Bioterrorism Preparedness and Response Act (PHSBPR)						

Table 7.1 (Continued)

Regulation or Guideline	CSO	Legal Counsel	SVP of Supply Chain	CIO	Dir. of HR	Other
Establishes national, state, and local preparedness and response strategies and procedures to protect U.S. food, water, and drug supplies. http://www.fda.gov/oc/bioterrorism/bioact.html						
Trade Act of 2002—Advance Electronic Information Requires advance transmission of electronic cargo information to U.S. Customs and Border Control regarding arriving and departing cargo. This consolidates the implementation strategy of the 24 hour rule and the implementation strategy of the Trade Act. http://www.cbp.gov/xp/cgov/import/communications_to_industry/advance_jnfo/						
U.S. Customs Container Security Initiative Places U.S. Customs officers at major foreign ports to prevent terrorists from accessing container ships. The incentive for foreign ports: In case of a terrorist attack involving cargo, program participants would be less likely to be shut down. http://www.cbp.gov/xp/cgov/border_security/international_activities/csi/						

(Continued)

Table 7.1 (Continued)

Regulation or Guideline	CSO	Legal Counsel	SVP of Supply Chain	CIO	Dir. of HR	Other
U.S. Dept. of Transportation's Pipeline and Hazardous Materials Safety Administration (PHMSA) HAZMAT Regulations Federal Hazardous Materials Regulations set forth transportation and packaging regulations for all modes of moving hazardous materials. http://hazmot.dot.gov/regs/rules.htm http://www.access.gpo.gov/nara/cfr/waisidx_04/49cfrv2_04.html						
U.S. Environmental Protection Agency's Water Infrastructure Security Affects community water systems. Organizations must certify and submit vulnerability assessments and emergency response plans. Provisions could one day be applied to factories that discharge into public water sources. Part of the U.S. Bioterrorism Act of 2002. http://cfpub.epa.gov/safewater/watersecurity/bioterrorism.cfm						

Use this table to determine how regulations and voluntary guidelines affect your organization, either directly or indirectly, who should be involved, to what extent, and who should carry them out.

Components of a Cost of Security Compliance Model

In the federal government's rule-making process, there are a number of milestones to enable impact assessment on your organization. Trade associations will be engaged early on, and typically, your legislative liaison or general counsel office will be tracking legislation or regulations of consequence to the company. In the final stages of rollout of a piece of legislation in the *Federal Register*, you will be able to identify the components of work required by the proposed regulation. Table 7.2 provides a template for consideration as you assess the potential cost of compliance impact.

Prospectively tracking the progress of security-related regulations and then estimating their financial and productivity impacts is an excellent way to work collaboratively with counsel and others in senior management. You are also demonstrating the blending of your professional knowledge with the financial objectives of the company.

The Implications of Noncompliance

The fact that regulatory compliance can be expensive is unquestioned. However, the notion that regulatory noncompliance can be far more expensive should be clear from the corporate failures of the past five to ten years. Enron and Global Crossing together lost $190 billion in market capitalization. Pfizer has lost $24 billion, and Hoffman-Laroche was fined 497 million Euros. Boeing has lost valuable Air Force contracts, and several noteworthy players in the financial services industry have individually paid millions in fines over the past several years. A company simply cannot accept the risk of noncompliance in today's regulatory environment.

What Are Some of Those Risks?

Company brand can be significantly impacted, resulting in loss of market share and reduced competitive position. After Sarbanes-Oxley, boards are comprised of increasing numbers of "independent" members who see their roles (and their personal liability) as more aggressive on the adequacy of internal controls and corporate integrity.

Fines can also be levied by the government. For example, in the initial decade of the Sentencing Commission Guidelines for

Table 7.2 Components of a Cost of Security Compliance Model

Cost Component	Unit Cost	Ext. Cost
Direct Costs (Assumes that the company using the model has an efficient time tracking system in place and the items under the proprietary staff time logged to compliance activities are defined in that system.)		
Billable time directly applied to compliance administration (Divide annual salary only by 2080 hours and multiply by 38% for hourly rate) Proprietary staff time logged to compliance activities. • Program planning and administration • Policy development of modification • Risk assessment • System engineering/construction documentation • Contract staff time logged to compliance activities • Consultant fees directly related to compliance • Training and awareness programs • Program development • Trainee participant time • Activities that can be directly allocated to auditing for ongoing compliance • Development and delivery of employee and agent awareness programs directly related to appliance with regulations • Development and ongoing administration and maintenance of required regulatory reporting • If security costs [e.g., account administration, access control list administration, etc.] • Other direct charges		
Capital Expenses to Meet Required Security Standards Determine local capital expense depreciation rates for one-year cost. See following equipment list for selected items: • Security equipment • Construction/installation/security system enhancement • Unique software development directly related to compliance • Other capital expense		
Estimated Loss of Productivity Due to Compliance Activities Redirected labor by specific persons, project delays, lost sales, etc.		
Indirect Costs Confirm with CPO/Legal if allocatable to impact: • Physical space costs		

(Continued)

Table 7.2 (Continued)

Cost Component	Unit Cost	Ext. Cost
• Cost of supervision • Recruitment costs • Administrative costs • Maintenance costs • Third-party licensing • Documentation maintenance • Awareness and education costs • Periodic filing costs • The cost[s] at change and recertification • Cost of repair		
Offset to Costs Recovery from increased cost to consumers, one-time assessments, or other recovery processes.		

Use this table as a template for consideration as you assess the potential cost of compliance impact.

Corporations (1991–2000), there were 1,494 cases brought to trial, 76% resulting in fines with an average of $2,069,675 and a high of $500,000,000. It is noteworthy that the regulatory environment for these cases was voluntary, whereas the 2004 revisions are mandatory. As a result, it may be anticipated that federal prosecutors will have far more measurable criteria to use to assess the level of conformance or nonconformance at the targeted organization.

Measurable Impact to the Bottom Line

Some of the risks of noncompliance can be measured against the bottom line in the following ways:
- direct cost of sanctions
- indirect multiplier impacts from compensation ordered to customers or others
- loss of program or other funding (venture capital or other)
- program suspension and related costs
- "reactionary" costs related to status reporting on deficiencies and corrective action
- costs associated with other programs having a dependency on the process deemed deficient
- partial adoption puts at risk insurance or bond coverage

- federal sentencing guideline implications
- loss of customers and market share
- vulnerability to class action suits

THE BOTTOM LINE: Security regulations are here to stay. Maintain your industry-specific contacts with regard to legislative and regulatory initiatives and work with your internal resources to influence policy at best; or, at least, you need to understand the cost and operational implications.

Highlights for Follow-Up

- What organization or executive is responsible for state and federal legislative initiatives, and how would you characterize your relationship with that office?
- Are you aware of anything in the works that may impact your company or organization, and to what extent are you influencing your company's strategy with regard to the implications of its implementation?
- What security-specific regulations apply to your organization now, and to what extent have you been engaged in their pre-implementation impact assessment and rollout?
- What is the real cost of security-related regulations to your company?
- To what extent can proposed or active regulations assist you in obtaining resources or influencing corporate policy in terms of voluntary compliance?

Key Terms

- Regulatory elements
- Security regulations
- Regulatory compliance strategy
- Legislation
- Regulation
- Voluntary guidelines
- Standards
- Security compliance model
- Noncompliance

8

INFORMATION SECURITY

Introduction

If you were to poll your top management by asking them to rank corporate assets, it is likely that information and the infrastructure around it would be at or near the top of every list. Information, specifically sensitive, private information, is the lifeblood of all business operations.

You may not have information security in your assigned responsibilities, but it is essential for all security personnel to have an appreciation of the criticality of this infrastructure in the health of the business. The integrity and availability of information goes to the heart of business efficiency, effectiveness, and reputation. As a security executive, you will invariably interact closely with your colleagues in the IT department. This chapter is intended to provide you and your team with a basic understanding of IT security to better enable your support for their mission.

Business Value

Assurance that sensitive, private information is verifiably secure is a fundamental requirement of business and a fiduciary responsibility of officers and directors. Without this assurance, shareholders, customers, and the viability of the business are collectively at risk, merely waiting to learn how devastating the compromise has been.

The Essentials

Information is a critical asset at increasing risk of loss or compromise. The heart of an information risk management program is an *ongoing* process of risk assessment. This involves an understanding of risk tolerance, knowledge of likely risks and threats, measured assessments of established controls, and executed plans to address identified vulnerabilities. The resulting information risk management strategy is focused on the preservation of confidentiality, maintenance of data integrity, and assurance of the availability of information for authorized users.

An effective information risk management program can only be assured through the diligence of every individual who has access to confidential information. Along with personal integrity, diligence is the one critical asset that touches just about every trusted individual in the enterprise. The notion of individual accountability is the model to be followed if information is to be truly secured. The key to proactive protection is the recognition that threat is truly dynamic. It is constantly changing and adapting to our efforts to safeguard vital information assets.

Critical Importance of Information Security

Information security is given critical importance within an organization if the following holds true:

- *You* decide it makes "business sense":
  - You and your customers care about privacy and confidentiality.
  - Information that has integrity and is available is critical for effective and timely operations.
  - Competitive pressures demand it.
  - It might even be an effective market differentiator.
- *Society* says it matters:
  - Gramm-Leach-Bliley Act (GLBA)
  - Sarbanes-Oxley Act (SOX)
  - Health Insurance Portability and Accountability Act (HIPAA)
  - California Breach Notification Bill (SB-1386 and AB-1950)
  - Federal Information Security Management Act (FISMA), the Payment Card Industry Data Security Standard (PCI DSS), the Personal Information Protection and Electronic Documents Act (PIPEDA), etc.

Most regulations are very vague, but they still have to be complied with. Long ago, the regulators understood that they could never hope to give actionable and implementable guidance about security controls that would work for all organizations. Consequently, the regulations say moderately clearly what needs to be protected, who is responsible for the protection, and, in general, what kinds of controls should be considered. It is up to each regulated organization to determine how the regulation applies to that organization, what controls make sense for that organization, and how to implement and operate those sensible controls.

Core Information Assurance Requirements

Confidentiality, integrity, and availability (CIA) represent the classic three-legged stool of information security. Be aware that responsibility for these three concerns cannot be readily given to a single person. Each is an important concern for multiple organizations, so many people will feel ownership for them. CIA is a great way to frame the challenge of protecting information, illustrated below:

- **Confidentiality:** Requirements that (some) information is to be kept private, secret, and restricted to specific parties. This requires business controls supporting access authorization and accountability.
- **Integrity:** Requirements that information must be accurate and authentic in content, currency/time, and source data. This requires business controls supporting change authorization and accountability.
- **Availability:** Requirements that information is to be available in the appropriate form when needed. This requires business processes supporting useful form and performance.

Information Has Value

Information has value to an organization's well-being and bottom line, which is why the information has to be protected and why certain things represent threats to information. The activities directed at understanding information value are determined from information risk assessment processes, which include considerations such as the following:

- What information do you have? (This requires an inventory-like exercise.)
- What defines the value of each information element? What are the likely consequences if the value is reduced or compromised?
- Who owns the information? The owner is the custodian and should be making the protection decisions.
- Where does it come from, where does it flow, where does it come to rest, where does it go?
  - Both inside and outside the enterprise (e.g., contractors and outsourcing)?
  - Both electronic and nonelectronic forms?
- What threatens the information?
- What controls currently offer resistance to the threats and how effective are those controls believed to be?

- What is the residual risk? Is the residual risk acceptable, and if not, what do you choose to do about it?

All too often, the value of information is poorly understood and rarely quantified. Therefore, most information-protection programs operate on gut-feel, seat-of-the-pants, and other judgment-based processes.

Information Moves at Warp Speed

This is not unlike people in a physical security program. Physical assets often stay in one place, retain their form for long periods of time, and are stable in other respects. On the other hand, people move around from one threat environment or control environment to another, which is a much more demanding protective challenge. Information not only moves around a lot during its lifecycle (one application to another, one firm to another, one machine to another, one network to another, etc.), it can do so at very high speeds and in a wide variety of forms and media. Once you have mastered herding cats, try your hand at ensuring information is protected throughout its lifecycle.

Key Assessment: What Is the State of Control?

How long would you be willing to operate your business with all the security controls turned off? How long before the consequences become catastrophic?

No control is perfect. A perfect control involves infinite cost. A perfect control almost certainly makes the information totally unusable, and therefore useless. Residual risk is a fact of life. No amount of technology can make up for incompetent, erroneous, or malicious human actions and behavior, if for no other reason than that people invent, build, install, and operate all controls. Almost always, someone (usually more than one someone) can circumvent, override, or reset the controls and do anything that is possible to and with the information, often unilaterally and without an audit trail. Your digital fate hangs on such people, and most organizations don't even know who they are!

Different executives and organizations have different appetites for risk and different tolerances for controls, in general. Perhaps they have more tolerance for the perceived inconvenience of even common sense controls. Avoid concluding that your control situation is unique. Repeatedly, it has been shown

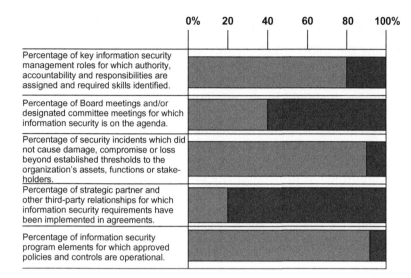

Figure 8.1 High Level Measurement of Information Security Program Elements. Any one of these that may be significantly lacking in compliance could contribute to a serious breach of information security.

that quite a small number of "styles" or methods of control can be defined that would serve in an enormous number of very different business circumstances.

What gets measured can be controlled. Without measurement and monitoring you have very little idea what the state of control really is. (See Chapter 16, "Security Measures and Metrics.") Measurement is something that is typically done very badly in most enterprises, government agencies, and the like. Although documenting the rate of attacks or similar event metrics may be useful, it is much more sensible to work on measuring the state of the control environment. What is the intended state of control? What is the risk-based measurement of the actual state of control? Are the controls actually there, and are they really working? If not, what will it cost and how long will it take to fix the problems?

Figure 8.1 provides an example of high-level measurement for five information security program elements. Note the issues being measured. Any one of these that may be significantly lacking in compliance could contribute to a serious breach of information security.

All information should not be equally protected. Having many variables implies one size does not fit all. Information values vary in the following ways:
- regulatory scope
- threats and vulnerabilities
- business models
- appetites for risk
- ability to fund controls
- cost of controls

Organizing the Information Security Program

How the information security program is organized is very important, because the organization model selected has to be consistent with the organizational model and culture of your enterprise. It should be decentralized if the business is decentralized, or as centralized as it can be if your firm's power model works that way. It is not possible to gather together in one organization all the resources that have some significant role to play in the information protection process. Rather, almost by definition, information protection is a cross-functional, collaborative undertaking that defies centralization.

The technical aspects of information security are very important and very complex. Specialists are necessary, and those specialists are likely to be part of the IT organization. Some sort of extended "organization" for the information security program is required in order to get the technical specialists into the mix. In most organizations, the information infrastructure is so distributed (top to bottom, inside and out, and geographically) that each custodial organization requires the assignment of trained and accountable information security administrators to oversee day-to-day adherence to policy.

If your background has not been in the IT world, you will find the CISO (chief information security officer) is likely to be a "techie." This is because most enterprises think information security is completely a technical problem, so they give it to the CIO (chief information officer), or more likely someone who reports to the CIO and brings a variety of technical types into the role. Therefore, most of the CISOs of the world have a technical background and have been tasked to manage information security as a technical function. If you are the non-IT security manager, your willingness to engage the technical organization in a coordinated protection strategy can go far to demonstrate that there are critical nontechnical security practices that serve proactive information protection.

We have discussed the potential of security committees to assure the exchange of information, coordination of risk management efforts, and basic security infrastructure teamwork. This is only one potential venue; but, as the senior security executive or as the CISO, your joint operational relationship is key to the effective administration of a proactive information protection program. Non-IT security professionals need to understand the range of information security risks confronting the company and their relative role in the protection scheme. Conversely, CISOs need to understand and engage their security operational colleagues in their protection and incident response strategy.

Information Security Infrastructure and Architecture

When every business unit is doing its own thing regarding choice and implementation of security processes and technologies, the company is in a losing game. There is a lot of power in "security infrastructure": security technologies implemented across an organization as common solutions and enterprise standards. The way in which all the security components relate can be referred to as the *security architecture*, which, in turn, must have clear and engineered relationships to other architectures (IT, network, application, data, etc.).

The notion of a network perimeter matters a lot. You may hear talk about "the disappearing perimeter." It certainly is changing, but it is not disappearing. Just as we envision effective physical security, there has to be a perimeter (think firewall) somewhere in the architecture, unless you intend for the asset(s) to be totally exposed. A perimeter that tries to protect a large collection of resources (such as an enterprise firewall) still has significant value. If there is no enterprise perimeter control environment, then each device, or smaller collections of devices, has to become totally self-defending to a degree consistent with its value. The perimeter has just been moved inward, but it still has to be there as a control concept. Your computer at home is a good example of a small domain, maybe even just one machine protected by a firewall and likely other protective tools.

Day-to-Day Operational Security

The 24/7 security operations organization can play a vital role in the information protection program. Providing a training program focused on the likely threats that may be discovered during tours can identify and eliminate—or illuminate—obvious vulnerabilities. Unsecured laptops, credentials left in the open, yellow sticky memos containing passwords, conditions contributing to fire or water damage, violations of policy, and other hazards to information integrity are all within the scope of a trained security officer. This engagement also makes the job of providing tours more focused on risk identification versus tapping a guard tour sensor.

Cyber Incident Response Planning

A cyber incident is a real, perceived, or threatened event that involves technology such as data, business applications, computers, networks, or electronic communications with the potential to have a major negative impact on the business. Cyber incidents may range in seriousness from no direct impact to customers to major disruption of business operations or significant impact to the company's reputation.

The purpose of the cyber incident response plan is to define the process to respond to cyber incidents, which significantly impact the company's critical business functions. It documents the procedures for responding to situations, which impact the company's ability to provide services to customers or to meet legal or regulatory requirements. The plan is limited to the response to cyber incidents after detection or identification and does not address ongoing preventative actions or detection techniques. Objectives of the cyber incident response plan are to supplement the cyber incident defense program by developing a response strategy that

- facilitates timely assessment of potential problems while ensuring a coordinated and comprehensive response to incidents that cross business units;
- minimizes the impact of cyber incidents on the company's ability to provide service while maintaining the company's public image and credibility;
- facilitates prosecution of offenders as appropriate;
- defines an organization to implement the response plan and includes definitions of the roles of the leaders and members;
- documents procedures to rapidly notify, deploy, and coordinate corporate resources to assess and respond to the incident; and
- documents the process to define how a decision to activate the plan is made and by whom.

In order to maximize overall effectiveness for preventing and responding to cyber incidents, a comprehensive, ongoing program with emphasis on prevention and early detection forms the foundation on which the response plan is based. In the event of a major incident, business unit senior management must be prepared to

- accept the consequences of the required responses in order to maximize the effectiveness of the response;
- support a comprehensive and cohesive response effort if required;
- take actions that are in the company's best interest, even though they may not be the best for the specific business unit, and which must be identified; and

- identify and understand roles of critical team members prior to an incident, for support from their management is essential.

Development of a cyber incident response strategy and related plans offers both the IT and corporate security teams an opportunity to identify shared and unique skills and responsibilities while building teamwork, which will serve beyond timely and effective incident management.

Never before has cyber security been more important than it is today. The world is not only being confronted with technology advancements on a daily basis, but is in the midst of an evolutionary event that has a global impact. The "bad guys" don't have to be in the same room; they can be on a different continent and obtain the same results—from a safer haven.

To provide for a secure future, both corporations and computer users must be constantly cognizant of the threats that are continually present and stalking their systems. They need to use safeguards (antivirus, anti-spam, anti-spyware, etc.) on their computers and be leery of scams and frauds. They must recognize changes in operation or other unusual characteristics of their computers and take corrective actions quickly.

Today and in the future, information assurance depends on an aware, accountable computer user, and that responsibility has to be set in policy, communicated, and enforced.

The image in Figure 8.2 displays many of the diverse threats and risks that confront an information protection program. The key to proactive protection is the recognition that threat is truly dynamic. It is constantly changing and adapting to our efforts to safeguard vital information assets.

Highlights for Follow-Up

- On a scale of 1 to 10, how dependent is your company on the IT infrastructure?
- Does your security strategy and planning reflect this level of priority?
- If you are not currently responsible for information security, is there a designated manager in IT or elsewhere who is?
- How would you characterize your relationship with this colleague?
- If you were the CISO, how would you respond to the same questions?
- Where the relationship may be less than mutually supportive, what steps might you take to move in a positive direction?

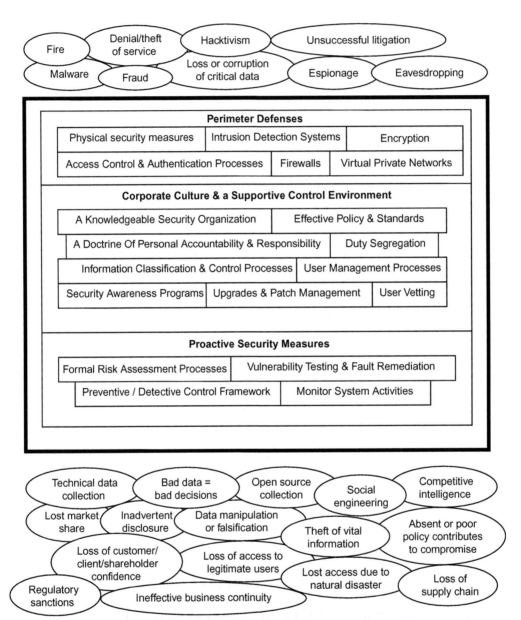

Figure 8.2 Information Protection Program Threats. The many and diverse threats and risks that confront an information protection program.

- Is the annual risk assessment program a joint effort between security and the CIO? How about other key stakeholders? Where are the gaps in this critical business process?
- Given that there is acknowledged interdependence between logical and physical security, do you believe this interdependence is acknowledged by current business practice and resource allocations?
- Has the current physical security deployment strategy (including first response) been effectively coordinated between security and IT? How about other key stakeholders, like facilities and business units with specific convenience or protection needs?
- If the 24/7 security operations group is responsible for first response to IT-related business continuity incidents, have there been adequate orientation, procedural training, and notification procedures made available?
- Is there an established cyber incident response plan that has been coordinated with business continuity, IT, risk management (if appropriate), and security?

Key Terms

- Information security
- Information assurance requirements
- Information security infrastructure and architecture
- Operational security
- Cyber incident response planning

9

PHYSICAL SECURITY AND FIRST RESPONSE

Introduction

Virtually every corporate security program contains some elements of physical security, premises protection, and security operations. Information security programs cannot securely exist without a protective envelope of physical and operational security. Critical and sensitive business operations also benefit from in-depth physical security and access control. Given the breadth and diversity of security hardware and software, a well thought out security strategy is essential.

You may not have physical security in your assigned responsibilities, but it is essential for all security personnel to have an appreciation of the criticality of this protection suite in the health of the business. The absence of effective physical security places every employee, visitor, and asset at risk. This chapter is intended to provide you and your team with a basic understanding of physical security to better enable your support for their mission.

Business Value

A case can be made that a proactive physical security program effectively supports business performance by mitigating employee and customer risk. A well-planned and secure business environment is a competitive advantage as compared to one that slows down and unnecessarily exposes the company to physical security threats.

Absence of reasonable and responsive security measures in the face of known vulnerabilities is a very serious risk. Purely from a liability protection standpoint, business cannot safely and securely exist without basic, if not in-depth, physical security. Modern technology and networking has enabled a tremendous range of protection options at an increasingly competitive price.

The Essentials

Virtually every company has some level of physical security associated with its business operations, including the following:

- A security cost is embedded in every lease.
- Insurance carriers (and many municipal codes) require certain protection measures above and beyond fire and life safety.
- Locks and alarms are an integral part of facility build-out.
- Various security procedures are employed in the protection of assets.
- Employee and invitee safety and security are basic expectations and legal precepts.

For the company as a whole, and at each specific site housing business operations, the risk profile will determine the need for more specific security measures. However, you will generally find that physical security operations represent a significant portion of the business security cost. Therefore, what should "an effective physical security program" cost? What level of investment will ensure the management of known threats? There is no single "best" answer that will suffice as a cost-effective model program. Assuming that every company brings to the "right" answer its own asset mix, range of threats, and perceived risk, how do I measure what is right for my company? To answer that question, we have to start with a solid understanding of what needs to be protected, against what set of probabilities, and how that protection needs to be tailored to mitigate risk at the lowest practical cost.

As we note throughout this book, security programs must be based upon a thorough risk assessment process. It is through this risk-oriented lens that specific threats and physical or operational vulnerabilities will be identified. The relationship of these exposures to company assets—people, information, facilities and mission critical products and processes—will define the options, their cost, and the operational implications.

A Caution:

Security options range from a fairly simple approach with few elements, to highly complex systems with multiple parts that have to be integrated and aggressively managed. At a high level, your options will depend on answers to these questions:

- What is the likelihood of what types of risk?
- How severe are the likely consequences, at best and at worst, of those risks?
- What are our estimates of financial impact, at best and worst?
- Which of these risks are we willing to accept, and to which do we choose to apply security measures?

- For each risk you choose to retain:
  - How would you rank order each risk in terms of severity?
  - What are the options to reduce our exposure to each risk?
  - What is the comparative initial and continuing cost of each option?
  - How would each option impact business operations?
  - Which option offers the highest level of confidence for mitigating the targeted risk while presenting the least impact to business operations?

It is possible to secure an asset with 100% confidence in the security measures you have chosen to apply. The problem is the degree to which your solution has adversely impacted the business and the confidence management has in security.

Perhaps, more than any other set of safeguards, physical security presents a face to the resident, visitor, and adversary. It may be imposing, conveying a fortress with increasingly discriminating layers of monitoring and control; it may be welcoming on entry, with highly selective controls at specific focal points of protection; or it may merely be a friendly concierge politely asking for your identification. If you have ever planned a comprehensive, integrated security system for a business that has to work seamlessly every day, you realize the range of opinions on the necessity of secure versus open access and the presence of big brother in the workplace. After 9/11, or a significant workplace violence incident, the number of changed views on the level of physical security desired is extraordinary.

Your Objective: An Integrated Solution

The purpose of design, in security or any other area, is to invent an order or arrangement of components and details of a system in accordance with a plan. In all cases, a system is designed for a purpose. In the case of an integrated security systems design, the design method is to select and incorporate the various technological and physical elements along with personnel and procedures into a unified system, which protects identified assets and controls risks by reducing or eliminating vulnerabilities based upon an identified threat.

The purpose of integration is to produce a complete, unified system, by bringing together individual parts. For the security manager, system integration is the art of fusing security equipment, facilities, personnel, and procedures together seamlessly in a manner that results in proactive asset protection. The result is a fully integrated security system that must respond effectively to dynamic threats and risks during crisis conditions and, at the same time, function imperceptibly during normal operating conditions. Whereas design generates the various security elements to respond to (or mitigate or prevent) a particular threat or risk, integration combines them into a workable, day-to-day system and overall security program strategy for effective asset protection. *Proper use and application of the integrated security design process is the single most important aspect in the defense against dynamic threats and potential catastrophic losses.* The process, when carefully and diligently adhered to, results in a fully integrated security program that incorporates all of the essential elements needed to effectively protect critical assets and control identified risks.

Physical Security at a Glance

Figure 9.1 displays the various elements involved in the administration of an integrated physical and operational security program. If you were planning a bottom-up retrofit of current systems or development of a responsive system at a new facility, you would do well to engage a qualified consultant with no ties to a specific hardware vendor. The preparation of design and bid documents, as well as the testing and acceptance process, is a complex undertaking. Except in rare circumstances, neither you nor your purchasing staff will have the time or expertise to develop the requisite documentation essential to project success.

Alignment with the Threat

Effective physical security is a relative term, dependent in large measure on management's understanding and acceptance of the gravity and sophistication of the threats arrayed against valued assets. Threats may be specified by regulation or your expert opinion. The most serious source of threat is from the knowledgeable insider who possesses access and knows where the vulnerabilities in protection capabilities may be exploited. Furthermore, any discussion about threat must be accompanied by an understanding of likelihood. One approach is to display your risk assessment findings something like the manner shown in Figure 9.2.

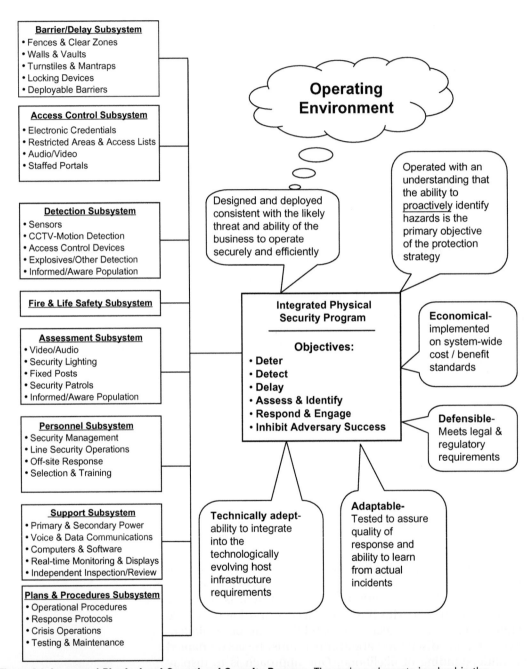

Figure 9.1 Integrated Physical and Operational Security Program. The various elements involved in the administration of an integrated physical and operational security program.

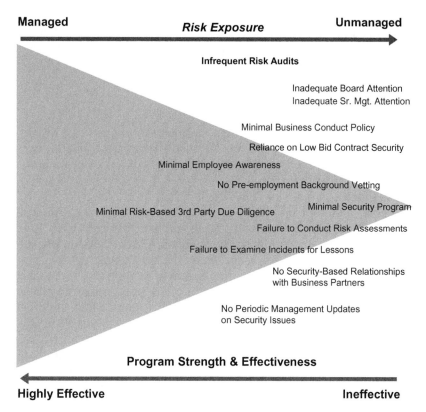

Figure 9.2 Threat Assessment Measuring Likelihood. Any discussion about threat must be accompanied by an understanding of likelihood.

Effective physical security has multiple objectives, including the following:

- **Deter**—Make protection visible enough to discourage the potential adversary.[1]
- **Detect**—Provide the capabilities necessary to ensure earliest (and most reliable) possible notification of the threat.
- **Delay**—Through the use of barriers, detection systems, or active surveillance, impose time constraints in the adversary's path to his or her objective.
- **Assess and identify**—Provide the capabilities to understand clearly and to reliably record the nature and extent of the threat.[2]

[1]A case may be made that the most effective security is *invisible*, especially when one considers the potential environmental impact of more highly visible security measures. This is a cultural issue that you will have to consider.
[2]This depends upon your assessment of likelihood and the potential need to successfully prosecute using reliable and defensible identification capabilities.

Physical security is in the eye of the beholder. You have the ability to convey a fortress image or be virtually invisible (yet still effective). Your test is to understand and be culturally sensitive to the unique needs of your company. Ensure that your security strategy has executive endorsement.

- **Respond**—Provide resources sufficient to mitigate the threat.
- **Inhibit adversary escape**—Provide detection, assessment, and positioning of response forces to minimize probability of adversary escape.

These terms are not meant to conjure up terrorists repelling down the sides of your buildings. The sequence of events for response to *any* attack incident has these elements. Obviously, each step will be graded depending on the value of the asset and the level of risk established between security and the asset owner.

A key point to make to management is that you *can* make your facilities virtually impenetrable. The only problem will be the business's inability to get anything accomplished. Finding the appropriate balance between being secure and insecure will be the challenge. Business people want convenience, openness, and absence of constraints on their work and the comfort of their invitees. The law expects a safe and secure workplace, and after a threatening incident, most employees want that sense of security as well, at least for a while.

A casual tour of the ASIS (American Society for Industrial Security) annual conference exhibit hall floor is enough to convey the expanse and diversity of the physical security inventory. What is clear is the convergence of physical security into the larger infrastructure of the organization. Modern electronic security is network-ready, and current open architecture standards facilitate communication among various components from different vendors across the corporate data infrastructure.

Differing, dated security systems, largely incapable of true integration, are a challenge often found by security executives when preexisting property has been acquired during various expansions. This situation may place extra burdens on a centralized monitoring capability and on the need for reliable maintenance. Where acquisition is in the offing, be sure to inject yourself into the due diligence of the infrastructure on the property, and inform the accountable parties on what needs to be done to bring the property up to your standards of protection.

There are excellent, expert resources available to assist in the planning and preparation of bid documents. Carefully consider how you will be (or are now) monitoring your suite of hardware.

Unfortunately, well planned, resilient, and reliable systems are worthless in the hands of untrained, unaware, and unsupervised central station or command center operators or unprepared response personnel.

Security Operations

As noted in Figure 9.1, an integrated physical security system effectively incorporates an operational element to establish a qualitative program management and response infrastructure. We discuss some of the noteworthy risk issues in Chapter 12, "Safe and Secure Workplaces," and in Appendix C we provide model procurement documents for selecting a contract guard force. This physical security operational element is the most visible component of a corporate security program and typically comprises the largest share of the security program budget. In many companies it may be the only security program having that label. More sophisticated investigations may be occasional and contracted out under the purview of legal. Likewise, information security becomes a mere operational element of the IT department. What is important to underscore here is the need to establish clear qualitative standards and expectations around these response resources, and to understand their role in the following: premises liability protection; security incident, emergency medical, and business interruption response; and operational management of the security technology infrastructure.

Owing to the budget visibility of security operations, economic downturn, downsizing, and other responses to business pressure, these resources are a potentially fruitful target. Management needs to be cautioned that such times often bring an increased potential for workplace hostility, theft, and sabotage, and reductions in first responder and physical security resources need to be carefully approached. What is that essential level of protection? What is the resource reduction baseline below which you believe the *cost of likely risk potential* will add to the cost of doing business?

If you refresh your understanding of risk assessment based on the steps discussed in Chapter 3, "Risk Assessment and Mitigation," and Chapter 4, "Strategic Security Planning," you have a handle on known vulnerabilities and risk trends. From this foundation you can demonstrate that at various levels of security resource reduction combined with the likely increase of people and property risk, your ability to prevent, detect, and adequately respond will be impacted at an unacceptable exposure to risk.

The Quality of First Response

The term "first responder" is justifiably at the center of the post-9/11 vocabulary. What is missing in these discussions and strategies is the fact that until public resources arrive, often it is a member of the corporate security team who is the first responder. Consider the following from a security executive (who wished to remain anonymous) who manages a global, proprietary security operation:

The rapid "quality" response goes beyond imminent life safety issues. I might add that in the age of heightened terror alerts, hoaxes, suspicious powders, and public sensitivity to air quality issues, having a trained staff that works collaboratively with facilities will go a long way to reducing risk, business impact, and employee anxiety. Taking certain measures to proactively contain a white powder substance, cordon off the area, and isolate exposed individuals, or to proactively shut HVAC air intakes when a fire rages next door (with unknown airborne contaminants), goes a long way to building credibility with public safety officials, employees, and C-suite executives when you can return to business as usual faster than would have been possible by watching and waiting.

As for defibrillators, as they become more ubiquitous, seconds matter more than ever. According to the American Heart Association (AHA) the chance of surviving a cardiac arrest decreases 10% with each passing minute. The victim is brain dead at seven to eight minutes. Even the best public safety response can't control traffic, weather, and "vertical response" time, a.k.a. elevators. Therefore, if security can be there in three minutes, that is a big difference. To complement response, we are now training all floor wardens on automated external defibrillators (AED) and CPR. The American Hospital Association made the training simpler (less than two hours); and, my thinking is, with these things in malls and airports, I'm putting them in our internal "public" areas. There is no measurement for the perceived quality of the security organization when the life of an employee or visitor has been saved by quick, qualified first response.

Now, consider this comparison of response times by trained on-premises security officers and local emergency medical technicians at ten locations throughout the United States (see Figure 9.3).

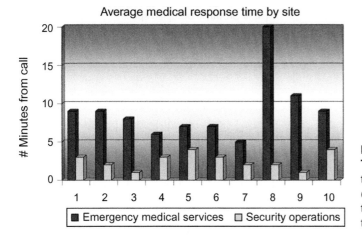

Figure 9.3 Average Medical Response Time by Site. Comparison of response times by trained on-premises security officers and local emergency medical technicians at ten locations throughout the United States.

All Space Is Not Created Equal

Your company's business processes have varying levels of criticality, some requiring complete redundancy to ensure seamless rollover upon interruption, and some capable of being restored in a matter of days or weeks. Plan your physical security strategy around those most-secure areas at the center of layered protection, with tailored protection suited to less sensitive spaces. Effective access control is a key element from the perimeter inward, for both outsider and insider adversaries. Assets move, often without security's knowledge, so it is important to keep that risk assessment current, especially for the most sensitive operations and spaces.

Physical Security as a Force Multiplier

The chart in Figure 9.4 illustrates how well-planned physical access control can be a force multiplier while directly contributing to the bottom line. In this case, while business space was rapidly expanding, security thought through how the combination of well-configured barriers, CCTV, and card access would have enabled significantly less growth in guard force headcount. Similar success has been achieved with 24/7 remote video monitoring. Two additional advantages are the elimination of some receptionist positions and depreciation of the equipment over a five-year period.

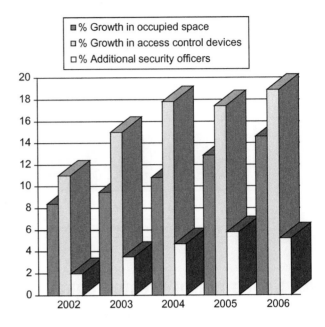

Figure 9.4 Physical Security as a Force Multiplier. Illustration of how well-planned physical access control can be a force multiplier while directly contributing to the bottom line.

Equipment Removal and Value of Risk Assessments

As businesses evolve and grow, physical security devices are deployed throughout the enterprise, but with what frequency are they removed when the risk dynamics they were intended to aid change? Be wary of the cost of ownership for devices that no longer add value because the assets they were intended to protect have been eliminated, moved, changed, or otherwise modified to change the protection objective.

Security Riding on the Corporate Network

Many of the legacy security systems you now possess originally communicated on dedicated wire installed from the device in the protected area to some sort of local controller and then to the on-site monitoring station. Pulling all this wire was a costly exercise. Now, with the capabilities of corporate-wide IT networks, much of the new device inventory can ride on this extensive network at significantly reduced cost and typically higher security. Consequently, you find a number of IT executives taking on the physical security program as a logical subsystem of the larger IT system. Many of the access control systems, network-ready CCTV, and other components require little bandwidth and, importantly, are scalable to facilitate growth. They are also attractive in that they enable smart-card credentials or biometrics to be employed for more secure desktop log on. A term in contemporary use for this broader integration of IT and security systems is *convergence*, which is often cited as revolutionary when it simply is an evolution, given the growth of dedicated networks throughout the enterprise.

A Note on Convergence

Over the past few years, there has been a growing interest and application of converged physical and IT security functions. We allude to this in Chapter 6, "Organizational Models." These discussions often focus upon organizational developments such as the following:

- integrated IT security and physical security systems
- unified auditing and response systems of physical and IT events
- systems for correlating physical and IT security events
- common access policy management and control
- common user provisioning
- single access credentials
- physical security solutions on IT networks[3]

There is a clear requirement for a converged security strategy and shared responsibility for corporate-wide security, regardless if physical and IT security (as well as contingency planning and other protection functions) are under a single executive or are separated.

THE BOTTOM LINE: Your physical security program effectively should balance responsiveness to known risks and an acceptable level of inconvenience to the business.

Highlights for Follow-Up

- If there were one fundamental improvement you could make to the physical security of your facilities, what would it be? How exposed are you with the knowledge of this need?

[3]Thanks to John McClurg, chief risk and security officer at Honeywell.

- Are your in-house first responders qualified to provide definitive care to victims of medical emergencies?
- Is there any opportunity to expand the use of security technology to reduce the level of manpower?
- Have you developed a policy or guidelines to influence the protection standards of your company's facilities and operations? Do you have a template for security system fit-out of new facilities?
- If you have objectively reviewed the security systems now in place, do you believe you have an effectively integrated physical security program?
- If you are under the scope of any state or federal regulations, are you now in compliance with applicable physical security, access control, and other operational security requirements?
- To what extent are you confident in the abilities of available vendors to execute your plans for electronic security system specifications and in their capabilities to upgrade and maintain your program consistent with the risk management profile you have specified?
- Evaluate your command center. How well does it provide operators with real-time information that they can effectively evaluate and act upon? How reliable is the system that collects and displays alarm and other essential aural and visual data? Does the head end essential to command and control provide 99.9% uptime reliability?

Key Terms
- Integrated solution
- Threat alignment
- Security operations
- First response
- Physical security
- Risk assessments
- Convergence
- Physical security
- First response
- Physical security program
- Threat assessment
- Force multiplier
- IT security

SECURITY TRAINING AND EDUCATION

Introduction

The professional development of you and your security team during this time of dynamic change is of utmost importance and must be a top priority for the security organization. There are a variety of developmental programs offered by professional associations, trade organizations, governmental agencies, and academic institutions to meet your organization's requirements and responsibilities. Many programs are offered online, requiring minimum disruption to regular business activities, and they range from certificate programs to university curriculums. These outside learning activities, coupled with internal and organizational development programs, will enhance the reactive and proactive activities of the organization.

Business Value

A security organization that understands and can respond to the needs of their customers in a timely manner, provides value-added service. Staffs that are poorly trained and educated will lack the skills and knowledge to properly respond to protection of asset issues (people, property, information, and reputation). Furthermore, a lack of understanding of current and future asset protection trends and the strategic plans of the parent organization will severely restrict the development of proactive programs. For example, a poorly trained emergency response team may result in unnecessary loss of life and property. Inadequate competencies by information security and business continuity teams impact the ability to foresee risk and response capabilities. Insufficiently prepared and trained investigators alienate the business entities and maximize potential recurrence of crime and misconduct with resulting exposure to potential liability issues. Highly trained staff and business units utilizing state-of-the-art asset protection programs may result in improved insurance coverage and deductibles directly impacting the bottom line.

The Essentials

At the core of any successful security program is an effective training and education plan geared at both security personnel and nonsecurity personnel.

Objectives of Security-Related Training and Education

All security-related training and education programs should contain the following:
- Job-related competencies and skills are identified and prioritized.
- Job performance and capabilities are enhanced.
- Training and educational programs are aligned with overall business strategies.
- Proactive requirements are identified and programs are initiated.
- Advancement opportunities are expanded, thereby increasing incentives for self-improvement.
- Pride and personal job satisfaction are enhanced.
- Cost savings are obtained through reduced turnover and in-house promotion versus costly external recruiting.
- Customer satisfaction is increased through demonstrated competency of security personnel.
- Liability risk and future losses are reduced.

Training Options

There is a wide range of professional development and job enhancement programs available. A search of the Internet or a review of appropriate trade and association publications will identify programs to meet a particular training objective or skill set. Professional association or academic certificate programs may require a fee. However, many governmental agency programs are free. Company programs in the areas of strategic planning, financial management, human resources policies, audit procedures, and information systems may be available and need to be considered. The support of senior management is demonstrated through employee incentives such as reimbursement upon successful completion, increased compensation, or annual bonuses for selected certifications such as emergency medical technician (EMT), certified fraud investigator, and other critical job-related skills. Completion of specialized certificate or academic programs should be considered during promotional opportunities. Undergraduate or graduate programs in various asset protection disciplines are offered locally or through online programs. Such programs may serve as a prerequisite for advancement or movement into areas requiring unique competencies and technical skills. The academic, training, and promotional policies of the security organization should follow the same requirements and incentives as other company business entities.

In-House Training

It is paramount that the security staff understands the core values, competencies, and objectives of the business. After current and future job-related competencies and skills are identified and prioritized, in-house developmental programs offered by HR and other business units need to be explored. These programs will not only enhance the knowledge base of the participant but also demonstrate to others a willingness to learn the operation of various business units. These partnerships will enhance the development of proactive programs and ensure a staff with current competencies. In special circumstances, it may be beneficial to detail a security professional to a critical or risk-prone business unit for a specified period to learn the unit's business processes, resulting in an asset protection program meeting the overall objectives of security and the unit. Participating in these in-house programs may enhance the development of multidisciplinary teams to protect assets and improve recovery or business-resumption time. For example, it is particularly important for the investigative staff to understand the beliefs of a particular business process that are arcane, mysterious, or secret, thus enabling improved understanding of fraud potential and the nuances when interviewing a person with a knowledge base in that particular field.

Certificate Programs

There are a number of certificate programs available through professional associations, government agencies, and academic institutions. These programs are usually designed to address a particular skill. Many programs are offered online and may be completed 24/7, while requiring minimum disruption to routine business activities and personal obligations. These programs may require participation involving several hours to several months. As an added incentive, some programs may include undergraduate or graduate academic credit, which may be applied towards a degree program. The objectives and requirements of each program should be carefully considered to ensure that it meets the employee's career development and business objective. Programs in homeland security, risk assessment, business continuity and recovery, fraud investigation, information security, and business practices may meet some of the security organization's needs.

Academic Programs

A number of renowned academic institutions offer undergraduate, graduate, or doctoral degree programs in security management, information systems, homeland security, or risk management. Many of these programs integrate theory from selected disciplines, particularly the social sciences and business, to understand crime causation, terrorism, crime control, and the administration and management of criminal justice and corporate security. Many programs allow the participant to take cross-disciplinary courses (supply chain, information systems, finance, product safety, business processes) to meet their personal objectives. Aside from the traditional areas of curriculum and study, many programs are enhanced by active outreach staffs connected with practitioners' concerns, applied research and theory, international or study abroad programs, and government grants addressing current issues. These programs should contain a strong academic emphasis, which also reflects the changing needs of the student, practitioner, and community. Institutions may offer a combination of undergraduate on-campus or online programs. Some institutions offer an entire graduate-level program online. Financial assistance may be provided through scholarships or company reimbursements upon course or program completion.

Development Plan

All employees should have a developmental plan, in collaboration with their supervisor, that meets department and HR policies. The developmental plan should be a part of the employee's file and reviewed on an annual basis or when a position change is made. Company assessment processes may help to identify employees with promotional potential or those in need of other skills. The formal performance review process should cover progress made against agreed upon skills and goals. The review should identify requirement shortfalls and address next steps for training or improvement.

Contractors and Vendors

If various components of your program have been outsourced, you should ensure that specified personnel skill sets and requirements are identified and mandated in contracts. This will require a close partnership with the business unit receiving the security service and the purchasing department or other entity responsible for supplier contracts and services. This may require criteria for pre-employment selection, pre-assignment training, and on-site or on-the-job training. The cost and hours of training must be clearly understood and stated in the contract. An audit of the training received by contract employees must be made on a regular basis, and the contract should include a breach-of-training penalty. The security manager should view the skill sets of contract employees, and they should be similar to proprietary personnel who have previously performed the tasks. Inability to perform a particular asset protection task should not be dependent on whether the responder is a contractor or company employee. Information security personnel, specialty investigators, and first responders are examples of employees possessing special skill sets. Security management needs to recognize that, when outsourcing, they still maintain the responsibility of providing the business with competent services.

Training Business Units in Security-Related Responsibilities

It has been emphasized that, in a decentralized business activity, each business unit has the primary responsibility for protecting its assets. However, by making this a partnership process, the protection of company assets is enhanced, and all employees believe that they are stakeholders in the process. The security organization must provide leadership and awareness to each business unit and be their "broker" in asset-protection initiatives. The units need to understand reactive and proactive activities and develop the sensitivity on when to alert the security organizations to threats beyond their scope of handling. The security organization may need to develop awareness programs or advise business units on outside training programs, as described earlier, to meet their particular risks. Business unit employees must be made aware of risks and be provided with the necessary skills sets to execute appropriate security tasks effectively. The business unit must understand that they are the first level of defense against threats and risk, which must be controlled at their level.

Of course, these activities and partnerships are highly dependent upon how the company has structured its security services. In some business models, the security organization is limited to a central staff function, essentially providing a policy framework and expert logistical support. In more decentralized models, the security organization may take a more "hands-on" approach. Regardless of the operating philosophy, the security organization must ensure that the business units or person with the primary asset protection responsibility have the required skill sets. Typical examples of jobs, which may be assigned to business units, are fraud detection or investigation, risk management, information-security administration, contingency planning, access control, loss prevention, and other unique risk-specific jobs. Regardless of the structure, reaching into business units to provide awareness and training maximizes the scope of the security program, obtains buy-in from stakeholders, and eliminates plausible denial on accountability.

Tracking Training Administration

It is important to maintain a training plan that not only provides for content but also records the targeted number of hours versus those that were actually provided (as shown in Figure 10.1). Such records are useful in demonstrating 111 regulatory compliance and as a defense should litigation for deficient security be an issue.

THE BOTTOM LINE: Given security's mission, the highest level of competence of every member of the team is essential.

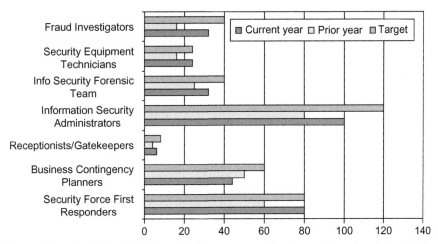

Figure 10.1 Hours of Security-Related Training. It is important to maintain a training plan that not only provides for content but also records the targeted number of hours versus those that were actually provided.

Highlights for Follow-Up

- How would you assess the work-related competencies and skills of key members of your team? Are you doing everything possible to address competency development and professional growth?
- Are you satisfied with the level of understanding of business process by investigative, information security, and contingency planning teams?
- Which incentives does the company offer for employees to pursue work-related training, professional certifications, and educational opportunities?
- Are you satisfied that the periodic performance review process provides adequate assessment of competencies and skills?
- Are you knowledgeable about in-house, governmental, and academic programs to address employee career development needs?
- Are your career development and training programs aligned with other business units and HR policies?
- Is there a clear understanding with company business units regarding security responsibilities? Has guidance been provided on training requirements and resources?
- Are you satisfied with the training provided to contract personnel? In what ways do shortcomings evidence themselves?
- Do outsourcing contracts contain selection and training criteria, and is the responsibility clearly delineated?

Key Terms

- Security-related training and education
- Training options
- In-house training
- Certificate programs
- Academic programs
- Security-related responsibilities
- Training administration
- Corporate security training and education
- Development plans
- Personnel development

COMMUNICATION AND AWARENESS PROGRAMS

Introduction

Just as the security policy provides the legal framework and sets expectations, the security awareness program keeps those expectations fresh and in front of those people who need to know and understand them. Awareness eliminates denial and focuses on accountability. Employees must share the responsibility for securing the company's reputation, its people, and its assets.

Business Value

There are multiple benefits to an informed and aware employee population, including the following:

- Employees understand their role in protection and are in the best position to see a hazard or vulnerability.
- Employees can more intelligently identify, prevent, and respond to potential issues.
- Management views security as a business partner.
- Employees understand the value of security for business.
- Management depends on security to educate, inform, and advise regarding security issues.

There are also consequences of an unaware population. The security department represented in Figure 11.1 understands that knowledge is critical to the notion of shared responsibility for protection. The survey portrayed was conducted both over the intranet and in brief, personal exchanges to determine respondent awareness of five basic security policies. As a result, the department now knows where and how to target increased awareness.

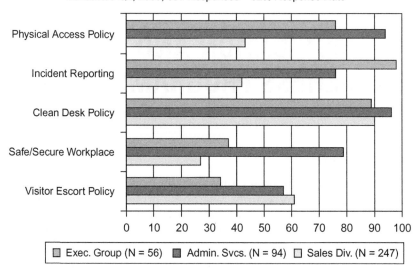

Figure 11.1 Survey of Security Policy Awareness. Results of a survey conducted both over the intranet and in brief, personal exchanges to determine respondent awareness of five basic security policies.

The Essentials

Customarily, your company will have an internal communications function that can help craft and deliver your message in ways that conform to current practice. The corporate intranet is an especially powerful medium to convey both urgent messages as well as the content of specific security awareness campaigns. Security should also have a slot in the orientation program for new employees. The focus of your program will be tied to risk exposure and the role that either the general population or a specific organizational group can play in mitigation. Urgency, such as with a virus attack, will influence the media used, but regardless, the purpose is to fix clearly the notion of shared responsibility and what new employees need to do to play a responsive role.

An excellent source of data on lack of awareness may be found in incident post-mortems. If your message is stale, absent, or the pitch did not work, this is the place to home in on improvements.

Your security communication program should include a smart mix of the following strategies and tactics.

Strategies

- Send messages that are targeted to different functions or owners.
- Create a visual identity, such as a logo for security that is included on all messaging.
- Consider a tagline.
- Focus security strategies on business issues.
- Use site or facility coordinators to assist in communications.
- Encourage employees to communicate with security.
- Quickly and professionally respond to any employee communications.
- Fully utilize the power and reach of the corporate intranet—get on employee desktops with important messages, but don't overdo this facility.

Tactics

- Communications should be short and easy to read and understand.
- Advertise awareness initiatives on the corporate intranet.
- Convey the benefits to business in every communication.
- Determine the best communication time schedules per audience.
- Provide a means to evaluate the effectiveness of the message.
- Regularly update information, for example with via a handbook or the intranet.
- Provide real-life examples, whether within the company or about competitors.
- Make security fun—use games or prizes to raise levels of awareness.

Security Awareness Approaches

Table 11.1 displays various types of security awareness approaches to several typical business risks usually found within the mission of a corporate security organization. Bear in mind that this is a baseline and does not include all factors of an awareness program such as constituencies, roles and responsibilities, and level of awareness by constituencies. Clearly, factors of an awareness program will also have items specific to the type of company and industry.

Table 11.1 Security Awareness Approaches to Typical Business Risks

Risk Category	Risk Issue	Countermeasure	Who Needs to Know?	Awareness Program Elements
Business Continuity and Resiliency	Business disruption	Business continuity plan.	All	Documentation, training exercises, company newsletters, leadership briefings
Business Continuity and Resiliency	Business disruption	Crisis management plan.	Corp. Security, BU Leader, Senior Management, BOD	Documentation, training, emails, exercise
Business Continuity and Resiliency	Business disruption	Disaster recovery plan.	Corp. Security, BU Leader, Senior Management, BOD	Documentation, training, exercises
Business Continuity and Resiliency	Risk mitigation gaps	Unified Risk Oversight™ team.	Corp. Security, IT, Audit, HR, Compliance, BU Leaders	Meetings, emails, documentation
Business Continuity and Resiliency	Outsourcing failures	Vetting program: Background check, security check, user references, compliance (if relevant)	Corp. Security, Senior Management, Legal	Meetings, documentation
Financial	Fraud/embezzlement	Fraud protection program: Prohibited activities policy, background checks, and audits.	All	Documentation, Intranet, leadership briefings
Financial	Unauthorized access to property, facilities, and systems affecting reporting integrity.	Facility access policy.	All	Documentation, emails, posters, leadership briefings
Financial	Unauthorized access to property, facilities, and systems affecting reporting integrity.	Role-based rules.	Corp. Security, Senior Management, BOD, BU Leader	Emails, documentation

(*Continued*)

Table 11.1 (Continued)

Risk Category	Risk Issue	Countermeasure	Who Needs to Know?	Awareness Program Elements
Financial	Disruption, losses, or reputation damage at key events.	Offsite event program.	Corp. Security, HR, BU Leader, Staff	Documentation, Intranet, leadership briefings
Human Capital	Accidents involving executives, employees, contractors, customers, guests, and visitors.	Environment, health, and safety program: Policies, standards, risk reporting, and audits.	All	Emails, Intranet, posters, training
Human Capital	Criminal victimization of executives, employees, contractors, customers, guests, and visitors.	Crime prevention program policies and standards including workplace violence program and ethics program: Prevention, response, remediation.	All	Email, Intranet, training
Human Capital	Victimization in high-risk (global/international) assignments period and travel.	Travel program: Assessment, prevention, response, remediation.	All	Documentation, Intranet
Information	Theft of exposed information.	Clean desk policy.	All	Emails, Intranet, company newsletters
Information	Inadvertent disclosure of customer information.	Risk reviews.	All	Documentation, emails, Intranet
Information	Inadvertent disclosure of proprietary information.	Classification scheme and audit.	All	Documentation, emails, company newsletters
Information	Misuse and information loss through Internet, email, IM, or other application usages.	Information systems usage policy.	All	Emails, Intranet, company newsletters
Information	Information loss through IT systems.	System monitoring processes.	Corp. Security, IT, HR, Legal	Emails, Documentation
Information	Unauthorized access to systems.	Authorized use policy and standards.	Corp. Security, IT, HR, BU Leader	Documentation, emails
Information	Unauthorized access to systems.	Role-based rules.	Corp. Security, IT, HR, BU Leader	Documentation
Information	Damage from virus, worm, Trojan horse, or bots,	Computer use/email policy.	All	Emails, Intranet, company newsletters

(Continued)

Table 11.1 (Continued)

Risk Category	Risk Issue	Countermeasure	Who Needs to Know?	Awareness Program Elements
Information	Loss through social engineering of sensitive or critical information.	Process for vetting external requests.	All	Poster, emails
Legal, Regulations, Compliance, and Liability	Regulatory compliance of ethics	Corporate governance program: Committee formation, assessment, policy, response, audit, whistleblower protection processes.	All	Policy sign-off, Intranet, meetings, company newsletters, leadership briefings
Legal, Regulations, Compliance, and Liability	Business regulatory compliance	Environment, health, and safety program including hazard reviews and post-event reviews.	All	Meetings, Documentation, training
Legal, Regulations, Compliance, and Liability	Security regulatory compliance	Compliance program: Assessment, controls, implementation, policies.	Corp. Security, IT, Audit, Senior Management, BOD, Legal	Meetings, Documentation
Physical and Premises	Loss of property, product, information, automated capability, dependent process, etc.	Property protection program: Processes, assigned responsibility, detection, investigation, recovery.	All, Law Enforcement	Documentation, emails, Intranet
Physical and Premises	Loss of property, product, information, automated capability, dependent process, etc.	Exception detection, reporting, investigation, mitigation, and recovery.	Corp. Security, Senior Management	Emails, Documentation
Physical and Premises	Loss of property, product, information, automated capability, dependent process, etc.	Authorized use policy and standards.	All	Intranet, emails, training
Reputation	Damage to brand reputation	Brand investigations/diversion period.	Corp. Security, Senior Management, BOD, Legal, PR	Documentation
Reputation	Counterfeit products in marketplace	Counterfeit prevention, detection, and reduction program period.	Corp. Security, Senior Management, BOD, Legal	Documentation, meetings, Leadership briefings

This is a baseline and does not include all factors of an awareness program such as constituencies, roles and responsibilities, and level of awareness by constituencies.

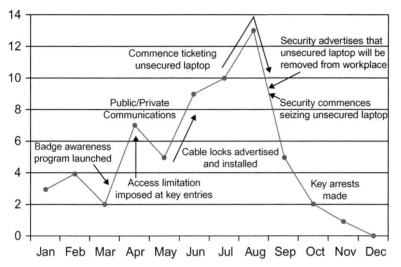

Figure 11.2 Combined Awareness and Security Program. An example of how an awareness program, combined with physical security enhancements, engaged the employee population to reduce costly and damaging laptop computer thefts.

In this arena, you are very much the same as any advertiser trying to sell a product or idea. You must know your audience. Furthermore, your delivery has to be tailored to the knowledge of what will grab them and create the solution or result you expect. Would you give a tri-fold brochure on information security classifications to the senior management team? No. However, you might spend some time with their administrative assistants, who really administer the traffic and are aware of what needs to be done to protect the executives.

Figure 11.2 displays an example of how an awareness program, combined with physical security enhancements, engaged the employee population to reduce costly and damaging laptop computer thefts. Commencing in January we see a spike in thefts and a post-mortem conclusion that they had been lost in spaces with poor access control discipline, which resulted in a focused and visible employee badge-display awareness effort. The next spike in April requires more rigorous access limitations and the engagement of local police and area businesses having similar problems. With a continuing loss experience in May and June, security developed a stick-on message that resembled a city parking ticket with an easily recognizable icon for unsecured laptops found during security tours. When combined with advertising that unsecured laptops will be seized if found on after-hour security tours, and several seizures with embarrassing supervisory consequences, employee awareness significantly contributed to hardened targeting and reduced loss experience.

Tailoring the Message

Examples abound of businesses failing to understand where the risks were housed and how to communicate with the residents of this space. For example, a company issues a strong message on trade secrets protection and then invites someone with a new gadget into the inner sanctum without being vetted and several years of development of a new, benchmark product go to the competition. The policy in this case was developed at the insistence of the audit committee, and when it was presented, it went into the legal files. Other reasons communication programs fail include the following:

- No communication strategy other than an intranet communication to all employees
- No focused training for those who might have access to this proprietary data
- No signature on a statement that acknowledges employees' obligations to protect
- No coordination of planning on-policy rollout, therefore
  - No survey to identify the location of all applicable materials
  - No retroactive security classification scheme for prior proprietary processes
  - No revision of contracts with vendors on requirements for protection of proprietary information or acceptance and sanctions for noncompliance
  - No understanding that third-party vendors had key information in their files
  - No rollout to the international divisions because of separation of oversight, due to tax issues

Most likely, you have a diverse employee and vendor population upon which you rely. If you have a multi-lingual population, should you not tailor your program to those individuals who have access and may fall within this employee group? How many employees do not have routing access to the corporate intranet?

You can complete this listing on your own, given your risk assessment. The message is that awareness of policy, rules, regulations, standards, accepted business practices, and other necessary information all succeed where the issuing authority thoroughly understands, in a detailed way, the risks associated with required security guidance. Furthermore, if you are uninformed, you will fail to understand the depth and breadth of dissemination of what you may think are "protected" materials.

THE BOTTOM LINE: Every employee has a role to play in the protection of corporate assets. Finding responsive ways to communicate this responsibility is a key building block in a proactive asset protection program.

Highlights for Follow-Up

- Are there any instances of internal investigations (or other incidents) where the subject indicated a lack of awareness of a policy that he or she is accused of violating?
- Are there indications from incident post-mortems or around any categories of loss investigation that lack of risk awareness contributed directly to the incident? How are you addressing incident follow-ups for awareness improvement?
- Is security included in the new employee orientation program?
- How are management's messages conveyed to employees? Is it via a corporate intranet or other electronic means? How can your messages be best conveyed for impact? Who in the corporate communications infrastructure could assist in crafting and delivering timely and impactful awareness materials?
- Have you ever conducted any sort of survey around the awareness of security policy or recommended practices by first-line supervisors and other mid-level managers? If you see more instances of security violations within a specific business unit, it may be fruitful to determine how aware and proactive these managers are about their responsibilities for securing corporate assets and setting appropriate models for their subordinates.
- If your company is outsourcing critical business processes, how are you being assured that your business partner is making their people aware of their responsibilities to protect their customer's interests?

Key Terms

- Security communication
- Awareness programs
- Strategies
- Tactics

12

SAFE AND SECURE WORKPLACES

Introduction

Employees and visitors have an expectation of safety and security when they enter our workplaces. Having clear policies to achieve this expectation, enforced by an aware and knowledgeable supervisory team, contribute to a work environment intolerant to abusive behavior, sexual harassment, or other intimidating conduct. Key executives have similar expectations but may resist the requirements of protection, an interesting challenge for the proactive security manager.

Business Value

There is no upside to failure to protect, especially in the face of what could happen without knowledgeable safeguards. Have a senior executive do a quick drill on what they would say to the press after a notable workplace violence incident that clearly could have been avoided.

The Essentials

Premises liability and other legal precedents surrounding deficient safety or security is a driving factor in the need to be aware of *preventable* hazards in the workplace. In some states, there is a legal concept of "one free crime and after that you are on notice." Regardless of the size or sophistication of the security program, there is a clear need to assess risk, eliminate vulnerability, and maintain accurate records on safety and security incidents.

Have corporate or outside counsel examine the legal precedents in your state or jurisdiction so that you understand the standards that have been applied around issues of premises liability and the obligation to protect employees and invitees. Federal employment law generally requires employers to maintain safe and secure workplaces.

Predictability of Risk

"Safe and secure" requires more than a physical security program. It requires a thorough understanding of risk dynamics. Environments and external influences are in constant change. One new unvetted employee with a tendency or history of violence can change the balance as clearly as a faulty or poorly maintained fire alarm system. Know the hazards, test the safeguards, and engage employees in awareness. When it comes to senior executives or their families who may be the focus of risk, carefully evaluate the vulnerabilities and understand how the various safeguard options might work within the executive's total environment.

The Policy Framework

We cannot imagine a CEO who would reject a stated commitment "to maintain safe and secure workplaces for our employees and invitees." This policy provides one of the principal pillars of the security program. While the prevention of violence in the workplace is a key concern, many other business risks are addressed by a set of security activities focused upon delivery of safe and secure workplaces that
- protect assets, or provides stewardship of company resources;
- protect against business interruption;
- provide safety, in response to medical and other emergencies;
- provide the protective perimeter around information assets; and
- engage employees in hazard awareness and contribute to employee morale.

Workplace Violence Policy

The sidebar represents a draft workplace violence policy that may be considered if none currently exists in your company.

Something like this sample policy, customized for your legal and cultural environment, is a basic requirement of employment law.

Workplace Violence Policy

[Designate company] desires to provide a safe work environment for all employees. Any safety or health hazards in the workplace should be reported to the individual's manager or the appropriate department, as identified below:

- To report an unsafe building condition, contact [designated person or department].
- To report an unauthorized person on premises, contact Corporate Security.
- To report a medical emergency, contact Corporate Security at [XXX-XXX-XXXX]. Calling the local emergency medical service (EMS) without first calling Corporate Security could result in a delay in the ability of EMS personnel to find the specific location of the emergency.
- To report all work-related injuries and illnesses, contact HR within 24 hours, regardless of whether the employee requires immediate medical attention. In addition, the manager must complete a Report of Injury form. This form is available from and is to be returned to [business unit] Human Resources, and a copy should be sent to [designated person]. For further information about this procedure, see the [name of policy document].
- To report any act or threat of violence, contact Corporate Security at [XXX-XXX-XXXX] or Human Resources. A Threat Assessment Team (TAT) has been formed to coordinate prompt investigations and provide advice in appropriate cases. The TAT includes individuals from [business unit(s)]. As part of striving to maintain a safe workplace, [company name] prohibits violence or threats of violence in the workplace, stemming from the workplace, or while otherwise representing the firm. The "workplace" is broadly defined to encompass buildings which [company name] owns and in which it leases space (including the parking lots, cafeterias, etc., which are affiliated with those buildings) and the areas where work is performed.

Violence includes physical altercations, fights, the use of firearms, explosives, and other weapons, and any other conduct which could cause injury or other damage. Threats of violence include acts of physical aggression or any statements that could be perceived as expressing intent to cause harm to an employee or to the Company. Threats can be direct statements or acts, as well as more subtle conduct, such as intimidating remarks or gestures, "stalking," or other menacing behavior. These threats must be taken seriously, and even comments that are intended as jokes may be inappropriate. Regardless of the laws of a particular jurisdiction, the possession of any dangerous substances, including firearms, explosives, and other weapons, is strictly prohibited in the workplace or elsewhere while conducting company business.

For purposes of this policy, protective sprays (e.g., pepper spray) will not be considered a prohibited weapon provided they are not inappropriately displayed or discharged in the workplace. Employees possessing protective sprays must comply with legal requirements governing their possession and use.

If an incident is imminent or under way, the manager is to use good judgment to endeavor to de-escalate the situation. If assistance is advisable, the manager should call Corporate Security. When at a location that is not routinely serviced by Corporate Security representatives, building security or the local police should be contacted, as appropriate.

Employees should immediately report any infraction to corporate security, their manager, and/or HR. If the report is made to the manager, the manager is responsible for taking action as appropriate and reporting any act or threat of violence to Corporate Security or HR. If an employee has committed a violent act or made a threat, the manager may immediately suspend the employee pending investigation.

As part of striving to maintain a safe work environment, [designated person or department] would like to be made aware of certain legal proceedings that could affect the workplace. Specifically, if an employee has obtained a restraining order or other similar order for personal protection, he or she is encouraged to notify Corporate Security, HR, or the manager. If Human Resources or the manager becomes aware of a restraining order, this information should be reported to Corporate Security. While Corporate Security, of course, cannot guarantee anyone's personal safety, it can suggest additional precautionary measures for the employee to consider, and it can assist in enforcing the order in the workplace. Employees may wish to contact Corporate Security if they are concerned for their personal safety, even if they have not secured a restraining order. The Employee Assistance Program under the auspices of Human Resources is also a resource for employees to consider. The following (see Figure 12.1) is an example of maintaining accurate records and informing management on the status of a safe and secure workplace.

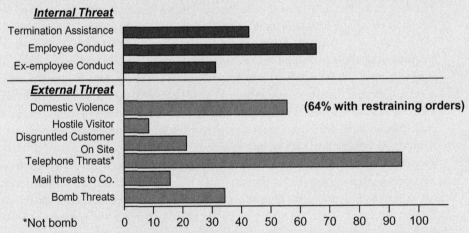

Figure 12.1 Workplace Violence: 2005. An example of maintaining accurate records and informing management on the status of a safe and secure workplace.

Protecting Key Executives and Key Individuals

In the global business environment, senior executives and key individuals travel extensively, increasingly to locations that may present a variety of likely hazards and personal risks. Some high-profile executives shun the presence of an executive protection detail, while others expect it as a perk or because they accept that the threat is real. Protection programs may be highly organized, comprising a cadre of dedicated and highly trained and potentially armed security personnel. Others may be limited to subscribed travel risk assessment services, case-by-case in-house or contracted protection details, and electronic monitoring of residences. All of these services and those detailed below require careful accounting to address tax implications.

The key focus is to tailor protection for specific corporate executives consistent with risk to the employee and co-workers (and their family members). Protection plans for the homes must change and evolve with the needs of aging children. An understanding of the threats and countermeasures posed to teens via the Web were nonexistent ten years ago but now are only a mouse click away for some unsuspecting teen or their absent parent who is an executive. With ID theft claiming more than 10 million victims a year and the proliferation of online shopping, banking, trading, and so on, harried executives or their caretakers must be knowledgeable of the latest trends concerning identity theft, spyware, keystroke logging, and other PC and network-based threats. It should be noted that personal risks at home could leak into the scope of potential concern to the security organization. Be prepared to incorporate these issues into your executive protection plan.

The greater the ongoing or infrequent risk, the greater or lesser the need to engage the executive in the potential for risk and the recommended safeguards. Certain industries such as financial services, pharmaceutical (e.g., animal rights), energy, and those with union activism may have a higher degree of exposure. Clearly, individuals at all levels working in foreign locales susceptible to kidnapping, bombing, carjacking, and terrorism need tailored protection. Regardless of the executives' potential or actual threat level, a common risk that they share is that of an acute health issue or accident. Given the hectic schedules that high-level executives such as CEOs keep, accompanied by the stresses involved with international travel (diet, sleep deprivation, etc.), for many executives, the chance of a health issue occurring is arguably greater than a targeted criminal attack. The executive protection (EP) program's tool kit must include basic or advanced medical training, again depending on individual risk profiles and the proximity of more qualified resources. Portability of an automated external defibrillator

(AED), advances in technology, and the rapid response of a well-trained staff can have life-saving benefits, whether the principal is traveling in Detroit or Delhi.

Executive Protection Program Options

As briefly noted above, the menu of protection options varies consistent with the perceived threat to the individual and acceptability to the executive.

Residence and Family Requirements

- The security team is familiar and acceptable to the executive and family (special attention to children's needs).
- Thoroughly vet and train household staff.
- Provide safe rooms (confidentiality is essential!).
- Securely monitor residences and selected office areas.
- Consider personal protection training or techniques, including protection devices for all family members or just the female members.
- If home is on corporate IT network or confidential information is stored there, designate a dedicated, secure area for limited access.
- Provide easy-to-use document-destruction equipment.
- Offer appropriate security coverage for valuable collections.

Offices and Business Environments

- Provide a low-profile, trained, and dedicated executive protection security cadre.
- Assess threat on an ongoing basis, given the public profile and notable issues associated with the executive, the family, and the company.
- Establish manned visitor control posts at access points to executive office areas or security-trained receptionists connected to the security control center.
- Vet background of selected personnel, such as personal assistants and others with special or unlimited access.
- Provide special handling for incoming packages and mail supported by knowledge of current (chemical and biological) hazards, not just letter bombs.
- In-house and external event organizers or communication services that are engaged in public relations and media activities related to the executive and family are aware of security issues.

- Keep a database of "persons of interest" or people with a past history of "reaching out" to executives either in person or via all forms of communication.
- Provide special protection for laptops and personal computers.
- Establish secure meeting areas that address the risks posed by compromising radio frequency (RF) emanations, visual surveillance, and leave-behind information or other assets.
- Consider sterile personal computer monitoring of groups, activists, etc., who would target an executive or their firm (e.g., Darfur, animal rights, eco-terrorists, or political activists focused on the company, etc.).
- Pre-position resources at contingency sites in the event of power outages.
- Pre-arrange strong relationships with local public safety officials.
- Be aware of social engineering risk to telephonic and logical (computer) communications.
- Provide special protection of communication devices and selected meeting areas to prevent covert listening.
- Establish special oversight of financial accounts to identify fraud, extortion, or identity-theft attempts.

Travel
- Security has the proposed travel itinerary for planning and risk assessment.
- Offer site-specific travel risk advisory services.
- Review pre-risk and tailored protection of housing and offices at frequently visited locations, with special attention to high-risk sites.
- Use key person kidnap and hostage insurance and related services.
- Offer awareness programs for corporate-travel personnel and recommend limited engagement of outside travel services.
- Offer security details for special events and travel as deemed appropriate.
- Provide armored vehicles and armed and specially trained drivers as needed.
- Provide coverage of communication devices used by executives (Blackberry, virtual private network [VPN], wireless hubs, etc.); availability of technical support while traveling may be limited or nonexistent.
- Pre-position emergency medical equipment or prescriptions as individually required. Be knowledgeable of what is and is

not allowed in some countries or likely to be questioned at an entry checkpoint.
- Arrange for specially prepared food in high illness-risk locations.
- Provide dedicated or interval ownership of aircraft to include emergency contact procedures for pilots or their tracking agents.

Dealing with Pushback

Many executives (or family members) will rebel at proposed protection, either occasionally or almost always. The security executive needs to be prepared to stand his or her ground and present the commonsense business case. Scare tactics will likely backfire. The one time you engaged an outside service who sent the highly visible car manned by the barely literate fellow with no neck to meet the executive will come back to haunt you.

Use the list of potential safeguards noted above (and modify as required to address your unique environment and executives) as a checklist and then develop a briefing for the appropriate executive. This will help drive the considerations to verifiable risks and engage him or her in a discussion on the risk exposure you have documented and the tailored options you have selected.

Maintain your vetted list of security resources. Use your colleagues in other companies who know of trusted and reliable resources in various locations. Where family members are involved, resistance will likely be minimal; but know the story of the person you are protecting when it comes to your recommendations, and be prepared with a solid rationale for your plans.

THE BOTTOM LINE: A case could be made that the security organization's first priority is to assure a safe and secure workplace while still enabling comfort, convenience, and efficient business processes. The challenge is finding that balance.

Highlights for Follow-Up

- Is the provision of a safe and secure workplace addressed within your company's business conduct or other policy framework?
- Where would you most anticipate a workplace violence incident within your company? Are you satisfied with the

safeguards you have in place? What other steps should you consider?

- How does your company handle notification of domestic restraining orders that include the workplace?
- What are the legal standards for a safe and secure workplace in the states in which you have staffed operations and/or visitor access?
- Do you provide escort services from the office for employees with active threats against them? What are the limits of that coverage, and are you comfortable with the legal liabilities attendant to such services?

Key Terms

- Predictability of risk
- The policy framework
- Workplace violence policy
- Protective spray
- Procedure
- Restraining orders
- Executive protection
- Residence and family requirements
- Offices and business environments
- Travel
- Dealing with pushback

BUSINESS CONDUCT

Introduction

The most serious and challenging adversaries confronting the enterprise are *knowledgeable, empowered insiders*. They capitalize upon weak internal controls and a lack of clear signals from the top that an expectation is integrity in everything we do.

The security executive is in a unique position to observe and potentially influence issues of corporate integrity and ethics. This perspective starts with the honesty associated with an individual's answers to a personal history statement in the background investigation, the values evidenced by the supervisor and manager in their leadership responsibilities, and when the individual employee makes the choice to "do the right thing."

Business Value

Reputation is everything in the marketplace. The security executive cannot be the conscience of the organization, but he or she can be the staunchest advocate for intolerance of wrongdoing.

The Essentials

Tracking business conduct cases and pointing out failures in controls and lapses in effective oversight provide undeniable signals to management that must be addressed. If *tested and legitimate* efforts to do this are quashed, seek other employment.

Know Your Adversary

Here are a few things to consider as you approach this thought process:
- What categories of employees or "trusted" vendors are in the most advantageous positions to damage the company's health and reputation?

- What specialized controls have been put in place to mitigate the potential risks from these individuals?
- Where your company has outsourced critical business processes or custody of assets (customer lists, trade secrets, etc.), what internal controls have you contractually imposed on risk from insiders, and what steps are you employing to be assured of the integrity of these assets?
- Consider engaging a small group of knowledgeable individuals in a business unit to discuss how an insider with access and desire might engage in a variety of criminal or risky activities. Then analyze the adequacy of controls to prevent, detect, and respond as required.

Corporate Hygiene

Much of what we see in corporate meltdowns due to ethical lapses or total absence of standards of conduct is within the scope of a business-astute security manager. We see the instances of internal investigations for travel and entertainment (T&E) fraud, sexual harassment, intranet abuse, workplace violence, substance abuse, and other events that strongly suggest the absence of ethically oriented oversight. As a professional, where are the boundaries of your investigation and reporting of these risks? Does top management support your ability to work collaboratively with HR, legal, and business units to find the facts in these matters?

Business conduct investigations are one of the most sensitive areas of security's engagement with the business. It's unfortunately true that when the subjects of investigation are lower-level hourly employees, there is little attention from top management. However, let the subject be a high-profile executive or one of the up-and-coming stars, and the security executive may be forced to walk a fine line with potential pushback from various directions.

Confidential reporting lines are a regulatory requirement and occasionally yield serious allegations of wrongdoing directed to senior staff.[1] Notification of general counsel is important if privilege is a consideration. Where allegations are found to be factual, and the investigation has yielded firm conclusions as to the extent of culpability, the employee's supervisor, counsel, HR, and security need to evaluate carefully the range of sanctions

---

[1] This function should be under the CSO. Many companies elect to place the confidential reporting line in human resources, where investigative competencies are lacking and the implications of the allegation may be missed.

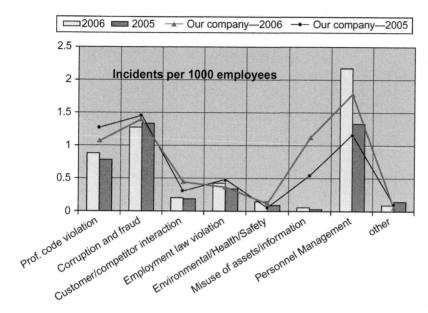

Figure 13.1 Confidential Hotline Reporting. Corporate confidential hotline calls compared to a national database.

with a view to consistency of application. Inconsistency in sanctions is a slippery slope opening a door to potential litigation and undesirable public notice. The absence of candor by investigative subjects should be seen as an aggravating influence on sanctions.

In Figure 13.1, a security department has compared their confidential hotline calls to the data from the Security Executive Council's "2007 Corporate Governance and Compliance Hotline Benchmark Report," which analyzed more than 277,000 hotline incident reports from more than 650 organizations across all major industries over a five-year period (2002–2006).[2] This enables a high-level peer group benchmark.

These cases will be benchmarks of management's stated commitment to ethical management. If you have done a highly objective, competent, and documented internal investigation, then it is the notable T&E fraud case involving a star that will test the commitment of management to "do the right thing." Work with the affected business unit and carefully draw the lines on your intentions. If appropriate solutions do not work at this level, escalate to whatever level is accountable. To the degree appropriate, keep your boss advised of legal advice.

[2]This report is available for download by registered users at https://www. securityexecutivecouncil.com/research/.

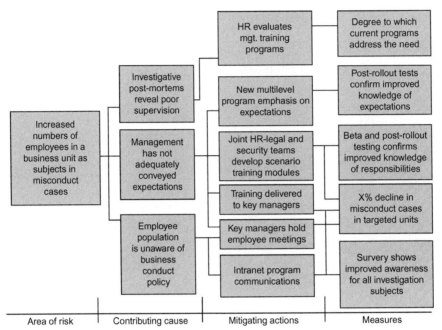

Figure 13.2 Continuum of Learning from Business Conduct Cases. Utilize investigative post-mortems to drill down on root causes of increased misconduct in this business unit.

Learning from Business Conduct Cases

Figure 13.2 shows the continuum of learning from cases. Rather than seeing this trend as an anomaly, security has utilized the investigative post-mortem process to drill down on root causes of increased misconduct in this business unit. Poor supervision has been exacerbated by a failure by top management to convey expectations and inform employees on business conduct policy. As a result, security and HR have collaborated to prepare and deliver training to address these gaps, and follow-up measures have demonstrated positive results in knowledge of expectations and reduced incidents of misconduct.

High-Level Policy or Guideline Statement

Make certain that there is a business conduct policy that guides business units and the governance infrastructure in addressing allegations of business misconduct or criminal activity. Work with HR, legal counsel, and senior management where these expectations are not clearly established and communicated to all employees and other applicable agents. A model business conduct and ethics policy may be found in Appendix E.

High-Level Survey of Reputation Risk and Business Conduct Policy

Use this survey to understand your organization's risk to reputation based on current business conduct policies:

- Has management clearly articulated their expectations on business conduct, ethics, and "doing the right thing" internally and with our shareholders and customers?
- Is there a way for employees and others to confidentially report suspected wrongdoing?
- How many allegations have been documented as reported and investigated with outcomes consistent with policy or stated expectations?
- What is the company's experience with regard to investigation of internal misconduct cases and the involvement of HR, legal, and other management units?
- Are appropriately placed senior managers aware of the regulatory requirements of your industry, and have requisite procedures been established to assure compliance with those legal expectations?
- Do any of your outsourced business processes involve assets that could adversely impact the business and shareholder confidence if those vendors were to misuse their access? Have your due diligence processes and contractual documents adequately protected the company from these risks?
- Are line business unit managers aware and adequately conveying expectations for business conduct and who to contact to address concerns on a timely basis?

Please note: Additional coverage of the high-level survey of reputation risk and business conduct policy may be found in Appendix E.

Sensitive Investigations

A caution on the assignment, production, and communication of internal investigations and other sensitive subject matter:

We allude to several types of security work products and their potential sensitivities throughout this book. Internal investigations, risk assessments, regulatory reviews, metrics indicating risk exposure, investigative reports, and a host of other documented matters may be discoverable and require special handling. Given the potentially litigious environment of employee law, premises liability, government regulations, corporate integrity, and other exposures, it is vitally important for security executives to thoroughly understand the protocols and legalities associated with the protection of sensitive internal communications. These risks underscore the importance of a healthy and trusting relationship between the CSO and corporate general counsel to include engaged outside counsel where appropriate.

The following are general guidelines that must be explored within each corporate setting and set of individual circumstances. Discuss the range of sensitive communications with counsel and set the protocols so that engagement is clear and timely.

There are two principle types of protected communications that involve attorneys:

1. attorney-client privileged communications, and
2. communications that constitute attorney work product.

Both of these can be present in communications to or from corporate security. Their potential utility should be considered whenever applicable and, in particular, prior to embarking upon an investigation that may have legal or regulatory implications for the company.

Attorney-Client Privilege

Attorney-client privilege is an evidentiary doctrine that protects certain types of communications from being obtained by the opposing party during the discovery process that attends litigation (or, in some cases, regulatory investigations). For example, it would preclude certain memoranda or reports from being produced or questioning during a deposition about oral conversations. The attorney-client privilege extends to confidential communications between a client and his or her attorney for the purpose of obtaining legal advice. The advice can be obtained at any time, and the privilege is not dependent on the client's being worried about pending or potential litigation. This privilege is absolute, unless the client waives it. A waiver occurs when the client conveys the substance of the privileged communication to a third party. The attorney-client privilege is relevant to security investigations when, for example, a corporate client decides to initiate an internal investigation to gather facts to refer to an attorney for the purpose of obtaining legal advice or to do a litigation risk assessment or compliance audit.

Attorney Work Product Doctrine

Attorney work product doctrine is an evidentiary doctrine that protects certain materials and reports from being produced during discovery. Attorney work product consists of reports or other written materials that were created by an attorney or at the attorney's direction in anticipation of litigation or for trial. In some respects, it is broader than the attorney-client privilege because it extends to materials that were collected or created by non-attorneys. In other respects, it is narrower, because it applies only to materials gathered in anticipation of litigation or preparation for trial. The protection afforded by the work product doctrine is qualified, and it may be overcome by a showing of significant need on the part of the opposing party. There is no automatic waiver of attorney work product if it is discussed with a third party, unless that communication means that it is likely that the opposing party would learn of it. Attorney work product is relevant to security investigations that have been initiated by an attorney in expectation of potential litigation or a regulatory inquiry or while preparing for a trial.

(Continued)

Some Practical Pointers for Sensitive Matters

Below are some practical pointers when conducting internal investigations and other sensitive subject matter:

- If one of the purposes for the activities of the security department is to enable the company to obtain legal advice, then contact the company's attorney before embarking on the activity. Explore whether the communications in connection with that activity should be privileged.
- If one of the purposes for the activity of the security department is because the company is concerned that litigation or a regulatory investigation may arise, or that information will be used in a trial, then contact the company's attorney before embarking on the activity. Explore whether the communications in connection with that activity should be attorney work product.
- Obtain appropriate documentation from the company's attorney whenever it is determined that communications should be privileged or should be considered attorney work product.
- Adhere to labeling requirements for all documentation as determined by the company's attorney.
- Address all communications in connection with the protected topic to the company's attorney.
- Do not discuss the substance of the security department's activities with anyone other than the team doing the work and the company's attorney. Other communications should be approved by the attorney or should take place in the attorney's presence.

Checklist for Conduct of Internal Misconduct Investigations[3]

Investigations of this type are often complicated, time-consuming, and time-sensitive. The correctness of the actions taken is dependent in large measure upon the quality of the investigation that the security professional conducts or leads. Well-conducted investigations are essential to protecting the organization legally, protecting the rights of employees, and observing the organization's human resources policies and principles.

The following materials are offered to assist security professionals to prepare for and conduct investigations into alleged violations of law or organization policy. By *investigating*, we mean fact-finding, often gathered for others who will make decisions based upon your work. Of necessity, we discuss at the outset the obvious fact that many issues do not require investigation, and many other issues require the consultation or involvement of persons other than those conducting the investigation. Some of the advice reflects lessons learned when the spotlight of litigation has been placed upon an investigator's practices.

The sensitivity of cases of this sort cannot be overstated, especially those that involve higher-profile employees or agents. Having investigative staff members who fully understand best practices in investigation, evidence gathering, confidentiality, interview techniques, and trusted relationships with legal counsel and human resources are highly valued assets.

Identifying Investigators

- Are special skills required?
- Should an attorney conduct the investigation?
- Are there actual or potential conflicts of interest that should be addressed?
- Are the proposed investigators objective and resistant to pressure?
- Will any party claim the proposed investigators are biased?
- Are the proposed investigators the individuals who can maximize the information obtained in interviews?

[3]The checklist for conduct of internal misconduct investigations is drawn from John Thompson's book, *The Compliance Response to Misconduct Allegations*, 2nd edition, Boston, MA: Elsevier, 2013.

Obtaining Documents

- Personnel files
- Telephone records
- Expense account records
- Personnel information on computer
- Appointment calendars
- Time cards
- Building entrance/exit records
- Computer and word processing disks (and hard drive memory)
- Electronic mail records
- Voicemail records

Planning the Investigation

- Minimize witness intimidation.
- Form an investigative team and divide duties.
- Establish a timeframe for completion of the investigation.
- Prepare confirmatory memorandum to complainant.
- Obtain and review relevant documents.
- Consider special investigative techniques.
- Identify interviewees.
- Establish an interview location.
- Arrange order of individuals to be interviewed.
- Prepare opening and closing comments.
- Prepare a set of written interview questions.
- Plan for multiple interviews of some individuals.
- Decide whether to obtain written statements.
- Take detailed notes of the investigation-planning process.

Procedural Interview Issues

- Provide a general description of the situation.
- Describe the purpose of the investigation and the interview.
- Make clear that the organization will not reach any conclusions until the completion of the investigation.
- Instruct the interviewee not to discuss the investigation.
- Explain what information you will share within the organization.
- Do not make any promise regarding the outcome of the investigation.
- Describe any organizational policies involved.
- Describe the seriousness of the issue under investigation.

- Indicate the penalty for providing false or misleading information, and tell the interviewee of his or her duty to cooperate in the investigation.
- Tell the interviewee that he or she is protected from retaliation for participation in the investigation.
- Obtain the identity of any other witnesses.
- Identify and obtain relevant documents.

Technical Interview Issues

- Make sure the interviewee is not recording the interview.
- Do not allow the interviewee to have an attorney present without consulting first with legal counsel.
- Nonemployees have a right not to participate in and to terminate any interview.
- The organization may require the cooperation of its employees in the investigation and interview process.
- Be careful not to invade the privacy of any individual.
- Even if the interviewee has no attorney present, assume that all parties are represented by and getting advice from an attorney.
- Assume that a verbatim recording of every interview will exist.
- Do not discuss your opinions or conclusions with any interviewee, and do not discuss your opinions or conclusions with anyone until you have completed the investigation.
- Do not unnecessarily divulge any information to interviewees.
- Assess the demeanor of interviewees as part of the overall credibility assessment.
- Avoid terms with criminal law implications.
- Avoid an appearance that you are investigating a violation of law or making legal judgments.
- Ask open-ended questions and then press for details.
- Identify hearsay and rumor.

Taking Notes

- Designate a primary note taker.
- Include date, location, time started and stopped, and identification of those present.
- Make sure notes are complete, and fill in information immediately after interview.
- Exclude interpretation, subjective comments, and conclusions.
- Write down objective evidence of demeanor of interviewee.
- Always write for the jury.

Taking Written Statements

- Seek voluntary statements.
- You may require employees to provide statements.
- Identify the topics the individual should discuss in the statement, but not the content.
- Statements should
  - include statement of being voluntary when appropriate;
  - discuss all pertinent topics;
  - be handwritten;
  - include a start and finish time at top of first page;
  - not skip lines;
  - have all cross-outs or erasures initialed;
  - have a concluding statement;
  - be witnessed by at least one person;
  - have signature and date of witnesses on every page; and
  - be provided to individual upon completion (as a copy).

Reporting Findings

- Avoid putting preliminary conclusions in writing, but any preliminary conclusions should be sent to legal counsel for the purpose of obtaining legal advice.
- Convene a meeting of the need-to-know group, and include legal counsel.
- If others need to see preliminary conclusions, ask legal counsel to send out those conclusions as part of an attorney-client privileged communication.
- After the need-to-know group meeting has developed a consensus, create a summary report of the investigation.
- Do not communicate any investigation results beyond the need-to-know group except with the advice of legal counsel.
- Have legal counsel review the investigation file once the investigation is over.

What Not to Do

- Do not ignore an "informal" complaint.
- Do not assume you will remember the case later—record it!
- Do not skip over opening and closing statements during the interview.
- Never assume innocence or guilt.
- Avoid terms with criminal law implications.
- Do not ask "yes" or "no" questions.
- Don't assume you can do it all—know when to seek professional help.

THE BOTTOM LINE: Discipline and ethical pursuit of detail are essential ingredients of internal business conduct investigations. Facts outweigh the rank of the subject. As soon as the management jury overlooks the evidence, you have lost the program.

Highlights for Follow-Up

- Remember that the knowledgeable insider is the most dangerous adversary you have! Engage those business units owning critical business processes in an intelligent discussion around how an insider (your own employee or a vendor) might engage in conduct with serious implications for the company's health and reputation.
- Engage counsel and HR (employee relations) in a review of current business conduct policy and the adequacy of business unit line management's knowledge of that policy and expectations for their oversight of an ethical business environment.
- Conduct investigative post-mortems to identify contributing causes and gaps in policy or other needs for improved conformance with high standards of conduct.
- Are you satisfied with the level of support you get from human resources (or others) in the investigation of employees in good standing? If not, what needs to be improved to create a more constructive relationship in these cases? How have you addressed this problem?
- Are sanctions in these internal cases applied consistently across the company and, if not, what legal exposure might that inconsistency present?
- Are you satisfied that the corporate business conduct policy adequately conveys the scope and clarity of management's expectations on conduct?

Key Terms

- Adversary
- Corporate hygiene
- Business conduct
- Policy statement
- Guideline statement

- Reputation risk and business conduct policy
- Attorney-client privilege
- Attorney work product doctrine
- Internal misconduct investigations
- Procedural interview issues
- Technical interview
- Written statements

14

BUSINESS RESILIENCY

Introduction

No matter who "owns" the responsibility for business continuity, the security executive will be right in the middle of response and should be in the middle of preparedness. We own the 24/7 incident reporting infrastructure, we are the first responders, and we maintain much of the physical and electronic monitoring of critical operations. If a vital process tips over, you will be in the harsh lens of crisis review.

Business Value

Being prepared for the possible is a competitive advantage. An uptime of 100% for critical business processes is not likely to be an achievable objective in these times of reliance upon a myriad of infrastructures we do not control, the foibles of weather, and the intentional or unintentional acts of individuals.

The Essentials

Formal planning for likely events is an essential part of business operations and has repeatedly demonstrated its value to organizations that have in-depth resources to respond to interruption.

Your Focus

If there were two lists for you to carry at all times, they would be your executive emergency contact list and those on the top two or three levels of most critical business processes. Understand the natural and manmade threats to those business processes that ensure your company is reliably online 24/7, and get on the record with the resilience of controls over preparedness and response. If you own business continuity, be in the middle of building competency around planning and testing.

Work closely with internal audit, the CIO, and business unit heads owning the most critical business processes. Remember that business interruption may be caused by hostile action of knowledgeable, disgruntled insiders and outsiders. Be aware of the effectiveness (or lack thereof) of security procedures within outsourced business processes, and be proactive on due diligence where critical processes are located in regions with highly unreliable infrastructures.[1]

High-Level Policy or Guideline Statement

It is the responsibility of every manager within this company to plan for emergencies that may impact employee safety and the availability of critical business resources to those supporting our customers' and shareholders' interests.

Consistent with this policy, the components of a business continuity program may include but are not limited to the following:

- A thorough and ongoing risk assessment and impact analysis process that includes estimation of maximum allowable downtime and acceptable levels of operational and financial losses, such as:
  - analysis of cost of business continuity operations compared to cost of downtime due to business interruption;
  - prioritization of potential disruption with rated likelihood of occurrence and potential consequences (Resource A = 0 downtime with full redundancy off-site, Resource B = X hours with equipped alternate site, etc.); and
  - a rigorous analysis and inventory of single points of failure (SPOF) in critical business processes.
- Decentralized, business unit accountability for contingency planning that includes:
  - training for contingency planners and other essential response elements.
- Written plan dissemination with periodic updates reflective of changes in business process, their criticality, and requirements for restoration of capability that includes:
  - clear accountability for action(s) to specify steps to be taken in planned events; and
  - crisis-stage procedures to assure timely evacuation and accounting of employees to specified assembly points;

[1]This includes, for example, corruption, personal risk, terrorism potential, difficult supply-chain logistics, verifiably unreliable support infrastructure, and costly security and support for ex-pat resources.

- recognition and incorporation of outsourced business processes to essential business operations, and the resilience of continuity planning within those contracted resources;
  - pre-positioning of hot and cold backup elements consistent with business process criticality and downtime limitations; and
  - provisions for insurance, site security, media communications, and coordination and communications with public sector first responders.
- Periodic testing of contingency plans with independent audit under the oversight of the board of directors that includes:
  - percentage of business units owning highly critical business processes should indicate percentage or number of fully competent business continuity planners;
  - the number of incidents where recovery was within the established time objective;
  - tested notification procedures upon indication of actual or potential interruption;
  - the percentage of most critical uptime business functions with tested and confirmed contingency plans;
  - the number and percentage of business units with up-to-date (or outdated) response plans;
  - alternate seats and pre-positioned resources required versus available and ready;
  - after-action reports indicate business function resumption occurred within defined timelines and planned results;
  - evidence that the severity of action items resulting from tests decreases; and
  - all action items related to employee safety are addressed through retesting.
- Business unit management financial incentives that are attached to positive business continuity planning and execution.

Track Business Continuity Readiness

The chart in Figure 14.1 represents a simple tracking metric you might want to consider for reporting on key readiness capabilities. Note that the highest level of business process criticality is AAA. You may label the zero downtime processes in other ways, but suffice to say there are multiple functions that must be off-site yet ready to recover should there be any interruption in continuity. While there are several other processes that might be identified, each of the seven items selected for tracking are interrelated in terms of a reliably responsive business recovery strategy.

Business Continuity Dashboard

Updated and tested business continuity plans for all Level AAA business processes	
Appointed and trained business continuity planning and response teams at all locations	
Progress in reducing single points of failure in Level AAA and AA functions	
Required service continuity plans for third-party vendors are tested and current	
Documented, current, and tested biohazard response plan for all facilities	
Electronic sensing, early warning, and all required crisis notification systems are 99.99% on-line	
Public Safety first responders demonstrate adequate response times over past 36 months	

Figure 14.1 Business Continuity Tracking. A simple tracking metric for reporting on key readiness capabilities.

NFPA Standard 1600

Be familiar with National Fire Prevention Association's NFPA 1600: Standard on Disaster/Emergency Management and Business Continuity Programs (2013).[2]

Influencing business units through a consultative approach builds bridges and facilitates business continuity planning and preparations. You also receive an improved understanding of those business processes that are most critical to the health of the company. This, in turn, will influence your protection and response strategy. For further information, see the Corporate Incident Reporting and Response Plan in Appendix F.

National Response Framework

The *National Response Framework* (NRF), last updated in 2013, is a guide that details how the nation conducts all hazards response—from the smallest incident to the largest catastrophe.[3] This document establishes a comprehensive, national, all-hazards approach to domestic incident response. The framework identifies the key response principles, as well as the roles and structures that organize national response. It describes how communities, states, the federal government, and private sector

---

[2]This and other NFPA standards can be found at http://www.nfpa.org/codes-and-standards/document-information-pages.

[3]FEMA's National Response Framework can be found at http://www.fema.gov/national-response-framework.

and nongovernmental partners apply these principles for a coordinated and effective national response. In addition, it describes special circumstances where the federal government exercises a larger role, including incidents where federal interests are involved as well as catastrophic incidents where a state would require significant support. It lays the groundwork for first responders, decision-makers, and supporting entities to provide a unified national response.

In addition to the NRF base document, the Emergency Support Function Annexes and Support Annexes are available online at the National Preparedness Resource Library (http://www.fema.gov/national-preparedness-resource-library). The annexes are a total of 30 individual documents designed to provide the concepts of operations, procedures, and structures for achieving response directives in order for all partners to fulfill their roles under the NRF.

The NRF is written especially for government executives, private-sector business, nongovernmental leaders, and emergency management practitioners. The NRF's clear, simple style makes the serious work of incident management understandable for newly elected or appointed government officials, for business executives, as well as for seasoned practitioners.

Regulatory Requirements

Many antiterrorism and other security regulations and guidelines require thorough contingency planning and countermeasure testing programs for those assets requiring targeted protection. Where countermeasures may be postulated potentially to fail, backup procedures must be in place to bring critical mission processes back online within established timelines.

THE BOTTOM LINE: Some form of business interruption is an area of risk that you can count upon. There is no substitute for knowing who and what you really need when the probable or improbable happens. Planning and being prepared is an obligation to shareholders, employees, and the community.

Highlights for Follow-Up

- Regardless of formerly assigned responsibility for business continuity, the security organization is a critical part of the early warning, crisis management, and response capabilities. What parts does your organization play in these areas of risk management, and are there value-added functions you could offer?

- Does your company annually conduct crisis management or business continuity exercises? What would you conclude if this sort of analysis has not been applied?
- The typical contingency planning processes require each business unit to priority rank their business processes by criticality ratings, the most critical requiring zero downtime. Use the resulting list to assure yourself that your security programs provide the requisite level of protection to these higher criticality processes.
- Have after-action-reviews been applied to the most serious business interruption events over the past three years? What was learned that has implications for your vision of the future security capability? What would you conclude if this sort of analysis has not been applied?
- Business is virtual, global, and increasingly risky. Know the potential risks your "partners" bring to the table before you sign on the dotted line. Hold them accountable for risk-specific standards, and then inspect to assure compliance.

Key Terms

- Business resiliency
- Assessing risk
- Business continuity
- Readiness
- National Response Framework
- Regulatory requirements

15

SECURING YOUR SUPPLY CHAIN

Introduction

Our businesses' operations are now largely dependent upon a variety of subcontracted business partners. What do we know of their security policies and procedures? How susceptible are their operations to natural, manmade, and political risks? What proprietary resources are we sharing that could be compromised? The list goes on. Go online and explore "supply chain risk management" and you will find scores of treatises on the critical importance of these chains and the variety of risks confronting them. Despite the plethora of information available on supply chain risk management, very few people recognize the risks we understand and deal with. Whose fault is that?

Business Value

Clearly, we need to expand our due diligence to include security-related risks. Our business operations must understand the full range of vulnerabilities that these distributed "partners" may introduce into our "trusted" business environments. We bring unique risk assessment skills to the table. As the company explores new relationships to assume processes formerly under your umbrella, make sure they include your capabilities in vendor selection and contractual requirements.

The Essentials

First and foremost, you must understand the array of risks to each link in the supply chain. If you are a regulated industry, you may be already under the aegis of post-9/11 security regulations, which universally mandate a documented examination of security-related risks. Armed with this information, you are in a better position to influence policy and the individual relationships.

Second, we cannot neatly categorize commonalities of supply chain requirements nor the risks confronting them.

Different companies with diverse supply requirements may operate in far less risky environments than others. All companies reliant upon vendors in politically risky countries—those having a high degree of commercial corruption, or areas with highly unreliable infrastructures—share in risk exposure to one degree or another.

Third, we have discussed the critical importance of our security strategy being aligned with the business strategy in Chapter 4, "Strategic Security Planning." If you have been successful in this essential alignment, you will be aware of emerging ventures and the targets of desired engagement. This awareness will enable your engagement with the business in *proactively* assessing risks. So much of the contemporary supply chain is found in locations where business practices, cultural mores, and political and physical risk are variables that require careful assessment and contingency planning.

Given the access to our most sensitive data, final product components or ingredients, and reputation that we are delegating to foreign and domestic business partners, why can't we find recognition of this potential exposure in the contemporary literature and corporate risk management strategy? This lack of foresight may have resulted in a government regulation such as the following.

An Example of the Elements of Supply Chain Risk Oversight: Customs Trade Partnership Against Terrorism, Shipment Guard (C-TPAT) Security Criteria for Importers

In November 2004, U.S. Customs and Border Protection (CBP) issued its Strategic Plan for Securing the Global Supply Chain, leveraging off from the voluntary criteria and best practices issued in 2002. The 2005 final rule outlined in Table 15.1 conveys a far more prescriptive approach to compliance than that of the original guidance. "Must" is now used far more frequently, and the criteria for importers have a broader scope of protection. This is a frequent practice in the evolution of government regulations. The benefit of proactive compliance is often lower cost controls that translate to customer loyalty and satisfaction.

To repeat our admonition on the diversity of supply chain risk, the list in Table 15.1 addresses a specific set of perceived institutional risks. It is not necessarily representative of the range of issues you may face in your business operations, but it

Table 15.1 Strategic Plan for Securing the Global Supply Chain

Security Element

Prepare Supply Chain Security Profile

Conduct comprehensive risk assessment of international supply chains and ensure that all partners meet or exceed the C-TPAT security criteria.

Develop written, verifiable processes for the selection partners including vendors, suppliers, and manufacturers. Identify all business partners and obtain documentation indicating whether or not each one is or is not C-TPAT-certified.

For those not eligible, obtain a completed security profile questionnaire or a written/electronic confirmation of conformance with C-TPAT criteria or equivalent World Customs Organization (WCO)-accredited security program from a senior partner.

Develop (and periodically apply) a documented risk assessment for all non-C-TPAT eligible partners for verification of compliance with security criteria.

Develop procedures to ensure that business partners have compliant security practices in place to enhance the integrity of the shipment at point-of-origin.

Conduct periodic risk-based reviews of partner facilities and security processes.

Where partners are certified by a foreign customs administration, obtain documentation on their status of participation.

Do business partner risk-based due diligence to include financial soundness, capability to meet contractual security requirements and identify/correct security deficiencies documented by an internal management team.

Use procedures to confirm container integrity and sealing at point of staffing.

Use procedures for control and affixing of high-security seals that meet or exceed PAS ISO 17712 to containers.

Use procedures for verification of physical integrity of containers prior to stuffing to include lock reliability and a recommended seven-point inspection of all surfaces.

Use written procedures for control of seals by designated persons, their affixing to containers, and a process for recognizing and reporting compromised seals and/or containers to CBP.

Use procedures for identification, challenging, and addressing unauthorized/unidentified persons.

Designate secure areas for container storage.

Use procedures for identifying, challenging, reporting, and neutralizing of unauthorized persons or access to containers and container storage areas.

Use application of access documentation and controls to ensure positive identification of employees, visitors, and vendors, and limiting access to only those areas required for duties.

Use procedures by management or security to ensure control of issuance and removal of all identification badges.

Use documented procedures for issuance, removal, and changing of access devices.

Use visitor photo identification, badge display, and escort procedures.

Use procedures for vendor identification and random screening of packages and mail.

Develop process for verification of applicant history information prior to hiring.

Develop process for prospective employee screening and, where job sensitivity warrants, periodic post-employment background investigation.

(Continued)

Table 15.1 (Continued)

Security Element

Use procedure for removal of logical and physical access for terminated employees.

Develop and apply security measures for the transportation, handling, and storage of cargo in the supply chain.

Use procedures in place to ensure that information from business partners is reported accurately and timely.

Use procedures in place to ensure all information (including computer-based) used in the clearing of cargo is accurate, complete, and protected against exchange, loss, or introduction of erroneous information.

Use procedures for positive ID of truck drivers delivering or receiving cargo.

Use control procedure for accuracy, security, and integrity of hard copy and computer-based documentation related to arriving cargo.

Use procedures for reconciliation of manifest on all pieces in arriving cargo and for verification of delivery orders for departing cargo.

Use process in place to investigate, resolve, and report to CBP all significant discrepancies, shortage, and overages.

Use procedures to investigate unauthorized access.

Develop and deliver security procedures for antiterrorism threat awareness program for all employees to include modules for personnel in ship/receive and mail operations areas and specific threat scenarios.

Conduct training and offer incentives to assist employees in maintaining cargo integrity, threat recognition, and protecting access controls.

Use cargo handling and storage area perimeter fencing.

Use interior cargo handling segregation area fencing.

Use procedures for inspection and repair of fencing.

Vehicle/personnel gates be manned and/or monitored.

Buildings to be constructed to resist unlawful entry. Inspection procedures to assure structural integrity for areas identified in the risk analysis as sensitive.

All external and internal windows, gates, and fences to be secured with locking devices. Make sure key management procedures are in place.

Ensure private vehicles are prohibited from parking in or adjacent to cargo handling and storage areas.

Ensure adequate lighting is provided inside and outside a facility, including exterior perimeter, entrances/exits, cargo handling and storage, and parking areas.

Alarm systems and CCTV should be utilized to monitor premises and prevent unauthorized access to cargo handling and storage areas.

Automated systems are to use individually-assigned accounts requiring periodic change of passwords.

Use process for investigation and application of disciplinary action for systems violations.

Prepare and deliver employee training on information security policies and procedures.

Install and monitor information security tools to identify intrusion, password compromise, access violations, and tampering of business data.

This 2005 final rule conveys a far more prescriptive approach to compliance.

is a good example of the steps you should consider in developing your supply chain security plans.

Multiple initiatives on the part of the U.S. government to assess and minimize the risks involved in the transportation of goods include the following:

- **The Advanced Manifest Rule (AMR)/Advance Cargo Information (ACI)**. These were instituted by U.S. CBP in conjunction with the Trade Act of 2002, and fully implemented in 99% of the ports by January 2005. It requires detailed cargo data for all modes to be submitted to U.S. CBP prior to arrival. An ocean container is allowed into the United States only if detailed contents information has been provided electronically to U.S. Customs at least 24 hours before the container is loaded on the ship at the foreign port of origin. The information is useful for pre-screening questionable containers prior to arrival to U.S. ports and for selecting containers for inspection at ports of departure and entry.
- **The Container Security Initiative (CSI)**. With the CSI, the U.S. government and more than 25 trading partner governments are pursuing supply chain security by pushing inspections and screening upstream to originating ports. This calls for pre-screening of containers coupled with fast tracking when the cargo reaches the United States.
- **The Customs-Trade Partnership Against Terrorism (C-TPAT)**. C-TPAT was launched in November 2001 with the guiding principles of voluntary participation and jointly developed security criteria, best practices, and implementation procedures. In exchange for the security investments they had made, C-TPAT partners receive reduced inspections at the port of arrival, expedited processing at the border, and other significant benefits, such as "front of line" inspections and penalty mitigation.
- **The Emergency Planning and Community Right-to-know Act (EPCRA)**. EPCRA was passed by the U.S. Congress in response to concerns regarding the environmental and safety hazards posed by the storage and handling of toxic chemicals. Among other things, it requires detailed information regarding hazardous materials to be given to the people in the community.
- **The Free and Secure Trade (FAST)** initiative. It allows low-risk goods transported by trusted drivers via trusted carriers for trusted firms to pass rapidly through border crossings while reserving inspection resources for unknown or high-risk shipments.

- **The Smart and Secure Trade-lanes (SST)** program. This initiative was established in October 2002 by the container shipping industry to ensure the security of cargo containers globally. SST's objective is to rapidly deploy a baseline infrastructure that provides real-time visibility, physical security through nonintrusive, automated inspection and detection alerts, as well as a complete audit trail of a container's journey from origin to final destination. In May 2003, the International Organization for Standardization (ISO) formally became involved with the SST program to gain insight for setting international supply chain security and visibility standards.

- External to the U.S. government security initiatives, the **World Customs Organization (WCO)**, a Brussels-based consortium of 169 customs administrations, which represent 99% of global trade, promotes trade facilitation by developing and promoting guidelines to help customs administrations work together to support rapid clearance of low-risk, cross-border shipments. Also, it has developed standard sets of customs data elements and guidelines for member countries to enable advanced electronic transmission of such data. Specifically, WCO members have developed the **Framework of Standards to Secure and Facilitate Global Trade (SAFE Framework)**, which outlines a strategy that aims to secure the movement of global trade in a way that does not impede but rather facilitates the movement of that trade.

A Focus on Supply Chain Security Has Multiple Benefits

A July 2006 report by the Manufacturing Institute, the research arm of the National Association of Manufacturers, entitled "Innovators in Supply Chain Security: Better Security Drives Business Value,"[1] analyzed the potential values of improved supply chain security and confirmed multiple benefits, as summarized here:

> *The goals of this study were to demonstrate that investments in supply chain security can improve organizations' business performance and, whenever possible, to quantify those improvements. We focused on collateral benefits of security*

[1]"Innovators in Supply Chain Security: Better Security Drives Business Value," The Manufacturing Institute, National Association of Manufacturers (NAM), Barchi Peleg-Gillai, Gauri Bhat and Lesley, July 2006, Stanford University, p. 29.

*investments to manufacturers and logistics service providers
(LSPs)/ocean carriers. Five major areas of improvement were
identified:*

- *inventory management and customer service*
- *visibility*
- *efficiency*
- *resilience*
- *customer relations*

*We received inputs from 11 manufacturers from a variety of
industries and three LSPs/ocean carriers, all considered in our
opinion to be innovators in the area of supply chain security.
The vast majority of companies were able to realize many
benefits from their security investments, with some of them
reaching very significant levels. Based on these inputs, we can
conclude that investments in supply chain security can help
organizations to improve internal operations, strengthen
relationships with their customers, and overall increase their
profitability.*

THE BOTTOM LINE: Your corporate supply chain may be your firm's lifeline in current business practice and customer service, and yet these potentially critical operations may be outside the scope of corporate security involvement. Find a mentor or an executive at risk and insert yourself and your resources into these business strategies.

Highlights for Follow-Up

- Which of the most critical business processes in your company rely in significant ways upon supply chain partners? To what extent have your partner selection processes incorporated a risk management strategy that includes security-related risk?
- What are the most likely risk scenarios that could significantly impact the top three most critical sources of supply? Do you have a role to play in any of these, and if so, have you effectively sold your risk management resources to those business units?
- Are you actively risk-profiling countries upon which you rely for the supply of essential products or services?

- To what extent have you identified and vetted in-country security (or other logistical) resources that may be engaged to assist in an interruption or other risk event in your critical supply chain?

Key Terms

- Supply chain
- Internal resources
- Business partners
- Supply chain security
- Voluntary government-issued guidelines

SECURITY MEASURES AND METRICS

Introduction

You need to be ready for these questions from on high: "How secure are we?" "What does security cost for each dollar of revenue?" "How much less risk do I buy with the budget you are requesting here?" Your company consistently tracks a variety of metrics, as do your shareholders and the marketplace. Security is rich with data that can demonstrate performance, value, and progress against specific risks. Understand the metrics that tell your story and positively influence the business.

Business Value

Metrics are measures that reflect contribution to the bottom line or an *agreed* indicator of success. They focus on the actions (and results of those actions) that organizations take to reduce and manage the risks of loss of reputation, assets, and business discontinuities that arise when security defenses are breached.

The Essentials

If we reverse-engineer a metric example, we can better visualize how we get from an area of risk to appropriate metrics. When we analyze a risk trend and dig for knowledge, we are able to focus on causes versus symptoms and develop countermeasures that are reliably measurable.

What Are Measures and What Are Metrics?

It's important to understand the differences between a *measure* and a *metric*, as explained below:
- **Measurement:** A single point-in-time view of specific factors generated by counting.

- Example: Number of life-safety vulnerabilities detected by security officers on tours.
- **Metrics:** A means of comparing a predetermined baseline of two or more measurements taken over time and generated from analysis.
  - Example: Change in number of life-safety vulnerabilities detected by security officers on tours since last reporting period.

What Are the Key Objectives for Our Metrics?

Objectives of a security measures and metric program should include the following:

- **Positively influence action, attitude, and policy:** Our metrics must inform, tell a story, and be capable of leading management to conclude that change in some form is required.
- **Materially impact exposure to specific risks:** If we are reporting on risk, we need to tell the story that will cause behavior modification and/or resource allocation.
- **Measure the success of our diverse programs:** We are consuming scarce financial resources. How are we demonstrating success in the objectives we set for our security programs?
- **Demonstrate security's value through clear alignment with business strategy and objectives:** Our metrics can focus on our value by clearly demonstrating that we are delivering on the first three objectives.

The chart in Figure 16.1 nicely lays out the response landscape for a specific area of security risk.

The steps are reasonably straightforward:

1. What is the specific area of risk you intend to attack?
2. Given your post-mortem analysis of this and related incidents, what have you concluded are the gaps in protection that contributed to these events?
3. Having analyzed and understood what happened and how these events occurred, what specific countermeasures will successfully mitigate future events such as these?
4. As you develop your countermeasures, how do you propose to measure their success in whatever terminology you may apply?
5. What are the results of your plans to mitigate these risks? What worked and what did not meet the mark you set and why?
6. How can you continue to use this information to educate the right people and implement the changes that are necessary?

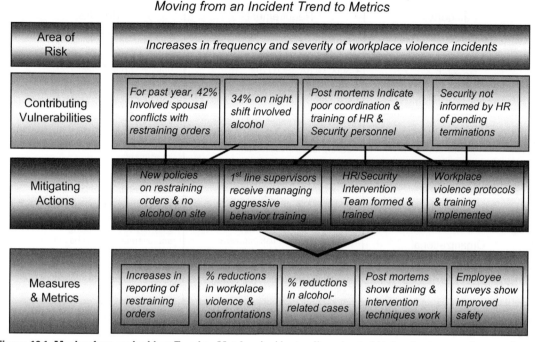

Figure 16.1 Moving from an Incident Trend to Metrics. Incidents offer a host of high-value lessons that may be translated into security initiatives with measurable results.

Incidents offer a host of high-value lessons that may be translated into security initiatives with measurable results. Metrics come alive when they are tied to reliable analysis, positive objectives, and reliable results. The real plus in a presentation like this is the objective of influencing senior management's awareness and causing resulting change in risky business processes.

Why Measure? What Are the Benefits of Measures and Metrics?

There are several good reasons to develop a measures and metrics program throughout security's service delivery processes, including the following:

- The businesses we serve live and die on metrics. Management expects us to demonstrate similar discipline.
- Risk is measurable, and *we are measured every day, incident-by-incident!* How is risk in your organization measurable? Where are the consequences of risk intolerable? What's the threshold? Is it a metric?

Categories	Requirements	Benefits
Regulatory	• HIPPA, FISMA • C-TPAT, MARSEC, MTSA • SOX, GLBA, ISO17799 • USSG, CIPAC-RPS • Etc.	• Reduce cost of compliance • Better assure compliance with regulatory requirements • Acquire good will with regulators • Compound improvements across related compliance elements
Financial	• Measure successes and failures of past and current security investments • Justify future investments • Demonstrate value in hard times	• Enable investment targeting to identified areas of need • Assure best value from security investments
Organizational	• Improve accountability to stakeholdors • Assure level of mission support • Determine Security program effectiveness vs. risk exposure • Improve customer confidence • Cost vs. benefit: Demonstrate leadership in contributing to the bottom line	• Instill confidence in leadership • Demonstrate improvements to stakeholders • Play key role in initiating improvement actions based on performance trends • Enable relevant, realistic, and appropriate security procedure modifications

Figure 16.2 Requirements versus Benefits. Comparison of the two against regulatory, financial, and operational categories.

- Your management likely has a scorecard on the security function. Is it yours?
- Finally, you need to demonstrate security as a *value center*, not a *cost center*. The value and influence of the security organization is directly proportionate to its *measurable impact* on the ability of the enterprise to manage and mitigate risk. Value indicators provide information on what or how much security programs are contributing to corporate health and profitability. Figure 16.2 presents a table that summarizes a number of tangible benefits.

Roles and Responsibilities

As Figure 16.3 shows, various levels in the organization have roles to play in an effective metrics program. The senior security manager has the responsibility to ensure that collection and analysis processes for our measures and metrics data are accurate and qualitative. A key point about the quality of the data you select to present: It must be *good* data! Good means the following:

- Regardless of the source, data must be quantifiable, repeatable (for trending), obtainable, and feasible to measure.

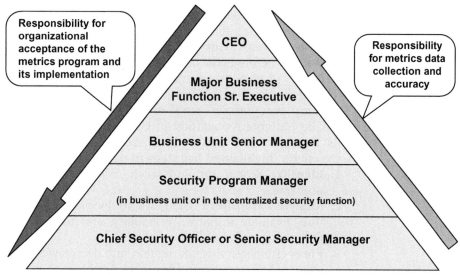

Figure 16.3 Metrics Related Roles and Responsibilities. IT Security Metrics Guidance, Hash and Grance, National Institute of Standards and Technology.

- Timely incident and investigation reports are competently prepared and reviewed by security management.
- Content of reports, logs, and other data sources are valid, accurate, and reliable.
- Your data resides in a platform that enables enterprise-wide data entry from all sources of incident and event data, query for trends, analytical searching, and interface with tools such as Microsoft Excel and PowerPoint.
- A data analysis process that enables and provides assurance of verifiable conclusions is essential.
- Ownership and accountability for data reliability is clear.

As you move up the organization, the need for accuracy increases as the data influences enterprise risk-management policy and business-process conduct. From the top down, the senior management team has the responsibility to buy in, and to assure organizational acceptance of the metrics program and implementation of the conclusions drawn from its results.

There is a definite need for security practitioners to see their metrics program as an integrated business process. It is not about simply counting or reporting; it is a key element of security risk management.

It's about Communication and Risk Management

As security executives, we are paid to be effective risk managers. The risk inventory confronting our organizationally diverse environments has substantially broadened and deepened in the past several years. Our counsel is increasingly sought in boardrooms and before audit committees, who are now held to higher standards of objective oversight. How do we communicate with these executives and others on the governance team? First and foremost, we communicate as managers and advisors on risk.

The National Association of Corporate Directors (NACD), in its Report of the NACD Blue Ribbon Commission on Risk Oversight,[1] highlighted five steps in risk management:

1. **Identify**—Search for and locate risks before they become problems.
2. **Analyze**—Transform risk data into decision-making information. Evaluate impacts, probability, and timeframe; classify risks; and prioritize risks.
3. **Plan**—Translate risk information into decisions and mitigating actions (both present and future) and implement those actions.
4. **Track**—Monitor risk indicators and mitigation actions.
5. **Control**—Correct for deviations from the risk-mitigation plans.

At All Times, Communicate!

Provide information and feedback that is internal and external to the project on the risk activities, current risks, and emerging risks.

Consider the aforementioned five steps. They all end with a need to present what you have learned, to convince with facts, *to influence.* "Brief me" means just that. Be brief and lead me to a conclusion.

Where Do I Find the Data for My Measures and Metrics?

We generate volumes of data every day. There are many sources for the data you will need to track and analyze as you identify the metrics you want to report. Figure 16.4 presents a

---

[1] Report of the NACD Blue Ribbon Commission on Risk Oversight, the National Association of Corporate Directors, 1828 L Street, Suite 801, Washington, D.C. 20036; p. 22.

dozen categories you should consider as you build a metrics program. Each of these also frames the focus of your analysis and reporting.

Presenting to upper management can be daunting and intimidating. These are individuals who live daily with statistics, graphs, slides, and other sophisticated briefing materials. They need focused dashboards to monitor the health and direction of their businesses. (Dashboards will be discussed in more detail later in this chapter, in the "Objective 4: Communicate Results" section.) Corporate cultures, individual executives, and committees all have their unique biases on the protocol of presentations, so it is difficult to identify one type or style. Suffice to say that if you pick Microsoft Office products and their associated tools, you're likely fit in the majority of corporate settings.

Business Alignment—Demonstrating Value to Management

When you consider the breadth of data that may be contained in the 12 file drawers shown in Figure 16.4, multiple

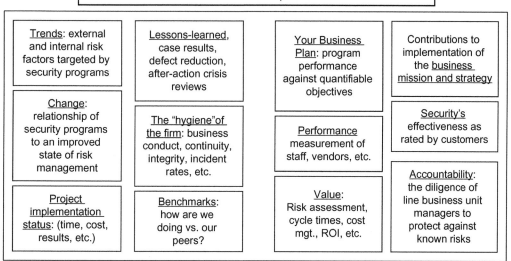

12 File Drawers for Actionable Metrics

"There are three kinds of lies: Lies, damn lies and statistics."

<u>Trends</u>: external and internal risk factors targeted by security programs	<u>Lessons-learned</u>, case results, defect reduction, after-action crisis reviews	<u>Your Business Plan</u>: program performance against quantifiable objectives	Contributions to implementation of the <u>business mission and strategy</u>
<u>Change</u>: relationship of security programs to an improved state of risk management	The "<u>hygiene</u>"of <u>the firm</u>: business conduct, continuity, integrity, incident rates, etc.	<u>Performance</u> measurement of staff, vendors, etc.	<u>Security's</u> effectiveness as rated by customers
<u>Project implementation status</u>: (time, cost, results, etc.)	<u>Benchmarks</u>: how are we doing vs. our peers?	<u>Value</u>: Risk assessment, cycle times, cost mgt., ROI, etc.	<u>Accountability</u>: the diligence of line business unit managers to protect against known risks

Figure 16.4 12 File Drawers for Actionable Metrics. Categories to consider when building a security metric program.

Table 16.1 Aligning Security with Business

Additions of Value	Reductions of Value
• Increased level of protection with improved controls and less cost	• Increased risk, to revenue-gathering activities
• Enhanced ability to satisfy customers with improved methods of protection	• Increased cost of security-related incidents
• Increased market penetration attributable to security measures	• Increased cost of insurance
• Increased recovery time to critical process interruption	• Increased notable audit findings attributable to security defects
• Increased integrity to revenue-gathering activities	• Increased risk, exposure from cost-reducing outsourced activities
• Increased recovery of losses	• Increased risk to customers in sensitive transactions and relationship management
• Increased confidence in effectiveness and need for security controls	• Increased risk of attack through less measurably-effective protective measures
• Increased engagement of employees in securing corporate assets	• Increases in employee interaction with time-consuming security measures

A list of 16 potential measures of security's alignment with core business strategies and objectives.

opportunities are presented to demonstrate ways in which metrics enable security to demonstrate its value. Consider as well the 16 potential measures of security's alignment with core business strategies and objectives shown in Table 16.1.

Pitfalls to Avoid

Here are several potentially career-threatening problems to avoid as you gather and evaluate your metrics and then prepare your presentation.

You are a fool when the following occurs:

- You have unreliable data and use it.
- You have reported on symptoms and not causes.
- You have only selected that which shines favorably upon you and your team.
- You don't have the courage (or backing) to tell the real story.
- Your metrics are irrelevant—you don't know your audience.
- Your data is not actionable—you have wasted their time.
- Your advertised accomplishments have gone the wrong way.
- You were right and nobody believed you, and now they look like fools.

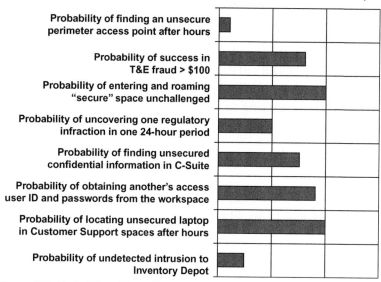

Figure 16.5 Probability of Loss. Based on vulnerability tests conducted 10/15/07 to 11/15/07.

Five Metrics You Might Consider

Each of the following objectives employs a theme to enable the presenter to tell a story to a specific audience. You are the arbiter of the metrics you will choose to maintain and how you will use them. The critical point is to pick those that best convey the story you want to tell and the result you seek to obtain. If you don't have a set of metrics on your department's performance, you give others the opening to use whatever measures they choose, without the benefit of your data and expertise.

Know your audience. What you measure and report may be extremely sensitive. Always classify and label your presentations according to its level of sensitivity (Figure 16.5.)[2]

---

[2]Our metrics may be particularly sensitive, given the litigious environments in which our businesses reside. When reporting on insider risk, internal vulnerabilities associated with privacy or customer data, cases subject to or involved with litigation, health, and safety issues, and so on, it is wise to seek guidance from legal counsel on classification of final presentation materials and to mark all in-process work as drafts with your highest level of handling standards.

The focus in the following objectives is to intelligently inform management on the potential for risk and loss in multiple areas of potential concern. Our primary aim is to recognize that these tests legitimately indicate vulnerabilities.

Objective 1: Measure Loss Probability

Have you ever heard "But it hasn't happened here" from someone you are trying to convince of your view of risk and to invest in improved protection? Here is an approach that can deliver some metrics calculated to provide verifiable estimates of probability of loss, given known vulnerabilities.

Risk Management Strategy

This is a test of likelihood or probability that certain goals would or would not be met based on multiple tests conducted over a four-week period. We have organized and advertised tests of policy-based or commonsense safeguards in a variety of protection categories. What you are presenting isn't hype or scare tactics. This data represents what is real, based on proactive tests against several test objectives you have advertised in your annual plan.

Think of the strategy in four levels or steps. First, protection programs and tactics are built around the achievement of clear, measurable results in terms of reduced exposure to risk—specify them! Second, by policy or accepted process, assessment programs *should be an essential component* of corporate governance with results presented—as required to senior management and internal audit processes and to include the audit committee. Third, risk and protection performance assessments are structured around measurable criteria of effectiveness (success or failure) for the element(s) evaluated and will be specifically measured on an advertised basis. Fourth, thoroughly analyze the data in your measures and report the results in a way that is responsive to management's format for action and accountability for results.

Where Is the Data?

The data is in the quality of risk assessments you routinely perform on the adequacy of key protection measures and to uncover gaps in the quality of internal controls around critical assets and business processes. If you have appropriately structured your ongoing recorded measures and planned your risk assessment processes to provide comparative metrics, you will have

- results of tests that yield a percentage of protection system or process failures and successes;
- incident post-mortem findings on gaps in protection measures;
- training records showing preparedness of key players;
- documented frequency and results of prior tests;
- recorded downtimes of critical systems or business processes; and
- specific benchmarks of protection system performance and test results for them.

Remember the objective. We want to use this to reinforce (or introduce) an attitude of understanding and intolerance! In the best of worlds, we want to hear, "I support your objectives in assessing these risks and the discipline you have provided in arriving at these results. I accept our responsibility to assure remedial action on each of these corporate risks and ask our general auditor to track the resolution of each of these findings."

Objective 2: Identify Perpetrator Attributes

Through incident post-mortems, identify attributes of perpetrators to inform management and aid in the formulation of preventive strategies. The chief security officer (CSO) possesses a unique risk-focused database that should be used to track key risk trends. This basic metric is used to alert management to ensure awareness and support for corrective actions and their effectiveness over an extended period of time.

Risk Management Strategy (Hypothetical Example)

This metric was started by security to highlight concern for the number of incidents attributable to insider employees. In partnership with human resources and legal, the CSO developed and applied a focused effort to develop, communicate, and applied a business conduct policy that has had a positive impact on employee misconduct. The following year, the company implemented a large-scale contractor program that resulted in a significant increase in inventory losses, systems abuse, and customer privacy violations. The services chosen for outsourcing often involve some of the most sensitive processes and information within the organization. The costs of compromise are potentially lethal. The rush for cost savings without a thorough understanding of the company's ability and commitment to

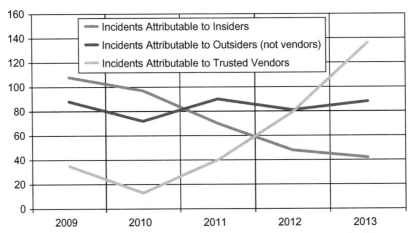

Figure 16.6 Tracking Source of the Threat. Use a metric similar to this one to keep track of how many threats come from various sources, including insiders, outsiders (not vendors), and trusted vendors.

protect their client is the stuff of the upper right corner of the *Wall Street Journal.*[3] Safeguards must be contractually imposed and monitored with the associated costs if these risks are to be managed.

In Figure 16.6, the obvious need to measurably reduce the number of incidents attributable to "trusted" vendors has not been addressed in spite of the CSO's prior reporting on this trend to procurement and business unit management. The solution involves more stringent pre-contract security reviews, audit engagement, periodic inspections, and procurement oversight. Escalation to the CEO and audit committee is the overdue and likely next step.

Where Is the Data?

Effective tracking of data on the three incident types in Figure 16.6 requires much more than security's investigative reports. Our internal business partners in HR, procurement, audit, and various managers overseeing outsourced programs all have data that represents the more complete picture; partnering with them gives us solid opportunities to influence policy and strategy.

These metrics require action and go to the fundamental measures of business reputation. The CSO in our hypothetical example understands the unique risk-management perch the

---

[3]The upper right corner of the *Wall Street Journal* was typically used to highlight a company involved in some sort of wrongdoing.

security role provides, what metrics are important, how to track it, and how to use it to successfully engage and influence senior management. The CSO understands that security is only a piece of the solution and is anxious to collaborate and partner with other members of the corporate governance team.

The trends in Figure 16.6 reflect very significant (and sensitive) data on the source of threats to the reputation and well-being of the company. The knowledgeable insiders are always the most serious threat, since they live inside the protective measures and have unique understanding of where the soft spots in protection vulnerabilities are located and how to use them to advantage. With outsourcing, we have brought a whole new population into this "trusted" realm: contractors and third-party business partners. You can bet that individual business units don't go around briefing senior management when they have insider misconduct, so it's important that security maintain the radar. Also, the multiple incident trends are what tell the story in this reputational risk area much more severely than individual cases.

What we want to achieve here is change. We need to eliminate likely denial. Success means a new or revised policy, and more security-aware business operations that contain the controls essential to these new ways of doing business.

Objective 3: Assess Business Unit Security

To assess the security of various business units and effectively communicate our findings and recommendations to business leaders. We are using metrics to engage in positive change. We want local management to be more focused on their responsibilities for reducing risk, rather than leaving it to us as the inspectors of last resort.

Risk Management Strategy

There are two ways to deal with business units' security trouble spots. One way is to bring them directly to the attention of the CEO and the audit committee. If we go this route, we may gain points for a "gotcha" that makes security look good in the eyes of upper management, but we will probably gain an enemy in the ranks who may remain a powerful thorn in the side of our objectives. A second way is to work prospectively with the business unit to assess and report on several key areas of risk exposure and collaborate on solutions.

The scorecard process is risky from an internal business relation's perspective; no line manager wants headlines highlighting his or her failure to protect the enterprise. This process must be a pre-advertised, coordinated, and accepted part of the corporate risk management strategy. When appropriately planned, incorporated as a consolidated part of the periodic metrics reporting process, and sold to participating line managers, it will be a powerful tool for addressing business units' perceived shortfalls with attention to specific areas of vulnerability.

We are not the corporate cops who get our headlines from nailing idiots who should know better. We are resident experts who have a unique perspective on operational risk, and we need to see ourselves as change agents intelligently using this unique knowledge. By informing the manager of this proposed assessment process and working with designated individuals in the business unit, we can create and present an honest report of past performance while still achieving a positive response from the manager.

This is similar to the process employed in an internal audit: We are coming, here is the focus, and we will work with you to identify deficiencies and help you correct them—all on the record. If you don't want to play, we will do our job and let the chips fall where they may. Few intelligent managers will refuse to participate when it's put to them in that way.

Where Is the Data?

Look at the categories of review of a fictional administrative services unit in the example annual business unit security card (Figure 16.7). Each one can point to a record to support the conclusions. In this example scorecard, a score of 1, 2, or 3 was assigned to 7 categories of security (1 is positive, 2 has both positives and negatives, and 3 is negative). A color rating system (green, yellow, and red) could also be used.

- **Maintaining an ethical environment:** In the example in Figure 16.7 there have been internal investigations that provide evidence that management has a low tolerance for misconduct and supports doing the right thing. Administrative services have been proactive in working with security as allegations have emerged, and they have supported sanctions where evidence supported them.
- **Protecting private information:** Periodic inspections and audits have shown poor controls in this area, according to the records of security and internal audit.

	Annual Business Unit Security Scorecard	

Business Unit: Administrative Services Accountable Executive: Paul Jones
Risk Manager: Charles Brown Scope: Corporate-wide

1	Maintaining an Ethical Environment	Excellent awareness and support for business conduct policy throughout the management team.
3	Protecting Private Information	Repeated notable audit findings. Frequent source of network virus. Poor laptop controls. Management insufficiently engaged in risk.
2	Maintaining Safe and Secure Workplaces	Propped doors and disabled access controls. Improvement in timely notification of emerging issues having workplace violence potential.
2	Plan/Prepare for Business Continuity	65% compliance with full plan testing for critical business processes needs improvement.
1	Employee Vetting	No hires of candidates or vendors with notable adverse backgrounds in the past year.
3	Vetting Third-Party Business Relationships	80% of all engagements in the past two years failed to conduct adequate risk-based due diligence.
2	Response to Security Incidents	Management's response to multiple incidents has been collaborative with good follow-up to address noted vulnerabilities.

Issue Resolution: All issues identified within this review have been addressed within a risk mitigation plan scheduled for completion by the end of Q2.

Figure 16.7 Annual Business Unit Security Scorecard. Use a scorecard like this one to annually review a specific business unit's security.

- **Maintaining safe and secure workplaces:** Security has advised administrative services for propped doors and disabled controls and the potential for workplace violence this vulnerable position creates. They are getting the point, so the scorecard acknowledges improvement with a score of 2.
- **Plan and prepare for business continuity:** Security can find no record of contingency plan testing for one-third of this unit's critical business operations, which raises concerns.
- **Employee vetting:** Security gives administrative services the results of background investigation findings, and hiring records show they are not hiring the bad guys security has identified.

- **Vetting third-party business relationships:** Security can find no record that more than one in five third-party relationships has been vetted for security or business risk.
- **Response to security incidents:** Where incidents have occurred, the business unit has responded well.

The final piece of data is the response by the business unit. If properly sold and executed, it will be difficult for them to push back if your data is solid. Negotiate a resolution. If they fail to appreciate the process and its implications, you can and should escalate.

Objective 4: Communicate Results

We are no different than any other business unit that is required to communicate its results to management periodically. Security departments often do not do that well and need to focus on those critical few measures and metrics that (1) management needs to hear, and (2) we may *or may not* want to convey.

Risk Management Strategy

There are two aspects to your risk management strategy at work here. First, you have an obligation to report, but the results may not shine favorably on you or your organization's performance. So be it. Welcome to metrics. Second, you have an obligation to inform management on key risk issues.

You need one or more dashboards (see Figure 16.6) to track your priorities. As you get comfortable with assembling the data of importance and various means of presentation, using simple applications of Excel or PowerPoint, you will develop ideas for broader and more specific uses.

Where Is the Data?

Figure 16.8 represents a basic CSO dashboard. Our CSO has selected five to six key measures relevant to the organization and the focus of reporting. This one speaks for itself. Target five key indicators that can represent a 15 to 20 minute briefing with the CEO or the senior management team. What do you want them to do with this information? What are you doing to address their issues, and is that metric here? What are the milestones of moving an issue from negative (red) to positive (green)? Pick your topics. Your focus will likely change from reporting period to reporting period, depending on the "hot" issues or a trend you want to update or highlight. The following

Security Department Dashboard

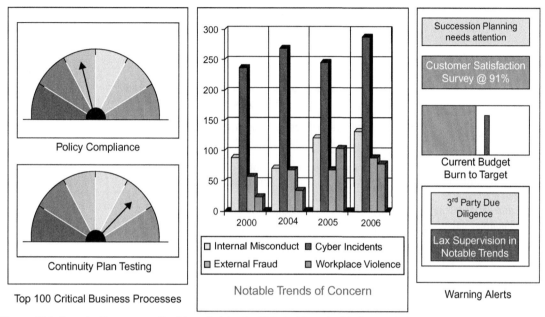

Figure 16.8 Security Department Dashboard. A basic CSO dashboard with five to six key measures relevant to the organization and the focus of reporting.

example offers a different, more comprehensive treatment of a CSO dashboard.

In Figure 16.8 we see a dashboard that uses several separate topical displays. The CSO has laid out a landscape that includes multiple metrics primarily focused on periodic updates on key areas of risk. At the left are two measures of policy compliance: one on the overall assessment of conformance with security policy, and the other on the current status of contingency plan testing. The former was gleaned from investigative results and risk assessments, and the latter is from current test results. At the center of the dashboard is a four-year analysis on four notable trends of specific concern to the CSO, again from incident results. On the right are two warning indicators that complement the notable trends, a quick look at the department's budget burn rate, and two color-coded status indicators on issues that management has stated as goals.

This is a likely 30 to 45 minute presentation upward to the CSO's boss who has specific issues that he or she wants tracked,

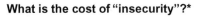

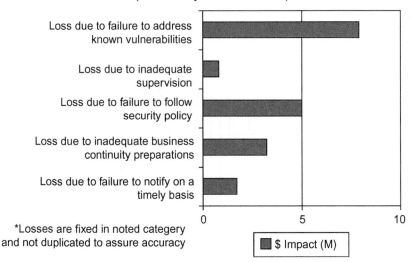

What is the cost of "insecurity"?*

(total current year to date = $18.5M)

Figure 16.9 The Cost of Insecurity. In this hypothetical example, what has occurred, what has been learned as a result, and what is being done to address each incident?

*Losses are fixed in noted category and not duplicated to assure accuracy

or one in which the CSO wants to focus management on a combination of discussion points. The format is easily adaptable to incorporate charts from your inventory, and to simple red/yellow/green indicators for selected measures. This format would also work well in a business plan update. All of the data to support the indicators should be readily available in your various databases.

Objective 5: Identify Loss Areas

Identify key areas of loss and inform key constituents on the causes to better assure awareness and accountability. Think about what you could do with a presentation like this. Are there any opportunities for increased awareness of actions that contribute to security-related incidents? How about ownership for improved risk management?

Risk Management Strategy

You report on losses due to various incidents. What have we learned from these incidents? How and why did they occur? How can we reduce our loss experience? Charting security-related losses is a bland exercise. The chart in Figure 16.9 attempts to plot knowledge gained from events and make the point that the lack of security or inattention to policy has consequences.

The five examples in the chart in Figure 16.9 could easily consume a half hour to hour presentation on what has occurred, what has been learned as a result, and what is being done to address each category of loss. For example, in "loss due to failure to address known vulnerability" the key word is "known." The risk had been previously identified and corrective action was not taken. Who failed to follow up? What process should be in place to better assure attention to known risks?

Where Is the Data?

Useful, actionable data is the output of a thoroughgoing program of incident post-mortems or lessons-learned analysis. This is not about taking prisoners; it is about learning to avoid future risk.

A presentation like this offers a tangible demonstration that we have learned from our mistakes and that business units are demonstrating improved ownership for protecting corporate assets.

Conclusion

Metrics are based on a firm foundation of performance objectives and designed to facilitate decision making, resource direction, and accountability. They provide the engine of influence and the substance of our business case for risk management.

Metrics are about building a process the CSO can use to ensure his or her focus is on target. Call it survival metrics. Begin with a thorough understanding of the security-related risks that confront the company and what measures are relevant to progress in managing them. Be able to demonstrate that the safeguards that are being employed are working. Secondly, when you meet with senior management, know what keeps them awake at night and the metrics that apply to reporting on these issues. Finally, make sure you understand the cost of protection versus the potential or likely cost of loss. These three skills will provide a broad portfolio of metrics and more effectively enable your ability to influence business managers.

Whatever metrics you decide to use, make sure they are SMART: Specific, Measurable, Attainable, Relevant and Timely.

THE BOTTOM LINE: If you are not measuring, you are not managing.

Highlights for Follow-Up

- What metrics are you currently providing to senior management?
  - If none, you are failing to demonstrate any value or ability to influence.
  - If you stopped providing them, would anyone inquire why and when they might see them again?
  - If you answered no or don't know, you are missing the mark, and you need to evaluate critically your security program, because it is likely that you have no idea how your areas of concern are performing.
- Assuming you do maintain security metrics, what are the top three weak spots in your measures and metrics program? What steps should you take to improve these areas?
- What are the most important metrics you need to manage your assigned resources?
- Which metrics have you successfully used to influence management action or policy?
- Which of the 16 contributions on business alignment shown in Table 16.1 can you demonstrate with your metrics? How well are you advertising these accomplishments? Of those you hadn't considered, which ones could you examine for development?

Key Terms

- Security measures
- Metrics
- Corporate readiness
- Impact on the bottom line
- Potential pitfalls

CONTINUOUS LEARNING: ADDRESSING RISK WITH AFTER-ACTION REVIEWS

Introduction

The notion of continuous learning is about growth and improvement from experience. In security, we live through incidents that can provide high-value information about the performance of plans, people, and processes, if we are willing to learn and be disciplined in our reviews.

Business Value

The value of after-action reviews for the business is to learn, to replicate processes done flawlessly, and not to repeat mistakes.

Essentials

Organizations that fail to learn from incidents are destined to repeat their mistakes. The after-action review, the incident post-mortem, or the lessons-learned analysis are all aimed at providing qualitative information on the *what, why,* and *how* of an event's occurrence. Because security organizations are at the center of crisis events, they are in a unique position to gather and record data critical to learning.

After-Action Review (AAR) and Incident Post-Mortem

The after-action review (AAR), originally developed for military use, is a formal review performed following an incident or event. It typically provides reviewers with insight into what happened, why it happened, and how to learn from the mistakes and successes following the incident.

The incident post-mortem, also known as the lessons-learned analysis, may be less formal, but it still requires a disciplined and objective review of events leading up to and taking place during and after a security-related incident. They seek to do the following:

- Identify root causes or previously unknown vulnerabilities that enabled the incident.
- Determine where policy or procedural voids or shortcomings exist.
- Assess how people and systems performed against planned standards.
- Measure the quality of response capabilities.
- Specify what needs to be fixed or improved.
- Offer objective tools for learning how to improve business processes.

These processes will lose their value if they become forms of investigative reporting that seeks to identify perpetrators and fix blame.

The security executive should assemble a team consisting of individuals who were involved in response to the event, from within business units that were affected, and individuals with other internal expertise who may be in a position to contribute to the examination and learning process. Ideally, team composition would not exceed eight people.

Know Your Audience

The incident post-mortem must be an objective and honest assessment of what happened as well as why and how to prevent recurrence. The process invariably uncovers previously unknown or known and overlooked vulnerabilities in the protection process. Depending on incident sensitivity, counsel may impose attorney-client privilege, or the results may be classified to protect findings from disclosure. However, it is also critical that a means be found to pass on learning and to inform and train those in a position to prevent similar incidents in the future.

Outline for the Incident Post-Mortem Management Plan and Briefing

1. Title and agenda
2. Key messages (2–3 key lessons from which we must learn)

3. What happened? Summarize
   a. the initial impact and awareness of risk exposure; and
   b. the incident timeline.
4. High-level analysis of incident and response, including our
   a. ability to anticipate an incident of this type and the consequence(s);
   b. initial understanding of the potential business impact; and
   c. initial activities to limit consequences.
5. What worked well and why?
6. What did not work well and why?
7. Threat diagnosis—what is the potential for recurrence?
8. What should we do differently?
9. Action plan—short-term efforts to
   a. update and prepare contingency plans and procedures to deal with similar incidents;
   b. reduce short-term risk and damage of reoccurrence; and
   c. resource requirements to address immediate vulnerabilities.
10. Action plan—long-term efforts to provide
    a. metrics for reporting on plans and accomplishments and
    b. resource requirements to address longer-term vulnerabilities.
11. Open items include
    a. specific task accountabilities;
    b. deliverable schedule; and
    c. anticipated benefits.

THE BOTTOM LINE: How do you explain an intelligent business not learning from something bad or unanticipated? Specific events provide a wealth of data on the root causes of risk and the failures and successes of response. Scrape until it hurts.

Highlight for Follow-Up

- How does your company approach examining its successes and failures? How might this influence your approach to the AAR process discussed here?

Key Terms

- After-action reviews (AAR)
- Incident post-mortems
- Lessons-learned analysis
- Review documents

APPENDIX A: RISK REVIEW ELEMENTS

Business Risk Environment

1. To what extent are there **pervasive** indications that integrity—doing the right thing—is a cultural expectation of the enterprise population?
    1.1. Is it part of employee orientation?
    1.2. Are there published value statements that encompass integrity/risk management?
2. Growth Issues (score 1–5):
    2.1. Pressure for performance
    2.2. Rate of expansion
    2.3. Inexperience of key employees
3. Cultural Issues (score 1–5):
    3.1. Rewards for entrepreneurial risk-taking
    3.2. Executive resistance to bad news—willingness to escalate
    3.3. Levels of internal competition
4. Information Management (score 1–5):
    4.1. Transaction complexity and velocity
    4.2. Gaps in diagnostic performance measures
    4.3. Degree of decentralized decision-making
5. Is there a communicated accountability model that holds business unit managers accountable for risk management, asset protection, and other security issues?
6. Are there indications that first-line managers are on top of poor integrity and climate issues?
7. Are controls around travel and entertainment (T&E) expenses, internet or intranet usage, or other behavior indicators in place and effective?
8. What procedures are followed for business conduct monitoring, investigation, and discipline?
9. Is there a means for employees to confidentially report potential ethical breaches, suspected criminal conduct, or other violations of policy?

Policy Framework

1. Are Business/Professional Conduct policies in place as an integral element of corporate policy? Are they clearly made part of line manager responsibility?
2. Is a security policy or similar guidance infrastructure in place and distributed?
   2.1. Does Internal Audit use it as a baseline expectation?
   2.2. Are new employees and vendors made aware of expectations on conduct and security as part of an orientation program?
   2.3. Are all elements of security-related risk incorporated in whatever guidance formats are utilized?
   2.4. Does the IT organization use information security policy for all aspects of systems development and implementation?

Threats

1. What are the postulated threat(s) *and likelihood of exposure* at the site(s) under review?
   1.1. Internal adversary—most serious; procedures-intensive countermeasures
   1.2. Information compromise, competitive intelligence
   1.3. Systems sabotage
   1.4. Theft
   1.5. Disgruntled ex-employee: not yet purged from access
2. Outsider adversary
   2.1. With (or without) knowledge of our security measures
   2.2. Terrorist or organized criminal
   2.3. Distributed denial of service, system sabotage, or hacking for malicious or criminal intent
   2.4. The Company as icon, disgruntled customer, violent spouse, etc.
   2.5. Crime of opportunity
3. Insider in collusion with outsider (extortion or selfish motive)
4. Natural disaster resulting in single building or regional outage
5. The Company (site) is a victim of collateral damage from attack elsewhere (infrastructure compromise)

Location Risk

1. FBI or other Crime Risk Score
2. Other high-profile/high-risk tenants in building
3. Adjacent or nearby risky properties that could impact the company
4. Space is in a corporate campus or served by on-site security or other support
5. Urbanization
6. Adequacy of life safety and other essential local response capabilities
7. Known response times versus first responder assets

General Data

1. Resident headcount
2. Square feet occupied
3. Most Critical Business Functions/Processes
    3.1. Ease/time to fail over to alternate site(s)
    3.2. Are all business-critical assets located here exclusively?
    3.3. Test frequency and results
4. Current assessment of business unit information security and business continuity staff influence and competence
5. Risk management assessment of competence of program
6. Other less business-critical functions
7. Adequacy of floor warden program, ratios, drills, etc.

Business Continuity Incidents

1. Total downtime of critical business processes here in past 12 months
2. Incident types
    2.1. Bomb threats
    2.2. Fire related
    2.3. Hazardous materials
    2.4. Power related
    2.5. Critical systems related
    2.6. Water related
    2.7. Weather related
    2.8. Other

Internal Risk

1. Prior workplace violence or issues of disgruntled insiders
2. Extent to which vendors or contractors have unsupervised access to sensitive space
3. Any issues associated with resident labor pools, background issues, etc.

Information Security

1. Components of the program
   1.1. Identification—Each entity must be uniquely identified: ask for credentials
   1.2. Authentication—Identities must be accurately confirmed: verify credentials
   1.3. Authorization—Control or limit access to resources: access based on need to know
   1.4. Confidentiality—Information must be kept private: we can keep a secret
   1.5. Data Integrity—Proof of no unauthorized changes: we keep accurate records
   1.6. Nonrepudiation—Parties are bound to their actions: a deal is a deal
   1.7. Accountability—All actions are auditable: we know who did what
   1.8. Administration—All of this is carefully managed: people make or break security
2. What is the policy infrastructure and application process? Internal Audit role?
3. How is logical access managed?
   3.1. Is access properly aligned with job responsibilities?
   3.2. When are transferring and exiting employees removed from access?
   3.3. Is there a single universal identifier for all with logical and physical access?
4. Observations on adequacy of proprietary information protection within interior spaces
   4.1. Labeling appropriate to sensitivity
   4.2. Storage (is there a clean desk policy?)
   4.3. Disposal and destruction process
       4.3.1. Cleaning vendors—issues?
       4.3.2. Shredders and secure containers deployed at key locations

   4.4. Awareness of policy
      4.4.1. Are there any indications of sloppy business practices around sensitive data?
5. What strategies and tactics are being utilized to protect the technical environment from intrusion, hacking, viruses, etc.?

Hazardous/Dangerous Material Issues

1. Jurisdiction
2. Response agency to threat
3. Company protocol approved by municipality?
4. Local response tests employees?
5. Third party testing agency available?
   5.1. Do they provide decontamination?
6. Extent to which incoming mail, courier, or common carrier deliveries are screened
7. Can base building air handling systems be *quickly* shut down if required
   7.1. Can the system be placed on full (100%) outside air?

Base Building Risks

1. Leased or owned?
2. If leased:
   2.1. Extent to which we are an anchor tenant
   2.2. Lobby and vertical attractions that impact public risk to Company spaces
   2.3. Visitor sign-in/sign-out process in place and enforced
   2.4. Does Property Manager have appreciation for security issues?
   2.5. Current square foot cost for security in lease?
      2.5.1. Comparison with Class A space locally?
3. Prior incidents:
   3.1. Is data available?
   3.2. CAP Index risk scores (if available)
   3.3. If problems occur, are they proactive on awareness?
4. Perceived or measurable competence of security vendor
   4.1. Security supervision and management
   4.2. Training provided prior to posting
      4.2.1. First responder qualifications
   4.3. On-site versus occasional
   4.4. Knowledge of resident issues and risks

5. Adequacy of staffing
   5.1. Any issues with current vendor that give concerns?
   5.2. Apparent turnover
   5.3. Communication and recording competencies
   5.4. Attention to detail
   5.5. Post coverage and awareness of procedures
6. Engagement of security vendor
   6.1. Apparent knowledge of tenant and local risk
   6.2. Ability to respond to changed threats
   6.3. Proactivity with tenants
7. Physical security
   7.1. Base building automated access controls
   7.2. Manned visitor and other access control posts
   7.3. CCTV, other safeguards that indicate risk-based planning
   7.4. Property introduction and removal procedures in place
8. Protection of critical allied systems:
   8.1. Ventilation and HVAC
   8.2. Incoming power and other utilities exposed to access
   8.3. Other building systems essential to business
9. Garages
   9.1. Access policy—limited versus virtually open
       9.1.1. Business versus off hours
       9.1.2. Access credential usage
   9.2. Approach to vendor access—open versus checking
   9.3. Deliveries—open versus checking
   9.4. Staffed security presence
   9.5. Limited automated access
   9.6. CCTV and/or duress capabilities
   9.7. Lighting adequacy
10. Is there a property removal process in place?
11. Are we dependent upon base building backup power or other vital equipment?
    11.1. Adequacy of protection at these locations

Owned Properties

Refer to all above (as appropriate) to owned space issues.
1. Card access authorization list review. Excessive? Purge process?
   1.1. What outsiders have access to our space? (cleaners, plants, building security and maintenance, etc.)
2. Are all critical spaces (Secure Areas) covered by appropriately configured electronics?
3. Is alarm management (nuisance alarms) being addressed?

Contractors

1. Access requirements? (background investigation, escort policy, etc.)
2. Are nondisclosure and confidentiality agreements executed?
3. Are due diligence examinations performed on (any or all) contractors and vendors?
    3.1. Is the sensitivity of the work to be performed a driver in a vendor risk review?

Background Investigation

1. Are pre-employment investigations performed on (all or some) employees and others with (physical or logical) access?
2. Are there clear and uniform suitability standards? What background elements are included?
    2.1. SSN verification
    2.2. National Credit check
    2.3. Military service
    2.4. Motor vehicle (if a condition of employment)
    2.5. Criminal or criminal litigation search
    2.6. Civil litigation search
    2.7. National corporate affiliation(s) search
    2.8. Online media search
    2.9. Education
    2.10. Registrations
3. Who performs the background checks? What quality management process in place?
4. What impact does the BI have on the hire decision? What are the derogatory rates?
5. What part does an executed personal history statement play in the process?

Data Management

1. What is the accountability model for report preparation and integrity?
2. How are incidents documented? Is it a consistent process to a central function?
3. Are incident and other workload data analyzed to influence resource allocation?

Business Continuity Planning

1. Program management model—accountability?
    1.1. Is there a policy that every business unit must have an up-to-date plan?
        1.1.1. Is there a hardcopy with senior management sign-off?
        1.1.2. Frequency for plan maintenance?
    1.2. What level is the contingency plan organization and local responsibility?
2. What is the high-level strategy for business interruption and recovery?
    2.1. Single site or regional outage?
    2.2. Regulatory or other implications for interruption?
3. Emergency notification procedures (pagers, published emergency notification lists, conference bridge process, etc.)
    3.1. What is the established routine for notification horizontally and vertically?
4. Are alternate sites provisioned for most critical processes?
    4.1. If contracted, what is the procedure for activation and risk of nonavailability?
    4.2. What are the proximity criteria for alternate sites?
5. Is there a program to identify and back up all vital records? (backup storage and frequency)
6. Identification of a hierarchy of critical business functions
    6.1. Documentation of systems, personnel, and resources to perform functions
        6.1.1. Is essential technology inventoried
    6.2. What is the downtime allowance?
    6.3. What are the critical interdependencies external to this business unit?
7. Are plans tested on an established basis? Frequency for each of the following:
    7.1. Call notification
    7.2. Walk-through/tabletop exercise
    7.3. Alternate site activation
    7.4. Full test
8. Employee awareness procedures (are all employees knowledgeable of what to do if?)
9. Is there a method for documenting expenses related to outage response?

Emergency and Crisis Management

1. Floor warden program in place and tested? Do all wardens know what to do if?
   1.1. Is there a clearly established hierarchy for evacuation orders?
2. Who comprise the crisis management team? Who is the decision-maker? Other member responsibilities?
3. Responsibility for media contact
4. Bomb threat procedures in place and understood?
5. What are the guidelines for kidnap or hostage and extortion?
6. Is there a plan for a cyber incident? What are the various responsibilities?

Security Awareness

1. How are employees made aware of security policy and practice?
2. Are there outward signs of a knowledgeable and compliant population?

APPENDIX B: SECURITY DEVICES, EQUIPMENT, AND INSTALLATION LABOR COSTS

A significant number of guidelines and regulations have physical security components that require estimating cost to procure and install. Table B.1, reprinted here from a previous publication of the Security Executive Council, displays the typical array of security devices that may be employed at a facility seeking to enhance physical security as a potential result of increased regulatory scrutiny. Installed costs are noted with three different labor rates to provide for regional diversity, and an annual inflation factor is noted in the footnotes. Equipment prices embedded in the estimates are typical of competitive products.

Table B.1 Summary of Security Device Costs

Description	Quantity		Installed Cost (Labor Rate: $50/hr)[A]	Installed Cost (Labor Rate: $65/hr)[A]	Installed Cost (Labor Rate: $85/hr)[A]
1. Site Work					
• Fencing — 7' Chain Link with 3 Strands of Barb Wire at a 45 degree angle	1×z	lf	$34.00	$35.00	$36.00
• Ornamental Iron Fencing	1	lf	$171.00	$173.00	$175.00
• No Trespassing Sign	1	each	$68.00	$69.00	$70.00
• Lighting — Exterior Wall-Mount High-Pressure Sodium	1	each	$364.00	$368.00	$370.00
• Lighting — Exterior Wall-Mount Low-Pressure Sodium	1	each	$396.00	$398.00	$400.00
• Lighting — Exterior Wall-Mount Incandescent	1	each	$141.00	$143.00	$145.00
• Lighting — Exterior Wall-Mount Metal Halide	1	each	$400.00	$402.00	$405.00
• Perimeter Lighting — 30' Pole-Mounted High-Pressure Sodium[B,E]	1	each	$2,145.00	$2,195.00	$2,245.00
• Perimeter Lighting — 30' Pole-Mounted Low-Pressure Sodium	1	each	$2,175.00	$2,225.00	$2,275.00
• Perimeter Lighting — 30' Pole-Mounted Incandescent[C,F]	1	each	$1,920.00	$1,970.00	$2,020.00
• Perimeter Lighting — 30' Pole-Mounted Metal Halide[D,G]	1	each	$2,180.00	$2,230.00	$2,280.00
• Parking Area Lighting — 30' Pole-Mounted High-Pressure Sodium[H]	1	each	$2,590.00	$2,540.00	$2,690.00
• Parking Area Lighting — 30' Pole-Mounted Low-Pressure Sodium	1	each	$2,730.00	$2,780.00	$2,730.00
• Parking Area Lighting — 30' Pole-Mounted Metal Halide[I]	1	each	$2,560.00	$2,610.00	$2,660.00
2. Access Control System Head End Components					
• Security Management System Server PC	1	each	$8,400.00	$8,520.00	$8,680.00
• Security Management System Software — up to 64 card readers[J]	1	each	$8,500.00	$9,700.00	$11,300.00
3. Access Control Components					
• Access Control Panel Controller	1	each	$2,900.00	$3,140.00	$3,460.00
• Alarm Output Board	1	each	$1,100.00	$1,160.00	$1,240.00

(Continued)

Table B.1 (Continued)

Description	Quantity		Installed Cost (Labor Rate: $50/hr)[A]	Installed Cost (Labor Rate: $65/hr)[A]	Installed Cost (Labor Rate: $85/hr)[A]
• Alarm Input Board	1	each	$1,300.00	$1,360.00	$1,440.00
• Network Interface for Access Control Panel	1	each	$650.00	$680.00	$720.00
• Access Control Panel Enclosure	1	each	$950.00	$1,010.00	$1,090.00
• Access Control Panel Power Supply	1	each	$800.00	$860.00	$940.00
• Lock Power Supply	1	each	$1,000.00	$1,060.00	$1,140.00
• Card Reader — Proximity (Surface Mount)	1	each	$350.00	$365.00	$385.00
• Card Reader — Proximity with keypad	1	each	$450.00	$480.00	$520.00
• Card Reader — Long-Range Proximity	1	each	$1,050.00	$1,095.00	$1,155.00
• Biometric — Finger Print Reader	1	each	$950.00	$995.00	$1,055.00
• Biometric — Hand Geometry Reader	1	each	$3,365.00	$3,410.00	$3,470.00
• Request to Exit Device — Wall Mount	1	each	$125.00	$140.00	$160.00
4. Door Hardware and Accessories					
• Electric Mortise Locking Device	1	each	$900.00	$990.00	$1,110.00
• Electric Strike Locking Device	1	each	$525.00	$585.00	$665.00
• Electric Cylinder Lock	1	each	$675.00	$735.00	$815.00
• Electric Exit Device	1	each	$1,700.00	$1,790.00	$1,910.00
• Electromagnetic Lock (Single Door)	1	each	$590.00	$650.00	$730.00
• Electromagnetic Lock (Double Door)	1	each	$880.00	$970.00	$1,090.00
• Door Hardware — Non-Electrified Storeroom Function	1	each	$475.00	$565.00	$685.00
• Electrified Keypad Lockset	1	each	$1,178.00	$1,268.00	$1,388.00
• Mechanical Pushbutton Keypad Lock	1	each	$550.00	$595.00	$655.00
• Mechanical Crashbar — with audible alarm	1	each	$725.00	$785.00	$865.00
• Delayed Egress Crashbar	1	each	$1,535.00	$1,625.00	$1,745.00
• Power Transfer Hinges	1	each	$425.00	$455.00	$495.00
• Door Cords	1	each	$85.00	$100.00	$120.00
• Pushbutton Exit Device	1	each	$152.00	$167.00	$187.00

(*Continued*)

Table B.1 (Continued)

Description	Quantity		Installed Cost (Labor Rate: $50/hr)[A]	Installed Cost (Labor Rate: $65/hr)[A]	Installed Cost (Labor Rate: $85/hr)[A]
5. Intrusion Detection Devices					
• Door Contacts Recessed	1	each	$70.00	$85.00	$105.00
• Door Contacts Surface Mount	1	each	$80.00	$95.00	$115.00
• Door Contacts — Industrial	1	each	$140.00	$170.00	$210.00
• Tamper Switches	1	each	$62.00	$77.00	$97.00
• Glass Break / Shock Sensors	1	each	$165.00	$195.00	$235.00
• Passive Infrared Motion Sensor — Wall Mount	1	each	$95.00	$110.00	$130.00
• Passive Infrared Motion Sensor — Ceiling Mount	1	each	$160.00	$190.00	$230.00
• Audible Alarm	1	each	$350.00	$365.00	$385.00
• Door Release Button	1	each	$155.00	$170.00	$190.00
• Duress Alarm Hardware	1	each	$80.00	$95.00	$115.00
6. CCTV Equipment					
• Video Matrix Switcher — 32 video inputs[K]	1	each	$10,615.00	$10,735.00	$10,895.00
• Matrix Control Keyboard	1	each	$1,245.00	$1,260.00	$1,280.00
• Fixed Wall-Mount Interior Color Camera	1	each	$650.00	$680.00	$720.00
• Fixed Wall-Mount Interior B&W Camera	1	each	$375.00	$405.00	$445.00
• Fixed Wall-Mount Exterior Color Camera	1	each	$850.00	$895.00	$955.00
• Fixed Wall-Mount Exterior B&W Camera	1	each	$525.00	$570.00	$630.00
• PTZ Wall-Mount Exterior Color Camera	1	each	$3,195.00	$3,255.00	$3,335.00
• PTZ Pole-Mount Exterior Color Camera	1	each	$3,395.00	$3,455.00	$3,535.00
• PTZ Corner-Mount Exterior Color Camera	1	each	$3,495.00	$3,555.00	$3,635.00
• CCTV Power Supply	1	each	$225.00	$255.00	$295.00
• Monitor 14" Color — CRT	1	each	$500.00	$515.00	$535.00
• Monitor 14" Color — Flat Screen	1	each	$1,400.00	$1,415.00	$1,435.00
• Monitor 20" Color	1	each	$850.00	$865.00	$885.00
• Monitor 20" Color — Flat Screen	1	each	$1,500.00	$1,515.00	$1,535.00
• Quad Multiplexer	1	each	$355.00	$370.00	$390.00

(Continued)

Table B.1 (Continued)

Description	Quantity		Installed Cost (Labor Rate: $50/hr)[A]	Installed Cost (Labor Rate: $65/hr)[A]	Installed Cost (Labor Rate: $85/hr)[A]
• 14" Monitor with built in Quad Multiplexer	1	each	$600.00	$615.00	$635.00
• Video Multiplexer (Color) — 16 inputs	1	each	$1,275.00	$1,320.00	$1,380.00
• VCR — Time Lapse	1	each	$950.00	$965.00	$985.00
• Digital Video Recorder — 8 Inputs	1	each	$7,295.00	$7,415.00	$7,575.00
• Digital Video Recorder — 16 Inputs	1	each	$10,795.00	$10,975.00	$11,215.00
7. Visitor Management System Components					
• Visitor Management PC	1	each	$2,195.00	$2,255.00	$2,335.00
• Visitor Management Software	1	each	$3,900.00	$4,020.00	$4,180.00
• Visitor Management Camera	1	each	$230.00	$245.00	$265.00
• Business Card Scanner	1	each	$560.00	$575.00	$595.00
• Driver's License Scanner	1	each	$775.00	$790.00	$810.00
• Signature Pad	1	each	$532.00	$547.00	$567.00
• Touch Screen Display	1	each	$2,825.00	$2,855.00	$2,895.00
• Temporary Badge Printer	1	each	$410.00	$425.00	$445.00
• Adhesive Badges — 100-count roll	1	each	$46.00	$46.00	$46.00
8. Photo ID System and Components					
• Photo ID PC	1	each	$2,195.00	$2,255.00	$2,335.00
• Photo ID Software	1	each	$1,400.00	$1,460.00	$1,540.00
• Photo ID Capture Camera	1	each	$1,676.00	$1,706.00	$1,746.00
• Signature Pad	1	each	$781.00	$796.00	$816.00
• Photo ID Lighting Kit	1	each	$475.00	$490.00	$510.00
• Tripod for Capture Camera	1	each	$147.00	$162.00	$182.00
• Color Badge Printer with Magnetic Stripe Encoding	1	each	$8,010.00	$8,025.00	$8,045.00
• Cleaning Kit	1	each	$84.00	$84.00	$84.00
• Ribbon and Consumables	1	each	$253.00	$253.00	$253.00
• PVC Badges	1	each	$4.25	$4.25	$4.25
9. Signal Transmission Components					
• Fiber Optic Transmitter — Video/ Data — Single Mode Fiber	1	each	$2,300.00	$2,360.00	$2,440.00
• Fiber Optic Receiver — Video/ Data — Single Mode Fiber	1	each	$2,300.00	$2,360.00	$2,440.00
• Fiber Optic Transmitter — Video/ Data — Multi-Mode Fiber	1	each	$820.00	$835.00	$855.00

(Continued)

Table B.1 (Continued)

Description	Quantity		Installed Cost (Labor Rate: $50/hr)[A]	Installed Cost (Labor Rate: $65/hr)[A]	Installed Cost (Labor Rate: $85/hr)[A]
• Fiber Optic Receiver — Video/ Data — Multi-Mode Fiber	1	each	$820.00	$835.00	$855.00
• Fiber Optic Transmitter — Video (Multiplexed) — Single Mode Fiber	1	each	$2,545.00	$2,560.00	$2,580.00
• Fiber Optic Receiver — Video (Multiplexed) — Single Mode Fiber	1	each	$2,545.00	$2,560.00	$2,580.00
• Fiber Optic Transmitter — Video (Multiplexed) — Multi-Mode Fiber	1	each	$1,845.00	$1,860.00	$1,880.00
• Fiber Optic Receiver — Video (Multiplexed) — Multi-Mode Fiber	1	each	$1,845.00	$1,860.00	$1,880.00
• Fiber Optic Equipment Rack	1	each	$1,100.00	$1,160.00	$1,240.00
• Wireless Transmitter / Receiver and Antenna (up to 1500')	1	each	$1,550.00	$1,625.00	$1,725.00
10. Communications Equipment					
• Base Radio with Antenna[L]	1	each	$2,076.00	$2,316.00	$2,636.00
• Hand-Held Radio	1	each	$291.00	$291.00	$291.00
• Master Intercom Station (allows up to 10 remote intercoms)	1	each	$335.00	$365.00	$405.00
• Remote Intercom Station	1	each	$99.00	$114.00	$134.00
• Master Video Intercom	1	each	$624.00	$654.00	$694.00
• Remote Video Intercom	1	each	$445.00	$460.00	$480.00
• Assistance Call Station — Surface Mount	1	each	$1,082.00	$1,127.00	$1,187.00
• Assistance Call Station — Surface Mount — with strobe light in enclosure	1	each	$2,325.00	$2,370.00	$2,430.00
• Assistance Call Station — Tower Mount — with strobe light	1	each	$4,625.00	$4,745.00	$4,905.00
11. Miscellaneous Equipment					
• Burglar Protection Safe — 20" W × 36" H × 17" D	1	each	$550.00	$550.00	$550.00
• Fire-Resistant Safe (2-hour rated) — 19" W × 28" H × 18" D	1	each	$800.00	$800.00	$800.00
• Burglar-Rated Fire Safe — 17 W × 34" H × 16" D	1	each	$1,900.00	$1,900.00	$1,900.00
• High-Security Padlock	1	each	$30.00	$30.00	$30.00

(Continued)

Table B.1 (Continued)

Description	Quantity		Installed Cost (Labor Rate: $50/hr)[A]	Installed Cost (Labor Rate: $65/hr)[A]	Installed Cost (Labor Rate: $85/hr)[A]
• C-TPAT High-Security Truck/ Container Bolt Seal — 500 count	1	each	$625.00	$625.00	$625.00
• Tamper Evident Seals — 1000 count packs	1	each	$88.00	$88.00	$88.00
• Annual Charge for Central Station Monitoring[M]	1	each	$550.00	$550.00	$550.00

[A]This data was generated in 2005 and should be adjusted for inflation.
[B]When using with CCTV, use 400W HPS flood light with quartz back-up on 30′ pole at 100′ intervals.
[C]When using with CCTV, use 30′ pole at 50′ intervals.
[D]When using with CCTV, use 400W metal halide flood light with quartz back-up on 30′ pole at 80′ intervals.
[E]Without CCTV, use 400W HPS flood light with quartz back-up on 30′ pole at 150′ intervals.
[F]Without CCTV, use 30′ pole at 80′ intervals.
[G]Without CCTV, use 400W metal halide flood light with quartz back-up on 30′ pole at 120′ intervals.
[H]Use 400W HPS area-type luminaire on 30′ pole at 100′ on center each way.
[I]Use 400W metal halide area-type luminaire on 30′ pole at 80′ on center each way.
[J]Assumes 80 hours of programming labor.
[K]Assumes 8 hours of programming labor.
[L]Include installation and tuning of base radio.
[M]Assumes monitoring of 64 alarm zones.

APPENDIX C: REQUEST FOR PROPOSALS FOR CONTRACT SECURITY SERVICES AT [SPECIFIC COMPANY LOCATION(S)]

Dear Sir or Madam:

Introduction

The **[Company]** is in the process of identifying, qualifying, and contracting with a Supplier to provide for Contract Security Services at **[Location(s)]**. You are invited to submit a proposal in response to this Request for Proposal (RFP). The intent of the selection process is to determine the Contractor who will meet the requirements of this RFP and offer the best service at the best price.

The remaining sections of this letter outline the requirements of the RFP, instructions to bidders, proposal contents, general information session, selection criteria, general conditions of the RFP, as well as several ATTACHMENTS which provide more detail regarding the scope of work, pricing requirements, and contractual arrangements.

General Information Session

A general information session and site tour for all participating suppliers has been scheduled for [set date] at [set time] and will be held at **[Location(s).]** Attendance is required. This will be the primary opportunity for all suppliers to address questions and concerns regarding this RFP.

Please RSVP by **Fax (or in person)** with the number of employees attending to the name and number listed immediately below. Prior to the general information session, questions for this RFP should be submitted by *Fax only no later than [set date and time]* to:

Name of Company Representative
Address
Fax #/Tel #

All questions will be compiled and addressed in a group fashion during the general information session. No further questions will be accepted in the time period after the general information session.

Instructions to Bidders

Proposals shall be submitted in an organized manner, and each copy (two copies are required) will be separately bound with sections appropriately tabbed and identified as follows:

PART 1	EXPERIENCE, CAPABILITIES, AND REFERENCES
PART 2	RESOURCES
PART 3	TRAINING
PART 4	FINANCIAL
PART 5	AGREEMENT

Information requested herein shall be furnished completely in compliance with the instructions. The information requested and the manner of submission is essential to permit prompt evaluation of all quotations on a fair and uniform basis. Accordingly, [**Company**] reserves the right to declare as nonresponsive and to reject any quotation in which material information requested is not furnished or where indirect or incomplete answers or information are provided.

Whenever repetitious requests of information occur anywhere in the RFP, SUPPLIERS need not repeat the information. Reference shall be made, however, to the exact location in the quotation where the information is already recorded. By submitting a quotation, SUPPLIER agrees that the quotation shall remain valid for ninety (90) days after the closing date for submission of quotations and may be extended beyond that time by mutual agreement.

Completed responses to this RFP are due at the locations below no later than [**set date and time**]. Any proposals submitted after this deadline may not be accepted or considered, at [**Company's**] sole discretion.

Two (2) copies of your proposal must be sent to:
Name of Company Representative
Phone
Fax

Proposal Contents

Experience, Capabilities, and References

Contractor shall provide a detailed description of its experience and capabilities to perform the work described in this RFP and shall list a minimum of three (3) references with a description of scope of work performed as well as the name and title of key Contractor personnel involved in the project. For each project listed provide a client reference, which shall include the name, title, address, and current telephone number of the individual directly responsible for the work.

Include any additional descriptive literature or information, relevant to the specification and/or services proposed that indicates unique qualifications, particular competence in this field, technical capabilities, proprietary techniques, or special resources. You should specifically indicate location and experience with Class A properties.

Resources

SUPPLIERS shall provide sufficient information and documentation to substantiate the following:

- Provide a key contact person at Supplier's management offices who will be accountable for the quality of this relationship and assure the competency and responsiveness of the on-site security team.
- Provide an on-site Manager who will be responsible for management of the overall relationship between the Supplier's firm and [**the Company.**] This person will be responsible for
  - maintaining the risk profile of the property, communicating and addressing identified hazards and security risks; establishing and improving post orders and operational procedures;
  - assuring the training, competency, and appearance of all assigned security personnel;
  - checking specific assignments, addressing operational inadequacies, and providing proactive leadership to assigned security staff;

- providing knowledgeable and responsive leadership in non-routine, emergency, and/or hazardous situations; and
- maintaining necessary communications and being accessible at all times during supplier's normal business hours.

This is considered a key person in the adequacy of the property's security program and the development and effective maintenance of this contractual relationship.

Training

SUPPLIERS shall provide sufficient information and documentation to substantiate the following:
- Provide qualified, trained personnel, properly supervised, in numbers sufficient to respond to day-to-day protective services and non-routine security incidents and consistently maintain the equipment in areas covered by the Contract.
- Enforce discipline and good behavior with Supplier's employees and take all necessary steps to assure that they are familiar with, and abide by, **[Company]** and Supplier safety, security and other rules and policies.
- Provide quality control measures for all work performed.

Financial

Contractor shall provide a copy of its most recent annual report.

Agreement

At the conclusion of this RFP process, **[Company]** intends to negotiate an agreement with one SUPPLIER to provide the aforementioned services. Exhibit C is the standard Master Agreement **[Company]** will use to acquire these products and services. If the SUPPLIER has any comments or exceptions to this Master Agreement, the SUPPLIER shall provide such comments or exceptions in its proposal. Submittal of comments shall not constitute acceptance by **[Company],** but shall be used in the selection process. Comments provided after submittal of the proposal may result in disqualification. The final agreement, once executed, supersedes all previous agreements for these products and services.

SUPPLIER must provide evidence of insurance as required in Article 5 of the Agreement.

[Company] may, but is not bound by any contract executed as a result of this process to enter into an Agreement for shredder services for a three (3) year period, and may extend for one (1) additional year upon mutual written consent of the parties involved, subject to the termination rights provided in the Agreement.

Selection Criteria

Quotations shall be considered from selected responsible organizations now engaged in the purchase and maintenance of shredders comparable with those described in this document.

A process has been identified to select the SUPPLIER or SUPPLIERS that best meet [Company's] needs. Proposals will be reviewed by designated [Company] representatives. Key factors that [Company] will use to determine the select list include, but are not limited to, the following:

Quality—Overall experience and capability of the SUPPLIER.

Personnel—Ability to provide highly trained and experienced personnel *with special consideration of on-site management/ supervisory personnel.*

Service—Willingness to provide immediate response to situations or concerns as they arise.

Pricing—Competitive pricing that will be guaranteed for the term of the Agreement.

Financial Stability—Sound financial condition.

Commitment—Willingness to work with **[Company]** in providing cost-effective quality service.

Contract—Willingness to execute **[Company's]** Master Agreement.

General Conditions of the RFP

Confidentiality. All materials contained in this RFP, or later distributed or referred to, including, without limitation, the descriptions of **[Company]** and its organization, systems and procedures, are the **[Company's]** property. The SUPPLIER agrees, by accepting this RFP, that it will keep all such materials and information in confidence within its company on a need-to-know basis, and will not provide duplicates of such materials or information or disclose such materials to any person outside its organization without the prior written consent of Heritage Property.

News Releases/Public Disclosure. News releases or public disclosure in any manner pertaining to this RFP or the selection of a SUPPLIER related to this RFP will not be made by any participating SUPPLIER.

Cost of Preparing Proposals. All costs incurred by the SUPPLIER in connection with responding to the RFP are the responsibility of the SUPPLIER.

Other. The written responses to this RFP will be an important consideration in the selection process. [**Company**], at its sole discretion, reserves the right to cancel or significantly modify the terms and provisions of the RFP if it is in its best interest to do so. If the RFP is significantly modified or amended by [**Company**] prior to the submission of the proposals, a change in the requested submission date for the proposal may be made accordingly.

RFP Timeline

The following schedule outlines [**Company's**] timeframe for selection of the Supplier(s):

Activity/Event	Target Date
RFP mailed to SUPPLIERS	[Specify date]
Bid Informational Meeting	[Specify date]
Proposals due to [Company]	[Specify date]
[Company] reviews proposals	[Specify date]
Final Contractor selection	[Specify date]
Agreement executed	[Specify date]
Contractor start date	[Specify date]

Please do not call or fax to determine the status or outcome of your company's Proposal. Timely notification will be made when final selections are complete.

We look forward to your continued participation in the proposal process. If you should have any questions or require additional information please contact me at [**(xxx) xxx-xxxx**] or [**designated alternate**] at [**(xxx) xxx-xxxx.**]

Sincerely,

[**Designated Representative**]

cc:[**Designated Alternate**]

APPENDIX D: WORKPLACE VIOLENCE INCIDENT RESPONSE GUIDELINE

Introduction

The templates in the series of toolboxes found in this appendix, which were developed by the Security Executive Council, are intended to introduce essential workplace violence prevention program elements such as awareness training, case management, response options, and crisis management. Its primary purpose is to present an overview of the components of a good baseline program with the focus being on essential elements needed to build a workplace violence prevention program rather than teaching about it.

Real research and initiatives in workplace violence began in the mid-1980s. National Institute for Occupational Safety and Health research provided a foundation from which workplace violence issues could be examined and risk reduction methodologies developed. Dr. Park Dietz and 3M Corporation, who developed a program and process for *Supporting a Nonviolent Workplace*, were pioneer thought leaders. To this day *Supporting a Nonviolent Workplace* is the only scalable offering developed out of research of a multidisciplinary cross-functional team approach. Dr. Dietz and the Threat Assessment Group (TAG) is the sole source licensed distributor of this process.[1] It is currently used by hundreds of global companies within the Fortune 500 and beyond.

The Security Executive Council has used *Supporting a Nonviolent Workplace* as a basis for further development of the security program components contained in this book. There is no product that is more cost-effective, customizable, and scalable than *Supporting a Nonviolent Workplace*, and the Council strongly recommends incorporating it into your program and utilizing it concurrently with the elements we are providing in this book.

---

[1]For more information about *Supporting a Nonviolent Workplace*, visit http://www.taginc.com/products/threat-management-supporting-a-nonviolent-workplace/.

Workplace Violence Prevention Program Template

Purpose

To provide a basic process for the handling of a workplace violence incident that can be adapted for use at all [**company**] sites.

Overview

[**Company**] sites should have a plan of action that will allow them to respond quickly and appropriately in the event of a workplace violence incident. The following guidelines will provide the framework for [**company**] site management to devise a plan for their individual sites in the event of a potentially violent incident.

There are three key components of a workplace violence response plan: (1) Proactive, (2) Planning and Preparation, and (3) Reactive Response.

Prevention and Early Intervention (Proactive) Toolbox

Proactive

Prevention and Early Intervention

Recognize early warning signs and behavioral indicators that identify troubled employees or troubling situations[2] and respond early and appropriately.

Measures and Resources

- Workplace Violence Training
  - Supervisor and manager training[3]
  - Troubled employee or troubling situations
    - Employee Assistance Program
    - Counseling
    - Administrative
    - Disability
    - Termination

---

[2]The terms "troubled employees" and "troubling situations" were developed for use with the *Supporting a Nonviolent Workplace* program, created by Dr. Park Dietz and 3M Corporation.

[3]See previous footnote.

Managing Potential Workplace Violence

- Establish policy management team
- Awareness education and training
- Corporate central reporting policy
- Effective security organization
- Intake and data entry
- Investigate all reports
- Risk assessment
- Situation classification
- Risk response options
- Security plan
- Case management and documentation

Preliminary Intake Information[4]

Name:
Address: Home   Work Location
Phone: Home   Work Location
Gender:
Date of Birth:
Supervisor/Manager:
Position:
Social Security #:
Date of Hire:
Height:
Weight:
Description:
EEO Classification:

	Make	Model	Color	License #	State
Vehicle 1	_____	_____	_____	_____	_____
Vehicle 2	_____	_____	_____	_____	_____

Employment Status: Currently working <u>Y N</u> STD ____
LTD ____

    Leave of absence ____ Layoff ____ Terminated ____
Retired ____

Marital Status: Spouse name
Spouse address and phone if different
Military Status:

---

[4]This preliminary intake form is available as part of *Supporting a Nonviolent Workplace* program and was created to assist in gathering pertinent information and guiding investigations in order to make appropriate decisions and take appropriate action. As with all of the *Supporting a Nonviolent Workplace* elements, cross-functional teams of experts collaborated on this material, and there are no other programs publically available to our knowledge that provide these types of resource materials.

Some Critical Elements to Consider In Determining Dangerousness

1. **THREATS**

   Did _____ make a direct threat?

   An implied threat?

   A conditional threat?

   A veiled threat?

   Did _____ *repeat* the threat in the presence of others or the interviewer?

   Does _____ have a clear reason in his mind for making the threat, however illogical?

   Does _____ admit to threatening others in the past

2. **PROJECTION ONTO OTHERS**

   Does _____ blame (project responsibility onto) others/another for any personal problems he or someone close to him may be having?

   Does _____ brood over perceived injustices or wrongdoings by specific others?

   Does _____ possess a violent attitude toward an administrative decision, policy, or action, and does he hold any specific other as the responsible party?

3. **FAMILY HISTORY/SOCIAL ENVIRONMENTAL FUNCTIONING**

   Have there been a series of *recent* events which have had a negative impact on _____ life? (Loss of job, status, significant relationship, family member, court case, etc.)

   Has there been a loss of structure in his life?

   Has _____ been recently released from a mental institution?

   A penal institution?

   History of chronic unemployment? Transience? Difficulty keeping jobs?

   Has _____ suffered repeated failure in his life?

   Does _____ have a history of hostility towards authority figures? (Home, school, employment, military, law enforcement, mental, penal, etc.)

   Does _____ have any social support system?

   Is there any evidence that _____ was physically, emotionally, or sexually abused by his parents, either directly or indirectly? By others?

   Was _____ exposed to violence and/or other anti-social behavior within his family setting? (Alcoholism, drug abuse/dependency, criminal activity, sexual perversion, etc.)

Does _____ discuss his "feelings of desperation"?

Is there evidence of violence towards other family members?

Are family members afraid of subject? Why?

Are associates afraid of _____? Why?

Does _____ accept violence as a means of solving his problems?

What has _____ reaction been to any/all of the above firings, lay-offs, criticisms, suspensions, expulsions, reprimands, etc.?

Does _____ have a history of threatening former bosses, co-workers, teachers, students, associates, friends, strangers?

Has _____ ever acted upon previous threats? How?

Do former bosses, co-workers, teachers, students, associates, friends, strangers, fear _____? Why?

Has _____ expressed his grievances to associates, seeking reinforcement? Their response? His reaction?

Did _____ grievances outline potential threats towards specific others? Method? How recently? Reasons?

4. CRIMINAL HISTORY

Is there any evidence of violence and/or threats of violence in _____criminal history?

Evidence of arrest for violent crime? Domestic violence? Violence/cruelty towards animals? Fire-setting? Burglary/criminal trespass? Property crime/vandalism?

Evidence of violence and/or threats of violence towards family, neighbors, co-workers, doctors, hospital staff, therapists, counselors, probation officers, police, teachers, students, etc.?

What is the most violent thing _____ has done? Circumstances?

How similar is current situation?

How recent, and what is the severity, and frequency of violent acts?

5. MENTAL HISTORY

Has _____ ever been diagnosed by a mental health professional as being *dangerous*?

Has _____ ever been diagnosed as being psychotic? Specific prior diagnosis?

Does _____ take any specific antipsychotic medication?

History of going off medication?

Does _____ state that he has a special mission to fulfill?

Does _____ state that he is only doing what greater powers are telling him to do? (Command hallucinations)

What are voices telling him? Do voices include identifiable others? How?

Has _____ ever heard voices commanding a certain act, and has he complied? Did acts involve violence?

Does _____ history indicate any homicidal fantasies involving authority figures? Identifiable others? Who? Why? When? What in fact happened?

Has _____ ever attempted/threatened suicide?

Does _____ feel that he has little to lose?

Does _____ express hopelessness ?

Do prior diagnoses by mental health professionals include terms such as explosive, impulsive, hostile, aggressive, unpredictable, deceitful, manipulative, poor control, "grudge against society," angry, homicidal, suicidal, distrustful, agitated, paranoid, or belligerent?

6. **INTEREST IN ASSAULTIVE, HOMICIDAL, OR SUICIDAL BEHAVIOR**

Is there evidence of a plan to carry out a threat or actual assault upon persons or property?

Does _____ appear to be mentally/physically capable of carrying out his threats or actual assault against persons or property?

Do behaviors and circumstances indicate that he *could* carry out threat/assault?

Have identified others been stalked? Their movements monitored? Itineraries investigated?

Has _____ collected personal data, photos, etc., reflecting obsession with identified other? Has he written stories, poems, created a diary dedicated to or centering around identified other?

Has _____ made reference to membership in any special organization, cult, association, etc., which advocates violence?

Does _____ have a history of attention-seeking behavior?

Desires for fame, notoriety, celebrity status? Power? Control? Positive or negative recognition?

7. DRUGS AND ALCOHOL ABUSE

History of drug/alcohol abuse?

Violence while under the influence?

Chronic abuser? Frequency of abuse? Recent change in pattern?

Does criminal history show evidence of alcohol or drug-related offenses?

Type of alcohol/drugs used? Quantity?

Does _____ procure and brandish weapons while under the influence of alcohol/drugs?

8. MILITARY HISTORY

History of insubordination, court martial, fighting, refusal to obey orders, other defiant acts?

Dishonorable discharge, bad conduct, undesirable discharge, or release for other than honorable reasons?

Circumstances of less than honorable discharge?

Any special skills acquired relevant to THREAT-ASSESSMENT? (Explosive ordnance, sniper training, SEAL training, Special Forces, RECON, etc.)

Prior military service in full combat?

Any grudges against government, society, or authority relative to military service?

9. WEAPONS OWNERSHIP/ACQUISITION

Does _____ own any weapons? Type? Number?

Recent attempts to purchase/procure? Borrow?

Evidence of recent practice at range or at isolated location?

Does _____ have weapons fixation?

Extensive weapons collection?

Weapons permit? Hunting license?

Prior weapons arrest or weapon-related crime?

Reputation for keeping a weapon on his person? At his residence? In car?

Is _____ known as a local "gun nut"?

Is _____ a subject of record to local or residentially historical ATF or USSS office? Local police, county, state, FBI, other?

10. MISCELLANEOUS

Does _____ initiate conversation regarding sexual themes?

Type? Detailed? Repetition of theme?

Has _____ exhibited any overt sexual perversity? Drawings?

Writings? Photos? Sexual paraphernalia? Type? Theme? Are interpretable materials obtainable?

Full descriptions of vehicles to which he has access? Evidence of rape kits within same?

Documented residence? Description? Prior residency? Appropriate checks prior to residences, schools, etc.

Hobbies, pastimes, ascertainable habits?

VCR ownership? Video club membership? Types of videos viewed?

Any other relevant subjects available for interview who might assist in providing insight into _____ personality?

How do others feel about _____ potential for dangerousness? To what degree? Why?

Victim — Suspect Internal Response Options

- Work schedule adjustments
- Time off
- Assignment change
- Travel/training
- Leave of absence
- Temporary/permanent relocation
- Job transfer
- Employment separation
- Re-employment
- Workers' compensation
- Disability
- Benefit extensions
- Outplacement
- EAP assistance
- Engage, win-lose, workers' compensation
- Disability

Planning and Preparation Toolbox

Planning and Preparation

Conventional physical security safeguards will deter, but not prevent, an armed intruder from gaining access. Corporate Security managers and staff are available to assist site management in devising a plan for specific locations.

It is important to approach the planning process as a team with your local authorities. As you enter into this partnership, you should identify strengths and limitations of the response plan. Work to refine the limitations of the plan. Discuss expectations. What should you expect to see happen in an incident, and what is the timetable for response and resolution. Be sensitive to the needs of the police department in the areas of familiarization with your facilities, types of chemicals being used, hazardous work areas, and electrostatic limitations. As part of your planning process, invite the police to tour your facility to get a firsthand look at your operation.

This plan should be developed as component of your other Emergency Response Plans. Many of the issues that must be dealt with during a violence situation can be handled through a typical incident command system. It is important to review these processes on a regular basis to ensure that those persons who work within the system understand their responsibilities.

Security Plans and Programs

- Facility security risk assessment
- Centralized incident reporting
- Local security responsibility assignment
  - Site security coordinator
  - Site security committee
- Local law enforcement liaison
- Notification and communication plan

Measures and Resources

- Facility preparation
- General guidelines manual
- Corporate security programs

Risk Assessment

- Risk rating assigned
- Best available method
  - Automated or subjective
  - Internal team
  - Consultants
  - Law enforcement

Security Plan

- Personnel Security Plan
- Facility Security Plan
- Emergency Response Plan

Law Enforcement Intervention Plan

- Damage control
- Corporate image
- Mitigate liabilities

Effective Security Organization

- Mission
- Adequately staffed
- Effectively organized
- Member of management team
- Assigned responsibilities
- Professional development

Police Preparation

- Police response times will vary for every jurisdiction and location. Establish approximately how long a response time should take.
- Many police departments are not equipped to manage a tactical situation. Establish which law enforcement agency will be responsible for oversight of the incident.
- The police will establish an inner and outer perimeter. They will also typically take care of traffic control as part of their overall management of the incident scene. The police may enlist company security to assist in this task.
- Identify a location for the police command center. It should be in a convenient location to your facilities, while at the same time not close enough to become a danger to the people working there. Identify a [company] representative to get location and phone number.

Facility Preparation

- Identify a [company] command center.
- Identify a single point of contact to represent [company] to communicate procedure information and brief police on the situation. This person must be empowered to make decisions. This person will interact with the police commander to provide necessary information and resources.
- Witnesses should be identified for police interviews. If possible, a separate staging area for the witnesses is desirable, or a dedicated phone line may need to be established.

- Electronic access capability to shut down and give police access cards.
- Determine who can lead police into buildings.
- Have building maps available for police review.

Identify Your Resources

- Incident management team members
- Security
- Facilities
- Medical
- Law enforcement

Trespass Policy and Badge Removal

- Person may be put on administrative leave due to an investigation until the investigation is finished.
- Trespass orders make it clear that the person is not supposed to be on [**company**] property.
- Person should sign trespass form, or it can be sent registered mail.
- Trespass notification should be in writing, rather than verbal: puts [**company**] and police in better position to take action if it is violated.
- Create a box on the restricted access notice that there is a trespass letter on file.
- If possible have police present when person is told, so it's on record at police department.
- For larger cases consider getting a court order.
- If person is given a trespass warning at the time of separation, create a form to have them read and sign, so the trespass warning can be on file.

Building Hazards

- Identify building hazardous materials, and determine if Material Safety Data Sheets (MSDS) are available and how police will react in hazard areas.
- *Reactive*

Prevention strategies directed at potential workplace violence situations will only reduce the possibility of an actual violent event. It is not possible to prevent all such incidents. It is important to identify and classify any incidents of violence or eminent danger as quickly as possible and be prepared to implement a specific plan of action.

The ability to continuously communicate detailed information about the incident will enable [**company**] and local authorities to provide a prompt and appropriate response.

Response Procedures

- Facility response
- Assigned responsibilities
- Crisis communication procedures
- Evacuation procedures
- Immediate protection
- Trauma counseling

Measures and Resources

- Administrative options
- Medical/psychological
- Termination

Reactive Response Procedures Toolbox

Intake and Data Entry

- Central reporting
- Master database
- Incident analysis
- Uniform quality control
- Incident tracking

Investigate All Reports

- Investigation appropriate to incident
- Broad-based to microscopic screening
- Uniformly objective
- Criteria-based

Threat Evaluation

- Internal
- Incident management team
- Law enforcement
- Forensic psychiatrist
- Profiling, psycholinguistics, specialists

Facility Response

- Notify the police immediately. Do not hang up the phone. Continue providing information for as long as possible without compromising your safety.
- Notify **[company]** Corporate Security at **[(xxx) xxx-xxxx]**, immediately after local notifications have been made.

Evacuation

- Decisions to evacuate are driven by the situation, although it is always better to get out of the building if it is possible to do so safely.
- The perpetrator is an intelligent threat. Unlike a natural disaster or fire, he or she knows where people will go and what they will do and may adjust the search for targets accordingly.
- One option to consider is making an announcement naming the perpetrator, and stating that he or she is in the building and is armed. Advise that everyone in the building should take appropriate actions to ensure their own personal safety.
- Lock as many interior office doors as possible in order to slow the perpetrator(s) progress, but not to hinder emergency egress by employees.
- Do not try to be a hero. Unnecessary injuries may be sustained if the perpetrator is encountered. Either hide or vacate the building.
- Security or police will lock-out elevators to try to contain perpetrator; trespass warning to perpetrator by police.
- Determine if the situation requires local resident evacuation.

First Aid

- Identify First Responders and prepare them to assist until Emergency Medical personnel arrive.
- Identify on-site medical staff and have them on scene and available to assist.
- If there is a "hot area," have police move the injured to a staging area.
- Ensure that adequate first aid supplies are available for emergency use.
- Identify a triage area for the wounded and injured. Determine capabilities of local hospitals for dealing with trauma-related injuries.

Perpetrator Information

- If perpetrator is a [**company**] employee or former employee, make every effort to gain information from supervisor and have supervisor and Human Resources manager available.
- Have EAP counselor available at the command center or by phone.
- Procedures for release of information will be streamlined to give information that will assist authorities, e.g., EAP files, medical files, attorney-client information.
- Supervisor to provide technical background and military background.

Communication

- The police will want the option of talking with the perpetrator via the telephone system. Determine if your telephone system can be used to pinpoint the exact location of the perpetrator inside the building.
- Identify and shut off fax communication; fax lines are analog lines and can be set up with a recording device.
- Secure communication line from negotiating center to perpetrator; set phone line of perpetrator to automatically dial the negotiating center when perpetrator picks up the telephone receiver.
- Radios, pagers, cell phones, and public address systems are other means of communicating with people in the affected area. Ensure that these devices are in working order and that you have access to telephone and pager numbers.
- Determine if all outgoing calls can be stopped. With the exception of 911 calls, outgoing calls will only exacerbate the situation.

Witness Call-In

- Utilize available resources that are already in place.
- Determine where to direct calls from family members.

Media Releases and the Press

- Expect that the press will probably arrive at the scene before, or at the same time, as the police.
- Identify one person to be liaison with the police.
- Identify an area to which the press can be taken. Ensure that Corporate Communications is apprised of the incident, so

that they can begin preparing appropriate news releases for the press. Identify someone to do this task.

- Media representative to gain police dispatch number.
- Press releases should be coordinated through the police public relations officer at the scene. This precaution is taken to ensure that no operational information is inadvertently released that could endanger the welfare of the police or employees involved in the incident.
- A [company] media representative should be located in the communication command center. Contact police immediately to determine where it is located and a dedicated phone line number.

Aftermath Trauma Counseling

- Ensure that Employee Assistance is notified via Human Resources. This will ensure that all effected personnel and their families will receive trauma counseling. This is an important part of the recovery process, and allows people to process and deal effectively with their emotions. Trauma counseling should be done at the earliest possible time.

APPENDIX E: CODE OF BUSINESS CONDUCT AND ETHICS TEMPLATE

[Company] is proud of its high standards of honesty and integrity in the workplace and in the conduct of its business affairs. It is the continuing policy of [Company] to maintain these standards and conduct business in an ethical manner.

The provisions of this Code of Business Conduct and Ethics apply to all directors, officers, employees, and agents of [Company] and its direct and indirect subsidiaries and affiliates, regardless of location. Thus, throughout the Code of Business Conduct and Ethics, the use of the term [Alternate or Abbreviated Company Name], or "company" refers to [Company] and its subsidiaries.

No corporate code of conduct can cover all relevant topics, and this Code of Business Conduct and Ethics may be supplemented (but not superseded) by divisional or departmental policy. Thus, in addition, employees are bound by various other corporate policies—such as the [Company] *Antitrust Compliance Policy*, policies on weapons, workplace violence, electronic mail, and Intranet usage—which are not included in this Code. Any questions regarding this Code or other policies governing conduct of [Company]'s employees should be directed to your manager or to the Business Conduct and Ethics Committee. The Committee consists of representatives from the Legal, Internal Audit, and Security departments.

The last two pages of this employee handbook are tear-out sheets. After you have read the Code of Business Conduct and Ethics, sign both the Acknowledgement and Certification and return to the Business Conduct Committee. We want everyone to understand the Code and have also provided space on the last page for you to pose any question or concern you may have to the Committee.

Any violation of the Code of Business Conduct and Ethics by employees will result in appropriate disciplinary action up to and including termination of employment. Violations by non-employees can result in termination of the business arrangement and barring the individual from [Company] facilities.

Company Assets

We all have an obligation to safeguard company assets, including exercising care in using company equipment and vehicles, as well as using company time for company business rather than for personal purposes. We all also have an obligation to bring to the attention of higher management any waste, misuse, destruction, or theft of [Company] property or any improper or illegal activity.

You may do so anonymously, if you so desire, by calling the Business Conduct and Security Hotline.

Compliance with Laws and Regulations

You must comply with all laws and governing regulations applicable in the country, state, and local jurisdiction where business is conducted. [Company] and its employees shall not violate the laws of any country, nor shall any employee assist a third party in violating the law.

The laws of many jurisdictions may impact a [Company] operation. These laws include not only those of the United States and of the country in which the operation is located, but those of other countries in which the operation conducts business. [Company]'s managers must comply with such laws and regulations, even though their competitors may not choose to do so.

Government Investigations

[Company] fully cooperates with government investigations. The [Company] Legal Department must coordinate such activities. If you are subpoenaed or contacted in any way by any U.S. or foreign government investigative agency, contact the Legal Department immediately. You should not respond to any governmental authority until you have had an opportunity to consult with [Company]'s Legal Department.

Laws Governing International Trade and Transactions

[Company] complies with all applicable U.S. laws governing imports, exports, and the conduct of business with foreign corporations.

Payments Outside of the Country of Residence

Company employees must comply with all applicable tax and currency control laws of the principal country in which they work. No employee shall be paid any commission or any other part of his or her compensation elsewhere than in his or her country of residence if the Company has knowledge that such payment would violate any local income tax or exchange control laws. The same goes for any payment to non-employees and unrelated entities for goods and services; no such payments should be made to such parties in a country other than that in which the party resides, maintains a place of business, or has rendered the services for which payment is made if the Company has knowledge that such a payment method would violate any local income tax or exchange laws.

If you have any questions in this area, consult the [Company] Legal Department.

Confidential Information

During the course of your employment, you may learn trade secrets or other confidential or unpublished information relating to [Company]'s or its customers' and suppliers' business, operations, research, or technology. You shall not use or disclose to any third party any such information, either during or after your employment, without the prior written consent of the company. Under no circumstances may you use or disclose such information for personal gain.

In general, you should only accept from sources outside the Company information that is released through normal, publicly accessible channels. Employees may not sign or enter into confidential disclosure agreements without review of the [Company] Legal Department.

Ethics—and the law—are involved here, and take precedence over competitive advantage. All employees should be aware that theft of trade secrets and economic espionage are crimes under federal and state laws and carry severe sanctions.

If you are ever unsure about what to do regarding the receipt, disclosure, or handling of confidential or trade secret information, or have questions about the application of the Code of Business Conduct and Ethics to competitor information, consult with your manager or a representative of the Business Conduct and Ethics Committee or the [Company] Legal Department.

Competitors' Information

From time to time, [Company] gathers information about the markets in which it does business, including information about competitors and their products and services. [Company] is committed to gathering this information honestly and ethically; however, we do not use, and we never encourage our employees to use, improper means to obtain our competitors' confidential or proprietary information or their trade secrets.

It is entirely proper to gather competitive information through surveys, market studies, competitive analyses, and benchmarking, as well as from published articles, advertisements, publicly-distributed brochures, surveys by consultants, and conversations with customers.

To avoid the appearance of improper conduct in the gathering of competitive information, you must not
- seek or receive such information directly from the company's competitors;
- misrepresent your identity in attempting to collect such information; or
- attempt to acquire a competitor's trade secrets or other proprietary or confidential business information through unlawful or unethical means, such as theft, spying, burglary, wire-tapping, deceptive relationships with competitor's suppliers, seeking disclosures by a competitor's present or former employee, or breach of a competitor's nondisclosure agreement by a customer or other party.

Employee Information

[Company] also protects the confidential information of its employees. You must not disclose any employee information (whether it be compensation or other personnel data, medical information, reasons for termination, or any other employment matter) to any third party unless required by law, and you must not disclose such information to anyone else in the company, except those with a demonstrated "need to know."

Conflict of Interest

Conflicts of interest occur when our personal activities and financial affairs conflict or appear to conflict with our responsibility to act in the best interests of [Company]. You must avoid personal situations that might be construed as conflicts of interest—*i.e.,* any personal interest outside the company that could make it advantageous for you to place such personal interest above your obligation to [Company].

You should not have any position with, or substantial interest in, any business enterprise operated for profit, the existence of which would conflict or might reasonably be supposed to conflict with the proper performance of your company duties or responsibilities, or which might tend to affect your independence of judgment with respect to transactions between the company and such other business enterprise. You must also first make available to the company any business opportunity that is related to any business activity of the company.

The following guidelines apply to most common conflict situations.

Employment

- If you are a full-time [Company] employee, your employment with [Company] must be your first priority. Any outside employment, investment, or other source of income must be secondary and must not interfere with the performance of your duties as a [Company] employee.
- You may not serve as an officer, director, partner, or consultant of, or work for, a supplier, customer, or competitor while working for [Company]; however, certain company officers and certain key employees may be allowed to serve as an officer or director of another company upon prior written approval from General Counsel and the CEO.

Finances

- You may not loan or borrow money or accept monetary gifts from individuals or organizations that do business with or compete with [Company].
- You may not buy or sell goods or services from or to any company in which you or a close family member may personally benefit from such purchase or sale.

Business Opportunities

- You should not make any investment that might affect your business decisions. For example, employees may not own or have a substantial interest in a company that is a competitor or one that has current or prospective business with [Company]. This prohibition does not apply to owning less than one percent of the stock of a publicly traded company.

Reporting Conflicts of Interest

Employees are required to disclose to the company any conflicts of interest they may have under the guidelines described in the Code of Business Conduct and Ethics. In the event of conflicts that arise during the course of employment, employees are required to report such conflicts by contacting a representative of the Business Conduct and Ethics Committee in a timely manner.

Dealing with Public Officials

Contacts with or gifts to public officials are subject to an expanding body of state and federal lobbying laws, rules, and regulations. As a result, all such contacts or gifts should be approved, in advance, by your regional government affairs manager. Payments to public officials to secure sales or obtain favorable treatment are strictly forbidden.

In no event shall gifts of substantial value or extravagant entertainment be permitted, since these actions could be construed as attempts to influence government decisions.

Foreign Corrupt Practices Act

[Company] complies strictly with the United States Foreign Corrupt Practices Act of 1977 that prohibits payments or offers of payments of anything of value to foreign officials (including employees of entities which a foreign government controls or in which it has a controlling interest), political parties, or candidates for foreign political office in order to secure, retain, or direct business.

Environmental Protection

It is [Company]'s policy to operate its facilities in compliance with all applicable environmental laws, regulations, and permits. This includes those governing the control, transportation, storage, and disposal of regulated materials as well as air emissions, wastewater, solid waste, hazardous waste, and storm water. All [Company] employees are responsible for performing their individual job functions in accordance with the company's environmental policies. The Company will not tolerate the falsification of data or the reporting of false information regarding environmental compliance to government agencies or within the Company. Employees shall respond promptly and professionally, in accordance with applicable procedures, to any potential threat to human health or the environment from the company's operations. Employees are also required to bring to [Company]'s attention any violation of the company's environmental policies. Retaliation against those who report violations in good faith will not be tolerated.

Equal Employment Opportunity

It is [Company]'s policy to provide equal opportunity in all aspects of employment. We forbid discrimination on account of age, race, gender, color, religion, national origin, disability, sexual orientation, or any other unlawful basis. We also forbid all forms of unlawful harassment. Discriminatory harassment includes any verbal or other conduct which disparages any individual or group on account of race, sex, or any other unlawful factor and which creates an offensive, intimidating, or hostile working environment. All forms of such conduct are prohibited—whether in the form of pictures, cartoons, teasing, jokes, e-mail, epithets, name-calling, offensive gestures, or other discriminatory behavior. Sexual harassment includes any unwelcome sexual conduct that is made a condition of employment or creates a hostile work environment. All forms of such conduct are prohibited.

Every employee is required to follow our policy against unlawful discrimination and harassment and to bring to the company's attention any action that does not comply with that policy or our commitment to equal employment opportunity. Supervisors and managers must be watchful for any signs that our policy is not being followed and must see that any possible violations are immediately referred for investigation, whether or not there has been a formal complaint. Retaliation against those who report violations of our policy in good faith is grounds for termination of employment.

Financial Records

[Company] has established and maintains a high standard of accuracy and completeness in its financial records. These records serve as the basis for managing the company's business, for measuring and fulfilling the company's obligations to shareholders, employees, suppliers, and others, and for compliance with tax and financial reporting requirements.

In the preparation and maintenance of records, all employees must do the following:

- Record and report information accurately and honestly.
- Comply with [Company]'s accepted accounting standards and practices, rules, regulations, and controls.
- See that all entries are promptly and accurately recorded and properly documented. Company records are subject to audit. No entry may intentionally distort or disguise the true nature of any transaction.
- Never establish any undisclosed or unrecorded funds or assets for any purpose.
- Maintain books and records that will fairly and accurately reflect our company business transactions. No transaction with a supplier, agent, customer, or other third party may be structured or recorded in a way that is not consistent with accepted [Company] business practices.
- Sign only those documents believed to be accurate and truthful.
- Devise, implement, and maintain sufficient internal controls to provide assurance that record-keeping objectives are met. Financial records should be maintained in accordance with the requirements of law and generally accepted accounting principles.

Gifts, Gratuities, Favors: Giving and Receiving

You must select and deal with those who are doing, or seeking to do, business with the company in a completely impartial manner, without any considerations other than the best interests of [Company] and the requirements of local, state, and federal law. This means you shall not seek or accept from any such person or firm any gifts, entertainment, tickets for sports or artistic events, trips, use of customer or supplier property or transportation or other favors that go beyond common courtesies consistent with [Company]'s ethical business practices. Acceptance of cash or gift certificates from customers or suppliers is absolutely forbidden. Any appearance of impropriety must be avoided. Prior disclosure to your supervisor, and approval by your facility manager or operating officer, who is not participating in the receipt of the gift, entertainment, or favor, are required for acceptances beyond common courtesies. There must be a business purpose for approval to be given.

This policy does not cover customer entertainment, such as accompanying the customer to dinner where a business discussion is held, except where such entertainment would be extravagant or excessively expensive.

Special Rules Apply to Federal, State, and Local Governments

Rules for dealing with federal, state, and local governments differ from those dealing with other customers. Failure to observe those regulations can result not only in loss of contract work and revenue, but in civil and/or criminal penalties as well. It is your responsibility to learn the applicable rules when dealing with a government agency.

Please refer to the section entitled *"Dealing with Public Officials"* for detailed information and guidelines.

Insider Trading

Federal securities laws prohibit your use of "inside information" when engaging, directly or indirectly, in transactions involving the stock of [Company], any company owned or controlled by [Company], or any other public company. Such laws also prohibit you from disclosing inside information to any other person so that they may trade or tip others to trade in a company's stock. "Inside information" may take many different forms and is broadly defined as any material nonpublic information about a company. Information is "material" if it would be likely to influence an investor's decision to buy, sell, or hold the company's stock, and is "nonpublic" until it has been made available generally to investors.

If you possess inside information about the company, you may not trade, directly or indirectly, in company stock (including exercising a stock option or changing your investment election with regard to any [Company] Stock Fund under your 401 (k) or Savings Plan), nor may you disclose such inside information to others, until such information has been publicly disclosed and the public has had sufficient time to absorb it (generally, two business days after its announcement). Similarly, you may not trade in the stock of any other company while in possession of inside information about such company obtained as a [Company] employee.

Certain employees of the company who have routine access to inside information are subject to trading approval processes and "blackout" periods described in the company's "Policy Regarding Inside Information and Trading in Stock." If you have a question as to whether you are in possession of inside information at any given time, call your division counsel.

Intellectual Property Rights

Employees must not take any actions that may violate the intellectual property rights of third parties.

It is [Company]'s policy to not knowingly infringe valid, enforceable patent rights or trademark rights held by others. If an employee is making, using, or selling a product about which the employee has patent or trademark infringement concerns, he or she should contact the [Company] Legal Department for advice and guidance.

[Company] does not knowingly infringe valid, enforceable copyrights held by others. Employees are prohibited from reproducing or distributing copyrighted materials (including printed publications, photographs, and music) not owned by the company unless permission is expressly granted by the copyright owner. [Company]'s policy is to comply with all laws and contractual obligations applicable to licensed software. This policy applies to software used, installed, or stored on any company-owned computer or related equipment, including equipment authorized for home use.

Political Contributions

Under federal law and the law in some states, corporate funds cannot be used for contributions to a political party, committee, organization, or candidate. Included in this prohibition are tickets to political fund-raising events, transportation, or other services provided at the company's expense.

No corporate political contribution may be made unless and until authorized in advance by [Company]'s vice president for government affairs

Workplace Safety

It is [Company]'s policy that its operations be managed to protect the health and safety of its employees and the communities where it does business. Sound operating practices will be followed to foster a safe working environment. At [Company], safety comes first.

Accident prevention is an operating responsibility. It demands the same management and control given to other aspects of improving efficiency in operations. Management at all levels will diligently enforce this policy.

The company requires employees to follow safe work practices in the interest of their own safety as well as that of fellow employees.

Employees are also required to bring to [Company]'s attention any violation of the company's safety policies and procedures. Retaliation against those who report violations in good faith will not be tolerated.

Reporting Violations and Policy Enforcement

Reporting Violations

[Company]'s Code of Business Conduct and Ethics provides an overview of the legal and ethical responsibilities of all employees. This Code is intended as a guide in making the right choice; however, we do realize that the right choice isn't always obvious. If you need help sorting out or resolving an issue regarding the Code, consult with any senior manager of the company, or call a representative of the Business Conduct and Ethics Committee.

If you have information or knowledge of any act or practice that is illegal or prohibited under this Employees Code of Business Conduct and Ethics, you must promptly report such matter to either your supervisor, facility manager, operating officer, the Legal department, representatives of the Business Conduct and Ethics Committee, or Corporate Security at **(xxx) xxx-xxxx**, or the Business Conduct and Security Hotline. Prompt reporting of violations by employees ensures the protection of the company's employees, assets, and customers. Failure to report a known violation of the Code may subject you to discipline, up to and including termination of employment.

The Business Conduct and Security Hotline was specifically created to provide employees with an avenue for confidential and anonymous reporting. **It is toll-free and available 24 hours a day, 7 days a week**. An independent service provider answers the Hotline, and you have the right to remain anonymous. The information you provide and your identity are kept in the strictest possible confidence. All issues reported via the Hotline are addressed promptly and fairly.

Policy Enforcement

All managerial personnel shall be responsible for the enforcement of and compliance with this Code of Business Conduct and Ethics, including necessary distribution to ensure employee knowledge and compliance. Supervisors will be evaluated, in part, on their effectiveness in implementing these policies in their respective departments, and disciplinary action may be taken against a violator's supervisor to the extent the circumstances of the violation reflect inadequate supervision or lack of diligence.

Selected employees will periodically be required to certify compliance with these policies in the Code of Business Conduct and Ethics Program. Failure of a selected employee to sign and return the Code of Business Conduct and Ethics Declaration will subject that employee to disciplinary action, up to and including termination.

Bringing suspected violations of this Code to the attention of management will not result in any form of retaliation or discipline as long as you are acting in good faith. "Good faith" doesn't necessarily mean you are right, but it does mean you reasonably and honestly *believe* you are accurate in your assessment and perception of the situation you are reporting. [Company] will not, however, overlook, condone, or allow to go unpunished the frivolous use of its policy for personal gain or vendetta.

The standards of this Code are important to the company and must be taken seriously by all of us. Accordingly, violations of these standards will not be tolerated and, in accordance with company policies and applicable collective bargaining agreements, will result in discipline up to and including discharge. In addition, reimbursement of losses or damages may be sought, or referral for criminal prosecution or civil action may be required.

It is never permissible to engage in any conduct that is a violation of the law or of a government regulation.

Acknowledgement

This Acknowledgment Is a Condition of Your Employment

I have received a copy of the [Company] Code of Business Conduct and Ethics and have fully read and understand my responsibility to comply with the Code. I am not engaged in and will not engage in any conduct that violates the Code, and will promptly report any violation of the Code or any applicable law of which I become aware.

I recognize that [Company] is committed to the guidelines contained in the Code and that any violation will result in appropriate disciplinary action, ranging from reprimand up to and including dismissal. I understand that I may discuss any questions or issues regarding the Code with any senior manager of the company or with a representative of the Business Conduct and Ethics Committee at Corporate Security at **(xxx) xxx-xxxx**. I further understand I may remain completely anonymous and report a violation of the Code toll-free through the Business Conduct and Security Hotline, 7 days a week, 24 hours a day, at **1-800-xxx-xxxx**.

___

Print or Type Name   Signature   Position

___

Facility Code Facility Street Address City/State Zip Code Date

Certification

This Certification Is a Condition of Your Employment
Conflict of Interest *(please choose the applicable category):*
___ I am not involved in any situation, and I hold no position or interest that would represent, or raise issues of, conflict of interest as set forth in the CONFLICTS OF INTEREST section of the Code.

___ I am involved in the following situations/I hold the following positions and interest that constitute, or raise issues of, conflict of interest *(list the nature of each situation, position, or interest, regardless of whether previously disclosed).*

___

Print or Type Name   Signature   Position

I have the following questions or comments, or wish to report the following violations:

___

___

Please complete, sign, and date
the Acknowledgement and Certification on the Previous Page
Fill out the above, if applicable
return to:

APPENDIX F: CORPORATE INCIDENT REPORTING AND RESPONSE PLAN

Planning Philosophy

Introduction

Every business is vulnerable to a serious incident that could affect business operations, damage community relations, create adverse publicity, or result in financial loss and civil liability. An incident could occur at any time, without warning, and range from a natural disaster such as a flood or wind storm to a man-made emergency such as sabotage or kidnapping.

Responding to each type of incident requires careful research; planning, preparation, and training to ensure that it is managed based on its specific and unique circumstances. But this should be accomplished by utilizing a process, infrastructure, and plan that is short, concise, and flexible.

Each company should recognize that significant risks exist regarding its ability to continue normal business operations following a serious, unexpected, disruptive incident. This vulnerability is a result of the company's level of dependency upon its operations processes, critical facility infrastructure, and electronic data systems. Risks to these services must be assessed on an ongoing basis. It is further recognized that response and recovery actions must be professionally and efficiently managed to ensure the safety of employees, compliance with regulatory requirements, and provide for a speedy restoration of business operations. The process to manage this requires a significant level of advance planning and preparation and involves a three-tier planning process.

- Tier 1 provides for the **Incident Reporting and Site Incident Response Plan,** which outlines procedures for reporting and responding to and managing incidents at the local level. The **Site Incident Response Team** implements the provisions of this plan.
- Tier 2 provides for the **Corporate Incident Response Plan,** which specifies operational procedures in responding to and managing incidents that significantly impact the

corporation. The **Corporate Incident Response Team** implements the provisions of this plan.

- Tier 3 provides for the **Corporate Crisis Management Plan**, which specifies corporate policy when dealing with incidents that could disrupt business operations or damage the corporate reputation. The **Corporate Crisis Management Team** implements the provisions of this plan.

Figure F.1 provides a graphical depiction of the Three Tier Management Strategy.

Objective

The objective of the tiered approach is to provide a structured response to all incidents in support of site management. The plan identifies guidelines to simplify and support the development of a well-structured and coherent concept that enables the organization to respond quickly and effectively to an unforeseen emergency, which could escalate and interrupt normal business operations. The process places the responsibility for managing incidents with local consequences with local

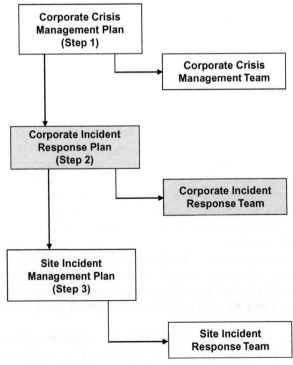

Figure F.1 Three-Tier Management Strategy.

management, yet provides for corporate support as the situation escalates. The Corporate Crisis Management Team or the Corporate Incident Response Team may assume oversight of crises that have regional, national, or international impact or exceed the resources of the local site.

Strategy

Every business can experience a serious incident that results in the disruption of normal business operations. This can range from a flood or explosion to a serious computer malfunction or information security incident. Management has the responsibility and need to recover from such incidents in the minimum amount of time possible. This recovery process requires preparation and planning. Figure F.1 outlines the planning strategy for managing incidents at all levels of the corporation:

- *Step 1.* Planning begins with the development of a **Corporate Crisis Management Plan** and the appointment of a **Corporate Crisis Management Team**. The responsibility for completing Step 1 usually resides with the Executive Management Committee (EMC), with oversight provided by the Board of Directors (BOD) if it is a publicly traded company. This program provides guidance and direction for managing incidents throughout the corporation.
- *Step 2.* A senior executive (i.e., chief legal officer) should be assigned responsibility for the development of a **Corporate Incident Response Plan** and organizations that provide representatives to the **Corporate Incident Response Team.** The purpose is to develop situation-specific response plans and identify subject matter experts as team members. These plans and response teams must be exercised semi-annually to ensure proficiency in managing and responding to incidents.
- *Step 3.* The development of the **Facility/Site/Building Incident Response Plans** and the establishment of **Facility/Site/Building Incident Response Teams** are the responsibility of the senior manager at each site. The purpose of these plans is to provide processes and procedures for reporting, responding to, and managing incidents/circumstances with local impact for that specific site.

Terms

Incident. A situation that requires an immediate reporting and response to protect lives, property, product, information, or business continuity.

Crisis. A crisis is any unplanned incident, event, occurrence, or sequence of events that has or could result in regional, national, or international consequences or that threatens business continuity.

Corporate Crisis Management Plan. The Corporate Crisis Management Plan establishes the requirement and development of Crisis Management Plans applicable to all levels of the corporation. It provides planning guidelines to ensure continuity and consistency in crisis planning, performance standards that meet acceptable performance levels, and protocols that are applicable to operations. Additionally, the plan provides assistance in managing serious disruptive events in a controlled and structured manner. It contains emergency contact details, strategies to mitigate the impact of an incident, and procedures to establish a communication process. Plans should be structured to address an "all hazards" classification and be easily adaptable to at any level of the corporation. The plan should include proactive measures to be taken in advance of, or in conjunction with, a crisis situation

Corporate Crisis Management Team. A decision-making body of senior corporate officers with cross-functional expertise in management, operations, and support services critical to managing the crisis and recovery operations.

Incident/Crisis Communications. A reporting and notification process that alerts the appropriate key operational personnel of an incident and the potential of escalation. This process should be established at all levels of the corporation.

Corporate Incident Response Team. A select group of staff content experts (at the department head level) with operational experience in managing real-time significant incidents as they unfold. The team is a support service to site management when the incident exceeds local resources.

References, if available, could include the following:

- Corporate Natural Disaster Plans
- Corporate Crisis Communications Plans
- Corporate Workplace Violence Plans
- Hazardous Materials and Spill Plans
- Business Continuity Plans
- Fire/Medical Emergency Response Guidelines

Senior management, at the direction of, or with approval of the Board of Directors, will develop and publish the Corporate Crisis Management Plan, identifying members of the Corporate Crisis Management Team. Local site management will develop a Facility/Site/Building Incident Management Plan and

organize, train, and exercise Facility/Site/Building Response Teams in the following areas:
- safety
- fire
- security
- medical
- environmental
- facilities
- local community emergency services

Responsible corporate staff groups will publish incident planning guidelines in the following areas:
- corporate crisis management guidelines
- incident/crisis communications guidelines
- natural disaster guidelines
- bomb threat plans and procedures
- workplace safety guidelines
- workplace violence response guidelines
- personal security guidelines
- investigations guidelines
- general security guidelines
- computer security guidelines
- kidnap and ransom response plans

Corporate Emergency Plan

Purpose

The purpose of the Corporate Incident Response Plan is to formalize processes and procedures in providing an operational response to incidents on the local, national, or international level.

Concept

A response should be available for any event that has the potential for escalating into a crisis situation that could affect personnel, equipment, property, product, continued operations, or corporate image. The management of such incidents must be clearly defined, responses organized, and scenarios tested. For ease of identifying actions to be taken, three separate and distinct assessments should be made at both the local and corporate level.
- **Situation Categories:** The magnitude of the incident and the impact it may have on the corporation is critical in

determining the required level of response. The impact of an incident is evaluated in four categories, from a local minor incident to major crisis that threatens the corporation. The level of response to any category may be tailored based on the magnitude of the incident.

- **Levels of Response.** The initial response to any incident is best managed at the local level. However, corporate support is available on request or when it has been determined that the incident exceeds local resources, or the long-term impact of the situation affects the entire corporation.

- **Incident/Response Analysis.** There is no unilateral relationship between a **situation category** and the **level of response.** The circumstances of the incident dictate the level of response required. (Example: A Category A incident should not automatically be associated with a Level 1 response. The response level should be tailored not only to the incident category but also to the specific situation.)

Categories of Incidents

The response to an incident will be dependent upon the magnitude of the situation. The corporation should plan for four classes of incident according to the impact they have on employees, equipment, property, products, continued operations, corporate image, and recovery efforts. Table F.1 outlines the four categories.

Levels of Response

The level of response should be commensurate with the severity of the crisis. The selection of response level should be based on the situation, and may be increased or decreased based on the situation. The responses outlined in Table F.2 identify the actions that should be considered as the crisis situation escalates.

Reporting

The **Corporate Crisis Management Team** should be charged by the Board of Directors and the Executive Management Committee with oversight responsibility for any emergency situation that has the potential to impact the Corporation. Timely communications and coordination between the incident site and the **Corporate Crisis Management Team** will ensure

Table F.1 Categories of Incident

Category	Description	Catalyst
A Local Incident	Minor damage to property or equipment No injuries Local community not effected No media coverage expected Operations continue as usual Minor accident or incident not involving fatalities Incidents of workplace violence not involving a serious injury or fatality Any incident that could affect community relations	Rain, snow, or ice storm Electrical storm High winds Confinable fire within site resources Intermittent power failures Equipment failure Power surge Minor flooding Industrial accident Labor/union dispute Activist activity Domestic dispute Employee confrontation
B Local Emergency	Accidents or incidents involving minor to serious injuries and damage to property or equipment Minor damage to community property Minor disruption of communications systems and local operations Brief hazardous chemical or vapor leak that does not require evacuation No health hazard to civilian population Suspected incidents of sabotage of equipment or product Incidents of workplace violence involving injury to one or more employees Any accident or incident that could result in media coverage	Severe rain, snow, or ice storm Electrical storm resulting in lightning strikes Gale winds Fire requiring external emergency response Power failure Flooding Industrial accident Labor/union dispute Activist demonstration Domestic dispute resulting in injury Employee confrontation resulting in injuries
C Corporate Emergency	Accidents or incidents resulting in life threatening injuries or major damage to property or equipment Significant damage to community property Potential health hazard to civilian population Temporary loss of communications systems Local operations temporarily halted Partial evacuation required Hazardous chemical or vapor leak Health hazard to local community	Tornado, hurricane, or earthquake Major fire or explosion Sabotage Exposure to toxic chemicals Explosion of any type Industrial accident Labor dispute Activist demonstration

(Continued)

Table F.1 (Continued)

Category	Description	Catalyst
	Partial shutdown of facility	Domestic disputes that carry over to the workplace and result in injury
	Sabotage of company property or equipment resulting in lost production time	Incidents of workplace violence that result in injuries
	National media coverage expected	
	Environment hazard probable	
D Corporate Crisis	Significant or multiple loss of life at a corporate facility, neighboring community, or accident site as a result of an incident originating at a corporate facility.	Tornado, hurricane, or earthquake Major fire or explosion Sabotage
	Significant threat or impairment of a facility due to an industrial accident.	High-risk exposure to toxic chemicals Explosion
	Product tampering resulting in serious injury or death	Industrial accident
	Serious off-site transportation/distribution incident or other company-related accident	Labor dispute Activist demonstration
	Incident that requires filing a report with EPA, OSHA, or any other state or federal regulatory agency	Domestic disputes that carry over to the workplace and result in severe injury or death
	Major destruction of company property by an act of nature or man caused incident	Incidents of workplace violence that result in a death(s)
	Act of terrorism	
	Kidnapping and/or extortion	
	Financial crisis (real or rumored) that has an impact upon company image	
	Action that results in significant negative attention from national and/or international media or any key stockholders	
	National and international media coverage	
	Total evacuation of facility	
	Severe impact on local community	
	Complete facility shutdown	
	Total loss of voice and data communications	
	Incidents that create a high probability of future lawsuits	
	Environmental hazard exposure	
	Incidents of product tampering	
	Disclosure of confidential information	

Table F.2 Levels of Response

Level	Site Response	Corporate Response
1	Activate the Site Incident Management Plan Provide first responder assistance as required Assess the circumstances of the incident Inform local officials as necessary Inspect affected equipment to determine cause and effect Return to normal operations as soon as possible Submit incident and after-action report to the Corporate Incident Response Team	Provide assistance as requested
2	Activate the Site Incident Response Plan Activate the Site Incident Response Team Implement the Site Emergency Response Plan Activate the Site Emergency Response Team Provide first responder assistance as necessary Request local emergency medical assistance as required Assess the circumstances of the incident Telephonically report incident to the Corporate Crisis Management Team Secure the immediate incident scene Advise local officials of incident and potential impact on the community Coordinate with Corporate Communications for media release Initiate inquiry to determine the cause and effect of the incident Return to normal operations as soon as possible Submit incident and after-action report to Corporate Crisis Management Team	Initiate the Corporate Incident/Crisis Communications Plan Assist with preparing media releases Place Corporate Emergency Response Team on alert to support the affected site Provide assistance and support as requested by the site
3	Implement the Site Incident Response Plan Establish a Site Emergency Control Center Implement the Site Emergency Response Plan Activate the Site Emergency Response Team Provide first responder assistance as necessary Evacuate and secure the incident scene	Implement the Corporate Crisis Management Plan Activate the Corporate Crisis Management Team Implement the Corporate Emergency Response Plan Activate the Corporate Emergency Response Team

(Continued)

Table F.2 (Continued)

Level	Site Response	Corporate Response
	Report situation in accordance with the Corporate Crisis Management Plan Account for all personnel Request local emergency medical assistance as required Assess the circumstances of the incident Advise local officials of the circumstances and the potential impact on the community Coordinate with Corporate Communications for media release Return to normal operations as soon as possible Submit incident and after-action report to Corporate Crisis Management Team	Coordinate directly with site management Corporate Security to investigate all incidents involving a death Coordinate logistical and procurement support Assist with human relations issues Determine potential impact on the corporation Assist with preparing media releases Assist with extraordinary financial support
4	Activate the Site Incident Management Team Establish a Site Emergency Control Center Implement the Site Emergency Response Plan Activate the Site Emergency Response Team Provide first responder assistance as necessary Evacuate and secure the incident scene Report situation in accordance with the Corporate Crisis Management Plan Account for all personnel Request local emergency medical assistance as required Assess the circumstances of the incident Advise local officials of the circumstances and the potential impact on the community Coordinate with Corporate Communications for media release Return to normal operations as soon as possible Submit incident and after-action report to Corporate Crisis Management Team	Implement the Corporate Crisis Management Plan Activate the Corporate Crisis Management Team Activate the Corporate Crisis Center Implement the Corporate Emergency Response Plan Activate the Corporate Emergency Response Team Coordinate directly with site management Corporate Security to investigate all incidents involving a death Manage all media inquiries Coordinate logistical and procurement support Assist with human relations issues Determine potential impact on the corporation Assist with extraordinary financial support

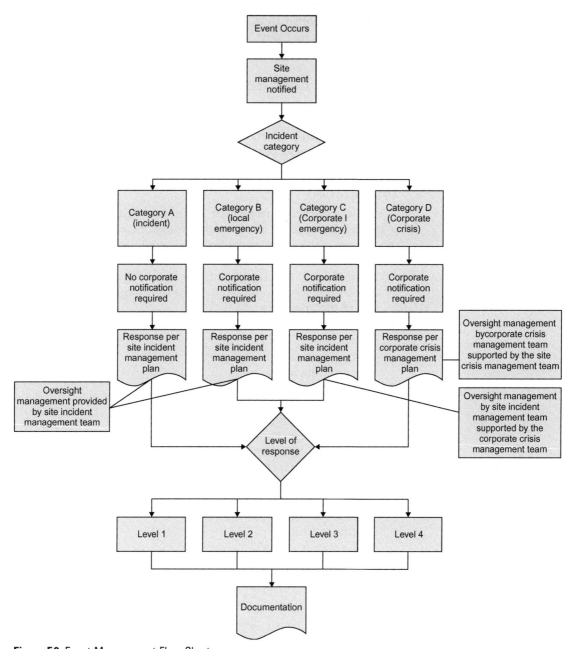

Figure F.2 Event Management Flow Chart.

optimum response to any crisis. Figure F.2 provides a diagram that identifies the Event Management Process.

Corporate Emergency Response Team

Purpose

The **Corporate Emergency Response Team** functions as the operational element of the **Corporate Crisis Management Team**.

Organization

The **Corporate Emergency Response Team** consists of a team leader and a core cadre. Subject matter experts in disciplines unique to the particular crisis may augment the team.

- Team Leader. A company officer from the affected business unit who has a working knowledge of the operational intricacies of the crisis site.
- Core Cadre. The core cadre should consist of representatives from:
  - corporate communications
  - corporate security
  - information technology
  - corporate safety
  - legal department
- Subject Matter Experts (augmentation). The following are examples of areas from which subject matter experts may be required to assist the **Corporate Emergency Response Team**:
  - engineering
  - procurement
  - risk management
  - transportation
  - human resources
  - environmental

Procedures

Specific actions to be taken by the **Corporate Emergency Response Team** will be dictated by the circumstances of the event. However, the following procedures should govern responses to every emergency:

- Category A (Incident)
  - Monitor the situation.
  - Be prepared to assist as requested or as directed.

- Category B (Local Emergency)
  - Draft press releases for local use.
  - Coordinate with **Site Incident Response Team** to assist in developing response strategies.
  - Provide logistical or procurement support as required.
  - Be prepared to assist as requested or as directed.
- Category C (Corporate Emergency)
  - Evaluate the situation to determine the composition of the **Corporate Emergency Response Team.**
  - Dispatch team within six (8) hours of the reported incident.
  - Integrate site and corporate team functions under site management with corporate oversight.
  - Develop an action plan addressing roles and responsibilities.
  - Coordinate with counterparts in the local community.
  - Address additional administrative or logistical support requirements.
  - Provide daily update reports to the **Corporate Crisis Management Team.**
  - Prepare final report identifying lessons learned to cope with future crisis situations.
- Category D (Corporate Crisis)
  - Evaluate the situation to determine the composition of the **Corporate Emergency Response Team.**
  - Dispatch team within three (3) hours of the reported incident.
  - Integrate site and corporate team functions under corporate management with site assistance.
  - Corporate Security to conduct a criminal investigation of any incident involving a death or a suspected sabotage.
  - Assume full responsibility for actions to be taken to address the emergency.
  - Develop an action plan addressing roles and responsibilities.
  - Coordinate with local, state, and federal agencies having an interest or jurisdiction over the investigative or recovery process.
  - Identify any potential violation of local, state, or federal law, rule, or regulation that could put the corporation at risk.
  - Address additional administrative or logistical support requirements.
  - Provide daily update reports to the **Corporate Crisis Management Team.**
  - Prepare final report identifying lessons learned to cope with future crisis situations.

Tactics

Each function represented by the **Corporate Emergency Management Team** should develop, maintain, and update a function specific plan identifying the processes and procedures to be employed when addressing an emergency. To ensure consistency and completeness in addressing response requirements, checklists should be developed outlining actions to be considered when addressing a specific type emergency. At a minimum, checklists should be developed in the following areas:

- Kidnapping/extortion
- Terrorism /sabotage
- Civil protest
- Labor strikes/work stoppage
- Industrial accident
- Fire
- Major chemical release
- Natural disaster
- Product recall
- Product contamination
- Transportation interruption
- Compromises of the corporate data network

Documentation

Each emergency will be unique. Valuable lessons may be learned for the experience gained in responding to and managing the emergency. Additionally, documentation of actions taken is important when a requirement exists to respond to regulatory agencies, criminal or fire investigators, or legal proceedings that may result. The following documentation should be maintained to document the corporation's response to the emergency.

- Chronology of events: a day by day identification of activities
- Chronology of media releases: a catalog of press and media coverage of the emergency
- Video or audio tapes of all press conferences provided
- Chronology of reports (written or verbal) provided by the **Corporate Crisis Management Team**
- Copies or transcripts of any written or verbal submittals to outside agencies
- After-Action Report summarizing all actions taken in response to the emergency and including the identification of any lessons learned that may be used to improve the corporation's response to emergencies.

APPENDIX G: CONSIDERING THE ESSENTIALS: QUESTIONS FOR PEOPLE AND PROGRAM DEVELOPMENT

Focus

We have tried hard in this book to assemble a set of topics that will be useful to our readers: the new security leader, a start-up security program, or a smaller corporation just considering the need and applicability of an asset protection program for their emerging risk management needs. Our intent is to provide a sampler of short but important subjects to give direction to this potentially diverse readership. Thus the following action-oriented questions taken from the end of each chapter are gathered here to enable review, provide grist for internal discussion and debate, or simply to facilitate a quicker read and perhaps send readers back for more information. We think how some of these questions may be answered *are* the essentials.

A Suggested Approach

Consider selecting one or two of the following questions or concepts and using each one as a security team exercise. Alternatively, use them to test the engagement of promising subordinates or as an exercise with a business unit risk management team. You may find a few you would want to toss to your CEO or other members of the senior management team. Be ready for the comeback: "That's your job. What do you think?"

1. Who are the two or three senior people you have met who see value in corporate security and understand what you want to accomplish? What is your plan for developing these relationships?

2. Based on your review and feedback from constituents, what is the most serious shortcoming of the program? What is your plan to address this, and on what schedule?
3. Who are the two strongest players on your team, and how do you propose to use them to measurably improve the program?
4. Who are your weakest players, and what is your plan to address these weaknesses?
5. Who among your constituents are going to be the hardest to satisfy, and why? How are you going to address this need?
6. If you had to identify one learning from your first 90 days, what would it be, and how will it influence your business plan and priorities?
7. If you accept the leadership competencies discussed in this book, where do you see your strengths and weaknesses? Which of these represents your best opportunity for influence and leadership in your first six months to a year on the job?
8. If you have arrived at this position on your own merits, you know where you need to grow and how to commence leading while this growth unfolds. Find a mentor who knows the business and has a reputation for being a real leader that people want to follow. What characteristics does he or she possess that you might emulate?
9. Keep your eye on the target. Listen and learn how to get things done in your corporate culture. A successful security program leverages results from its understanding of the culture.
10. Never forget that those you lead are watching.
11. Where does the program stand with regard to the five keys to leadership and influence? Which of these do you believe are the most important for your business planning? Which are most important for your personal development?
12. What did you learn about yourself and your needs from your Next Generation score?
13. Understand the risks you own and those in which you share responsibility for some phase of management or elect to defer.
14. Anticipate! Understand the potential source of the risk event(s) and how it would likely occur.
15. Be aware of the impacts of emerging economic and strategic pressures on the business, and how developing corporate plans may impact the risks you should understand better than others in the management team.
16. Advertise advice and requirements.
17. Establish ownership for risk management and response.

18. Offer assistance in installing and training on protection measures. Test their effectiveness frequently, and then provide feedback on results. Escalate if you don't see measurable improvement, then repeat the test.
19. Establish key performance indicators appropriate to your programs.
20. Establish key risk indicators appropriate to the security of your company's business operations.
21. Are your services seen as a cost or value center? Go back and review the stakeholder statements you collected during the Task Assessment in Chapter 1. Don't rely on your frequent customers, and look for feedback from executives where security is less known.
22. What is your candid appraisal? If you have results that demonstrate aligned value, how have you missed telling the story? If you see a real lack of alignment with business objectives, what steps might you take to better deliver?
23. How would you approach a proposal to outsource the current portfolio of proprietary security services to achieve potentially significant savings?
24. Do any of the alignment examples noted in Chapter 4 resonate with you? Using these topics as a starter, how do your security programs provide clear indications of alignment with the business?
25. Has your security mission been articulated and accepted by senior management?
26. What approach within your corporate culture would best enable implementation of a set of high-level security policies? (Or you could use "business practices" for a less controversial term.)
27. Which standards or practices under the eight business objectives is the security program currently performing? Which ones do you think would be value-added for your program and the company?
28. What constraints would exist for the implementation of each one?
29. How might those barriers be overcome? Of those services currently being delivered, to what extent are they at a standard of performance acceptable to you?
30. Are you satisfied that the security program is being effectively marketed and sold within the company?
31. How are you measuring program acceptance or buy-in and knowledge of shared responsibilities?
32. Where are the biggest gaps in the security program's marketing strategy, and what would be required to fill these gaps?

33. Using whatever criterion you believe is appropriate to your company, how would you rate your ability to access senior management for nonemergency communications?

34. Do you believe your current organizational model yields the best results for influence and senior management access? Why or why not? If not, what would be required to make this more impactful?

35. If one does not currently exist, would a security committee work in your company? If so, how might it be organized and sold?

36. How does your management react to the receipt of bad news? How does this or other factors influence your preference on placement of the security organization?

37. What organization or executive is responsible for state and federal legislative initiatives, and how would you characterize your relationship with that office?

38. Are you aware of anything in the works that may impact your company or organization, and to what extent are you influencing your company strategy with regard to the implications of its implementation?

39. What security-specific regulations apply to your organization now, and to what extent have you been engaged in their pre-implementation impact assessment and roll-out?

40. What is the real cost of security-related regulations to your company?

41. To what extent can proposed or active regulations assist you in obtaining resources or influencing corporate policy in terms of voluntary compliance?

42. On a scale of 1 to 10, how dependent is your company on the information technology (IT) infrastructure?

43. Does your security strategy and planning reflect this level of priority?

44. If you are not currently responsible for information security, is there a designated manager in IT or elsewhere who is?

45. How would you characterize your relationship with this colleague?

46. If you were the CISO, how would you respond to the same questions?

47. Where the relationship may be less than mutually supportive, what steps might you take to move in a positive direction?

48. Is the annual risk assessment program a joint effort between security and the CIO? How about other key stakeholders? Where are the gaps in this critical business process?

49. Given that there is acknowledged interdependence between logical and physical security, do you believe this interdependence is acknowledged by current business practice and resource allocations?
50. Has the current physical security deployment strategy (including first response) been effectively coordinated between security and IT? How about other key stakeholders, like facilities and business units with specific convenience or protection needs?
51. If the 24/7 security operations group is responsible for first response to IT-related business continuity incidents, has there been adequate orientation, procedural training, and notification procedures?
52. Is there an established cyber incident response plan that has been coordinated with business continuity, IT, risk management (if appropriate), and security?
53. If there were one fundamental improvement you could make to the physical security of your facilities, what would it be? How exposed are you with the knowledge of this need?
54. Are your in-house first responders qualified to provide definitive care to victims of medical emergencies?
55. Is there any opportunity to expand the use of security technology to reduce the level of manpower?
56. Have you developed a policy or guidelines to influence the protection standards of your company's facilities and operations? Do you have a template for security system fit-out of new facilities?
57. If you have objectively reviewed the security systems now in place, do you believe you have an effectively integrated physical security program?
58. If you are under the scope of any state or federal regulations, are you now in compliance with applicable physical security, access control, and other operational security requirements?
59. To what extent are you confident in the abilities of available vendors to execute your plans for electronic security system specifications and in their capabilities to upgrade and maintain your program consistent with the risk management profile you have specified?
60. Evaluate your command center. How well does it provide operators with real-time information that they can effectively evaluate and act upon? How reliable is the system that collects and displays alarm and other essential aural and visual data? Does the head end essential to command and control provide a 99.9% uptime reliability?

61. How would you assess the work-related competencies and skills of key members of your team? Are you doing everything possible to address competency development and professional growth?

62. Are you satisfied with the level of understanding of business process by investigative, information security, and contingency planning teams?

63. What incentives does the company offer for employees to pursue work-related training, professional certifications, and education opportunities?

64. Are you satisfied that the periodic performance review process provides adequate assessment of competencies and skills?

65. Are you knowledgeable about in-house, governmental, and academic programs to address employee career development needs?

66. Are your career development and training programs aligned with other business units and HR policies?

67. Is there a clear understanding with company business units regarding security responsibilities? Has guidance been provided on training requirements and resources?

68. Are you satisfied with the training provided to contract personnel? In what ways do shortcomings evidence themselves?

69. Do outsourcing contracts contain selection and training criteria, and is the responsibility clearly delineated?

70. Are there any instances of internal investigations (or other incidents) where the subject indicated a lack of awareness of a policy that he or she is accused of violating?

71. Are there indications from incident post mortems or around any categories of loss investigation that lack of risk awareness contributed directly to the incident? How are you addressing incident follow-ups for awareness improvement?

72. Is security included in the new employee orientation program?

73. How are management's messages conveyed to employees? Is it via a corporate intranet or other electronic means? How can your messages be best conveyed for impact? Who in the corporate communications infrastructure could assist in crafting and delivering timely and impactful awareness materials?

74. Have you ever conducted any sort of survey around the awareness of security policy or recommended practices by first-line supervisors and other mid-level managers? If you

see more instances of security violations within a specific business unit, it may be fruitful to determine how aware and proactive these managers are about their responsibilities for securing corporate assets and setting appropriate models for their subordinates.

75. If your company is outsourcing critical business processes, how are you being assured that your business partner is making their people aware of their responsibilities to protect their customer's interests?

76. Is the provision of a safe and secure workplace addressed within your company's business conduct or other policy framework?

77. Where would you most anticipate a workplace violence incident within your company? Are you satisfied with the safeguards you have in place? What other steps should you consider?

78. How does your company handle notification of domestic restraining orders that include the workplace?

79. What are the legal standards for a safe and secure workplace in the states in which you have staffed operations and/or visitor access?

80. Do you provide escort services from the office for employees with active threats against them? What are the limits of that coverage, and are you comfortable with the legal liabilities attendant to such services?

81. Remember that the knowledgeable insider is the most dangerous adversary you have! Engage those business units owning critical business processes in an intelligent discussion around how an insider (your own employee or a vendor) might engage in conduct with serious implications for the company's health and reputation.

82. Engage counsel and HR (employee relations) in a review of current business conduct policy and the adequacy of business unit line management's knowledge of that policy and expectations for their oversight of an ethical business environment.

83. Conduct investigative post mortems to identify contributing causes and gaps in policy or other needs for improved conformance with high standards of conduct.

84. Are you satisfied with the level of support you get with human resources (or others) in the investigation of employees in good standing? If not, what needs to be improved to create a more constructive relationship in these cases? How have you addressed this problem?

85. Are sanctions in these internal cases consistently applied across the company and, if not, what legal exposure might that inconsistency present?

86. Are you satisfied that the corporate business conduct policy adequately conveys the scope and clarity of management's expectations on conduct?

87. Regardless of formerly assigned responsibility for business continuity, the security organization is a critical part of the early warning, crisis management, and response capabilities. What parts does your organization play in these areas of risk management, and are there value-added functions you could offer?

88. Does your company annually conduct crisis management or business continuity exercises? What would you conclude if this sort of analysis has not been applied?

89. The typical contingency planning processes require each business unit to priority rank their business processes by criticality ratings, the most critical requiring zero downtime. Use the resulting list to assure yourself that your security programs provide the requisite level of protection to these higher criticality processes.

90. Have after-action-reviews been applied to the most serious business interruption events over the past three years? What was learned that has implications for your vision of the future security capability? What would you conclude if this sort of analysis has not been applied?

91. Business is virtual, global, and increasingly risky. Know the potential risks your "partners" bring to the table before you sign on the dotted line. Hold them accountable for risk-specific standards, and then inspect to assure compliance.

92. Which of the most critical business processes in your company rely in significant ways upon supply chain partners? To what extent have your partner selection processes incorporated a risk management strategy that includes security-related risk?

93. What are the most likely risk scenarios that could significantly impact the top three most critical sources of supply? Do you have a role to play in any of these, and if so, have you effectively sold your risk management resources to those business units?

94. Are you actively risk-profiling countries upon which you rely for the supply of essential products or services?

95. To what extent have you identified and vetted in-country security (or other logistical) resources that may be

engaged to assist in an interruption or other risk event in your critical supply chain?

96. What metrics are you currently providing to senior management?
    a. If none, you are failing to demonstrate any value or ability to influence
    b. If you stopped providing them, would anyone inquire why and when they might see them again?
    c. If you answered no or don't know, you are missing the mark, and you need to critically evaluate your security program, because it's likely you have no idea how they are performing.

97. Assuming you do maintain security metrics, what are the top three weak spots in your measures and metrics program? What steps should you take to improve these areas?

98. What are the most important metrics you need to manage your assigned resources?

99. Which metrics have you successfully used to influence management action or policy?

100. Which of the 16 contributions on business alignment shown in Table 16.1 in Chapter 16 can you demonstrate with your metrics? How well are you advertising these accomplishments? Of those you hadn't considered, which ones could you examine for development?

101. How does your company approach the process of examining its successes and failures? How might this influence your approach to the AAR process discussed here?

ABOUT THE CONTRIBUTING EDITOR

George Campbell served until 2002 as the chief security officer (CSO) at Fidelity Investments, the largest mutual fund company in the United States, with more than $2 trillion in customer assets and 32,500 employees. Under Campbell's leadership, the global corporate security organization delivered a wide range of proprietary services including information security, disaster recovery planning and crisis management, criminal investigations, fraud prevention, property and executive protection, and proprietary security system design, engineering, and installation. Since leaving Fidelity, Campbell has served as a content expert for product/content development for the Security Executive Council, of which he is a founding Emeritus Faculty member.

Prior to working at Fidelity Investments, Campbell owned a security and consulting firm, which specialized in risk assessment and security program management. He has also been group vice president at a system engineering firm that supported government security programs at high-threat sites around the world. Early on in his career, Campbell worked in the criminal justice system, and served in various line and senior management positions within federal, state, and local government agencies.

Campbell received his bachelor's degree in police administration from American University in Washington, D.C. He served on the board of directors of the International Security Management Association (ISMA), and as ISMA's president in 2003. Campbell is also a long-time member of ASIS International. He is a former member of the National Council on Crime Prevention, the High Technology Crime Investigation Association, and the Association of Certified Fraud Examiners, and is an alumnus of the U.S. State Department's Overseas Security Advisory Council.

ABOUT ELSEVIER'S SECURITY EXECUTIVE COUNCIL RISK MANAGEMENT PORTFOLIO

Elsevier's Security Executive Council Risk Management Portfolio is the voice of the security leader. It equips executives, practitioners, and educators with research-based, proven information and practical solutions for successful security and risk management programs. This portfolio covers topics in the areas of risk mitigation and assessment, ideation and implementation, and professional development. It brings trusted operational research, risk management advice, tactics, and tools to business professionals. Previously available only to the Security Executive Council community, this content—covering corporate security, enterprise crisis management, global IT security, and more—provides real-world solutions and "how-to" applications. This portfolio enables business and security executives, security practitioners, and educators to implement new physical and digital risk management strategies and build successful security and risk management programs.

Elsevier's Security Executive Council Risk Management Portfolio is a key part of the **Elsevier Risk Management and Security Collection**. The collection provides a complete portfolio of titles for the business executive, practitioner, and educator by bringing together the best imprints in risk management, security leadership, digital forensics, IT security, physical security, homeland security, and emergency management: Syngress, which provides cutting-edge computer and information security material; Butterworth-Heinemann, the premier security, risk management, homeland security, and disaster-preparedness publisher; and Anderson Publishing, a leader in criminal justice publishing for more than 40 years. These imprints, along with the addition of Security Executive Council content, bring the work of highly regarded authors into one prestigious, complete collection.

The Security Executive Council (www.securityexecutive-council.com) is a leading problem-solving research and services organization focused on helping businesses build value while improving their ability to effectively manage and mitigate risk. Drawing on the collective knowledge of a large community of successful security practitioners, experts, and strategic alliance partners, the Council develops strategy and insight and identifies proven practices that cannot be found anywhere else. Their research, services, and tools are focused on protecting people, brand, information, physical assets, and the bottom line.

Elsevier (www.elsevier.com) is an international multimedia publishing company that provides world-class information and innovative solutions tools. It is part of Reed Elsevier, a world-leading provider of professional information solutions in the science, medical, risk, legal, and business sectors.

INDEX

Note: Page numbers followed by "*f*", "*t*" and "*b*" refer to figures, tables and boxes, respectively.

24/7 security operations organization, 101

A
Access, 66–72
Access control, 117–119
Actionable metrics, 183*f*
Advanced Manifest Rule (AMR)/ Advance Cargo Information (ACI), 173
Adversary, 149–150
After-action review (AAR), 197–198
Alternative organizational models, 62–64, 63*f*
Antitrust Compliance Policy, 241
ASIS (American Society for Industrial Security), 114
Asset protection, 44
Asset protection programs, 122–123
Attorney-client privilege, 154
Attorney work product doctrine, 154
Awareness program, 135*f*

B
Background investigation, 207
Base building risks, 205–206
Baseline program elements, 60
Board-level risks and response research, 32, 33*f*
Brand exposure, 42
Brand recognition, 50
Business-aligned program elements, 60
Business alignment, 45–47, 183–184, 184*t*
Business case, building, 9–16

Business Conduct and Ethics Committee, 241
Business conduct cases, 152, 152*f*
Business conduct investigations, 150
Business conduct policy policy statement, 152–155
reputation risk and, 153–155
Business continuity incidents, 203
Business continuity planning, 208
components of, 164–165
Business continuity tracking, 165, 166*f*
Business controls, effective, 29
Business drivers, 41–42
Business enabler, 20
Business objectives, 53–56
Business open architecture, 42
Business practices, 51–52
Business resiliency, 163
policy statement, 164–165
Business risk environment, 201
Business strategist, 20
Business strategy map, 11

C
C-suite engagement, 23
C-TPAT (Customs-Trade Partnership Against Terror), 79, 173
California Breach Notification Bill (SB-1386 and AB-1950), 96
CCTV, 118–119
Certified fraud investigator, 122–123

Code of Business Conduct and Ethics, 241
certification, 253
company assets, 242
compliance with laws and regulations, 242–243
confidential information, 243–244
conflicts of interest, 244–246
dealing with public officials, 246
environmental protection, 246–247
equal employment opportunity, 247
financial records, 247–248
gifts, gratuities, favors, 248–249
insider trading, 249–250
intellectual property rights, 250
policy enforcement, 252
political contributions, 250
reporting violations, 251
workplace safety, 250–251
Communication and risk awareness program, 23
Communication program, 130–131
Components of a Cost of Security Compliance Model, 90, 91*t*
Confidential hotline reporting, 151, 151*f*
Confidentiality, integrity, and availability (CIA), 97
Consolidated service model, 64, 64*f*

Container Security Initiative (CSI), 173
Contingency planning, 164–165
Continuous learning, 197
Contractors, 207
Control Objectives for Information and Related Technology (COBIT), 82–83
Converged physical and IT security functions, 119
Core management philosophy, 22
Corporate crisis management plan, 256, 258
Corporate crisis management team, 256, 258
Corporate culture, 11
Corporate emergency plan, 259–266
  categories of incidents, 260, 261t
  event management, 265f
  incident/response analysis, 260
  level of response, 260, 263t
Corporate emergency response team, 266–268
Corporate hygiene, 150–151
Corporate incident response plan, 255–257
Corporate incident response team, 255–256, 258
Corporate intranet, 129–130
Corporate leadership, 19–20
Corporate risk management program, 22
Corporate security map, 12f
Corporate security potential impact/cost, 37t
Corporate security program, 62f
  potential benefits, 10t
Corporate security work breakdown structure, 66–67
Corporate security work functions, full-service, 68t
Cost of insecurity, 194f
Crisis, 258

Cross-disciplinary courses, 124
CSO dashboard, 193f
Customs-Trade Partnership Against Terrorism (C-TPAT), 79, 173
Cyber incident, 102
Cyber incident response plan, 102–103
  objectives of, 102
  purpose of, 102
Cyber security, 103

D
Dangerousness, 228–239
Data management, 207
Dated security systems, 114
Department of Homeland Security (DHS), 42

E
Electronic security, 114
Emergency and crisis management, 209
Emergency medical technician (EMT), 122–123
Emergency Planning and Community Right-to-know Act (EPCRA), 173
Enterprise policy influencer, 20
Enterprise risk assessments (ERA), 32
Enterprise risk management (ERM)
  framework, 3
  structure, 4f
ERA (Enterprise risk assessments), 32
Essentials, 269–277

F
First response, 116
Foreign Corrupt Practices Act, 246
Framework of Standards to Secure and Facilitate Global Trade (SAFE Framework), 174
Free and Secure Trade (FAST), 173

G
Global business risk environment, 62, 63f
Global supply chains, 42
Gramm-Leach-Bliley Act (GLBA), 96
Guidelines see Voluntary guidelines

H
Hazardous/dangerous material issues, 205
Health Insurance Portability and Accountability Act (HIPAA), 96

I
Incident, 257
Incident/crisis communications, 258
Incident post-mortem, 31, 197–199
Incident reporting and site incident response plan, 255
Information, value of, 97–98
Information assurance requirements, 97
Information protection program threats, 104f
Information Security, 204–205
Information security
  architecture, 101
  importance of, 96
  infrastructure, 101
Information security program, 41–42
  high-level measurement of, 99f
  organizing, 100–101
Information security standard, 82–83
Insurance carriers, 108
Integrated physical and operational security program, 112f
Integrated security systems, 110–111
Integrated solution, 110–111

Internal misconduct investigations, 156–159
Internal risk, 204
ISO 17799, 82–83

K

Key performance indicators (KPIs), 36
Key risk indicators (KRIs), 36

L

Legislation, 78, 81
Legislation, Regulations, Voluntary Compliance, and Standards (LRVCS) Breakdown, 78–79
Lessons-learned analysis, 198
Location risk, 203
Locks and alarms, 108

M

Management model, 21
Marketing strategy, 49–50
Measures, 177–178
Metrics, 178
Mission statement, 51, 52f

N

National Association of Corporate Directors (NACD), 182
National Response Framework (NRF), 166–167
New employee orientation program, 129–130
Next Generation score, 24–26
Next generation security leader, 24–26, 25f
NFPA 1600 Standard, 82–83, 166
Noncompliance, 90–93
    impacts, 92–93
    risks of, 90–92

O

Organizational constituents, 1–2
Organizational leadership, 19–20
Organizational model, 62
Owned properties, 206

P

Partnerships, value of, 23
Performance review process, 124–125
Physical security program, 111
    aligning, 111–115
    equipment removal, 118
    and first response, 116
    as force multiplier, 117, 118f
    integrated program, 112f
    and IT security, convergence of, 119
    objectives, 113–114
    risk assessment, 118
    threat assessment, 113f
Policies, 51–52
Policy framework, 201–202
Professional development programs, 121
Program characteristics, 60–62

Q

Qualitative risk analysis and reporting program, 22–23

R

Regulation management worksheet, 83–89
Regulations, 75, 82
Regulatory compliance strategy, 79
    elements of, 80f
Regulatory elements, 76
Regulatory requirements, 167
Relationship manager, 20
Request for Proposal (RFP)
    general conditions of, 223–224
    general information session, 219–220
    instructions to bidders, 220–221
    proposal contents, 221–223
    selection criteria, 223
    timeline, 224
Residual risk, 13–14
Responsible, Accountable, Consulted, Informed (RACI) methodology, 83, 84t

Restraining orders, 142
RFP (Request for Proposal), 219
Risk appetite, 44
Risk assessment, 29–30
Risk group and security committee leadership, 20–21
Risk management, 36–38
    anticipation, 36
    communication and, 182
    execution, 38
    preparation, 36–38
    steps in, 182
Risk management guide, 20
Risk mitigation, 36–38, 42
Risk quantification, 33–36, 34f
Risk review elements, 201

S

Safe and secure workplaces
    policy framework, 140
    predictability of risk, 139–140
Sarbanes-Oxley Act (SOX), 96
Security, as value center, 180
Security, goals of, 42
Security architecture, 101
Security awareness, 209
Security awareness approaches, 131–135, 132t
Security awareness program, 135f
Security budget cost elements, 7t
Security committee
    advantages of, 64–65
    membership of, 65
    results-oriented measures, 65
Security communication program
    strategies, 131
    tactics, 131
    tailoring message, 136
Security device costs, 212t
Security Executive Council (SEC), 24
Security executives, 41
Security infrastructure, 101
Security issues, 41
Security leader, 20–21, 42

Security leadership
  core competencies, 20–21
  organizational influence and
    Impact, 21–23
Security measures, 177–178
  benefits of, 179–180, 180*f*
  data sources, 182–183
  objectives of, 178–179
  in reducing risk, 45
Security metrics, 177–178
  avoiding pitfalls, 184
  benefits of, 179–180, 180*f*
  data sources, 182–183
  objectives of, 178–179
  potential metrics, 184
  related roles and
    responsibilities, 180–181
Security operations, 115
Security planning and program
  development, 44–45, 45*f*
Security policies framework,
  21–22
Security policy awareness,
  survey of, 130*f*
Security professionals, role of,
  79–90
Security-program objectives,
  46–47
Security programs, 7–8, 41–42
Security regulations, 76–78
Security-related costs, 5, 108
Security-related training and
  education, 127*f*
  academic programs, 124
  certificate programs, 123–124

developmental plan, 124–125
in-house training, 123
objectives of, 122
outsourcing contracts, 125
security-related
  responsibilities, 125–126
training administration, 126
training options, 122–123
Security riding on corporate
  network, 118–119
Security strategic issues, 44
Security strategy alignment, 44
Shared responsibility, 129–130
Site incident response team,
  255
Smart and Secure Trade-lanes
  (SST) program, 174
Standard security practices,
  53–56
Standards, 82–83
State of control, 98–99
Strategic management process,
  43*f*
Strategic Plan for Securing the
  Global Supply Chain, 171*t*
Strategic planning process, 45*f*
Strategic security plans, 41
Strategic security program,
  43–44
Supply chain risk, 170–174
Supply chain risk management,
  169
Supply chain security, 174–175
Supporting a Nonviolent
  Workplace, 225

T
Team leader, 20
Thought leader, 20
Threat alignment, 111–115
Threat assessment, 30–31, 30*f*,
  113*f*
Threats, 202
Three-tier management
  strategy, 255–256, 256*f*
Training and education,
  127*f*

U
Unified risk oversight (URO),
  4–5, 65–66

V
Voluntary guidelines, 78–79,
  82
Vulnerability assessment, 31

W
Workplace executive protection,
  144–146
Workplace violence policy,
  140–141, 141*b*
Workplace violence prevention
  program, 226–227
  planning and preparation,
    232–233
  proactive, 226
  reactive response, 236
World Customs Organization
  (WCO), 174

Printed and bound by CPI Group (UK) Ltd, Croydon, CR0 4YY

08/05/2025

01864904-0001